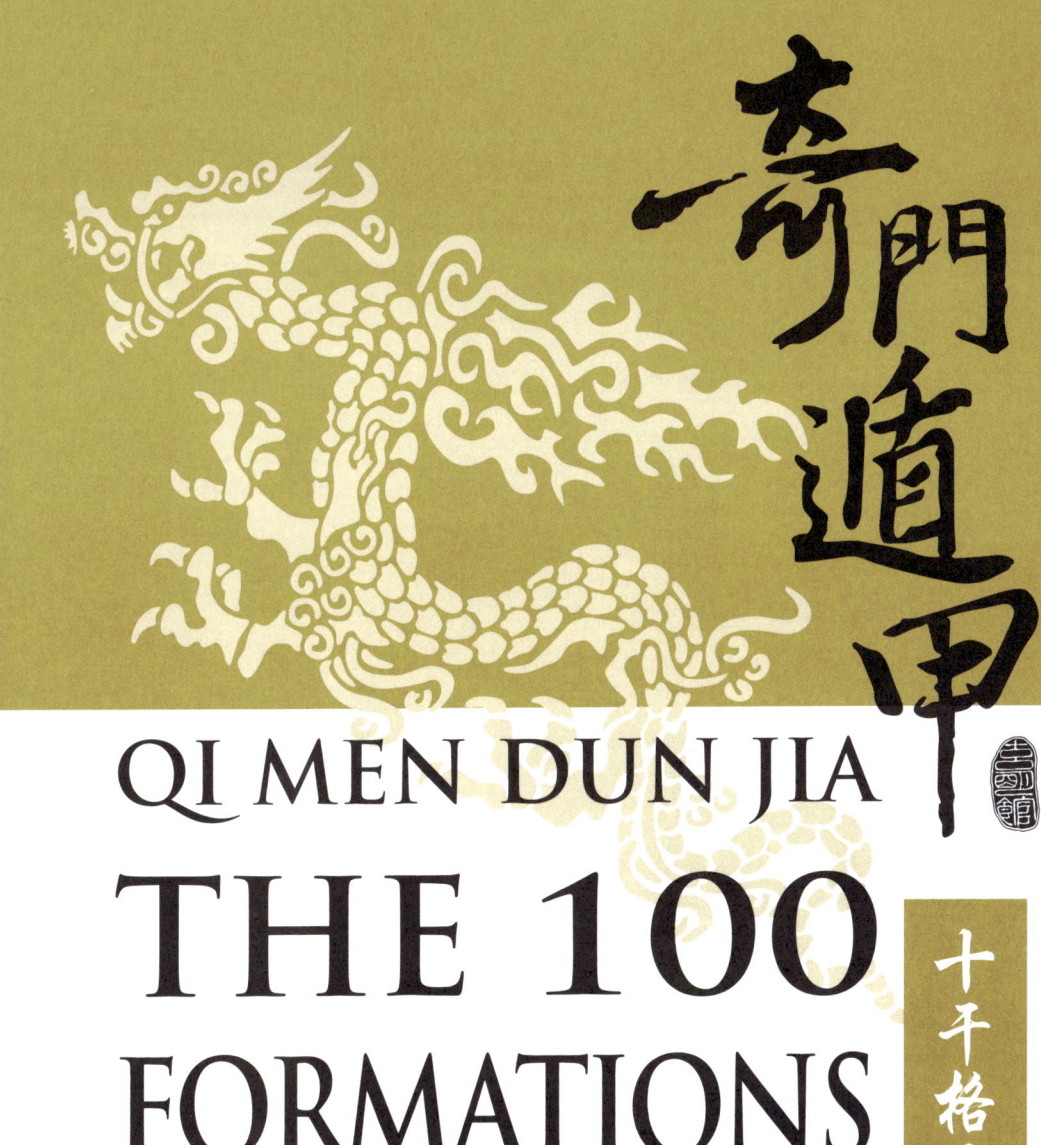

QI MEN DUN JIA

THE 100 FORMATIONS

Joey Yap's Qi Men Dun Jia - The 100 Formations

Copyright © 2014 by Joey Yap
All rights reserved worldwide.
First Edition June 2014

All intellectual property rights contained or in relation to this book belong to Joey Yap

No part of this book may be copied, used, subsumed, or exploited in fact, field of thought or general idea, by any other authors or persons, or be stored in a retrieval system, transmitted or reproduced in any way, including but not limited to digital copying and printing in any form whatsoever worldwide without the prior agreement and written permission of the author.

The author can be reached at:

Joey Yap Research International Sdn Bhd (939831- H)
19-3, The Boulevard, Mid Valley City,
59200 Kuala Lumpur, Malaysia.
Tel   : +603-2284 8080
Fax   : +603-2284 1218
Email   : info@masteryacademy.com
Website : www.masteryacademy.com

DISCLAIMER:

The author, Joey Yap and the publisher, Joey Yap Research International Sdn Bhd., have made their best efforts to produce this high quality, informative and helpful book. They have verified the technical accuracy of the information and contents of this book. However, the information contained in this book cannot replace or substitute for the services of trained professionals in any field, including, but not limited to, mental, financial, medical, psychological, or legal fields. They do not offer any professional, personal, medical, financial or legal advice and none of the information contained in the book should be confused as such advice. Any information pertaining to the events, occurrences, dates and other details relating to the person or persons, dead or alive, and to the companies have been verified to the best of their abilities based on information obtained or extracted from various websites, newspaper clippings and other public media. However, they make no representation or warranties of any kind with regard to the contents of this book and accept no liability of any kind for any losses or damages caused or alleged to be caused directly or indirectly from using the information contained herein.

Published by Joey Yap Research International Sdn Bhd.

Table of Contents

Preface	6
Introduction	9
The Five Areas Of Qi Men Dun Jia	11
The Brief Origins Of Qi Men Dun Jia	13
How Does Qi Men Dun Jia Work?	15
Qi Men Formations – 100 Combinations	16
How to Obtain Your Qi Men Chart for Analysis	18
QI MEN DUN JIA-THE 100 FORMATIONS	**33**
Jia 甲 **(Yang Wood)**	35
Yi 乙 **(Yin Wood)**	67
Bing 丙 **(Yang Fire)**	99
Ding 丁 **(Yin Fire)**	131
Wu 戊 **(Yang Earth)**	163
Ji 己 **(Yin Earth)**	195
Geng 庚 **(Yang Metal)**	227
Xin 辛 **(Yin Metal)**	259
Ren 壬 **(Yang Water)**	291
Gui 癸 **(Yin Water)**	323

About The Chinese Metaphysics Reference Series

Reference Series

The Chinese Metaphysics Reference Series of books are designed primarily to be used as complementary textbooks for scholars, students, researchers, teachers and practitioners of Chinese Metaphysics.

The goal is to provide quick easy reference tables, diagrams and charts, facilitating the study and practice of various Chinese Metaphysics subjects including Feng Shui, BaZi, Yi Jing, Zi Wei, Liu Ren, Ze Ri, Tai Yi, Qi Men and Mian Xiang.

These series of books are intended as reference text and educational materials principally for the academic syllabuses of the **Mastery Academy of Chinese Metaphysics**. The contents have also been formatted so that Feng Shui practitioners and other teachers of Chinese Metaphysics will always have a definitive source of reference at hand, when teaching or applying their art.

Because each school of Chinese Metaphysics is different, the Reference Series of books usually do not contain any specific commentaries, application methods or explanations on the theory behind the formulas presented in its contents. This is to ensure that the contents can be used freely and independently by all Feng Shui Masters and teachers of Chinese Metaphysics without conflict.

If you would like to study or learn the applications of any of the formulas presented in the Reference Series of books, we recommend that you undertake the courses offered by Joey Yap and his team of Instructors at the Mastery Academy of Chinese Metaphysics.

www.masteryacademy.com/estore

Titles offered in the Reference Series:

1	The Ten Thousand Year Calendar
2	The Ten Thousand Year Calendar (Pocket Edition)
3	The Chinese Metaphysics Compendium
4	Dong Gong Date Selection
5	Earth Study Discern Truth
6	San Yuan Dragon Gate Eight Formations Water Method
7	Plum Blossom Divination Reference Book
8	The Date Selection Compendium - The 60 Jia Zi Attributes

BaZi Structures & Structural Useful Gods Reference Series

9	Metal
10	Wood
11	Water
12	Fire
13	Earth

BaZi Hour Pillar Useful Gods Reference Series

14	Metal
15	Wood
16	Water
17	Fire
18	Earth
19	Xuan Kong Purple White Script
20	Ode To Mysticism
21	Ode To Flying Stars
22	Secrets Of Xuan Kong
23	Eight Mansions Bright Mirror
24	The Yin House Handbook
25	Water Water Everywhere

Qi Men Dun Jia Series

26	Qi Men Dun Jia Compendium
27	Qi Men Dun Jia Ten Thousand Year Calendar
28	Qi Men Dun Jia 540 Yang Structure
29	Qi Men Dun Jia 540 Yin Structure
30	Qi Men Dun Jia Year Charts
31	Qi Men Dun Jia Month Charts
32	Qi Men Dun Jia Day Charts
33	Qi Men Dun Jia Forecasting Methods Wealth And Life Pursuits (Book 1)
34	Qi Men Dun Jia Evidential Occurrences
35	Qi Men Dun Jia Destiny Analysis
36	Qi Men Dun Jia Feng Shui
37	Qi Men Dun Jia Date, Time & Activity Selection
38	Qi Men Dun Jia Annual Destiny Analysis
39	Qi Men Dun Jia Day Charts (San Yuan Method)
40	Qi Men Dun Jia Forecasting Methods People And Environmental Matters (Book 2)
41	Qi Men Dun Jia The 100 Formations
42	Qi Men Dun Jia Strategic Executions
43	Qi Men Dun Jia Sun Tzu Warcraft

Xuan Kong Da Gua Series

44	San Yuan Qi Men Xuan Kong Da Gua Ten Thousand Year Calendar
45	San Yuan Qi Men Xuan Kong Da Gua Compendium
46	San Yuan Qi Men Xuan Kong Da Gua 540 Yang Structures
47	San Yuan Qi Men Xuan Kong Da Gua 540 Yin Structures
48	Xuan Kong Da Gua 64 Gua Transformation Analysis 1 - Fixed Yao Method
49	Xuan Kong Da Gua 64 Gua Transformation Analysis 2 - Flying Yao Method
50	Xuan Kong Da Gua 64 Gua Transformation Analysis 3 - Six Relationships Method
51	Xuan Kong Da Gua Xuan Kong Five Element Structures
52	Xuan Kong Da Gua Xuan Kong Leaning Star Structures
53	Xuan Kong Flying Star Period 1 - 5 Natal Chart Analysis
54	Xuan Kong Flying Star Period 6 - 9 Natal Chart Analysis
55	Xuan Kong Flying Star Secrets of the 81 Combinations
56	Xuan Kong Flying Star Purple White Script's Advanced Star Charts
57	San Yuan Qi Men Xuan Kong Da Gua Advanced Charts 540 Yang Structures
58	San Yuan Qi Men Xuan Kong Da Gua Advanced Charts 540 Yin Structures

Preface

The mystical nature of Qi Men Dun Jia will always be seen as an inscrutable art form of ancient Chinese Metaphysics by its many practitioners and students. Considered one of the highest forms of metaphysical arts in China, it is still used worldwide today for business, crime-solving, marriages, health, military endeavours, and personal fortune. Its versatility and practicality is what enables it to continuously stand up to the test of time, enduring not only as a mystical form of divination, but also as a modern tool to empower and equip people for decision-making.

Those who have studied Qi Men Dun Jia would have come across its many different Structures, which are all unique and representative of an outcome of their own. Of course, a Qi Men Chart is by no means simple. A whole host of Structures exist within a Chart, but not all of them have to be studied at once. This book will focus on the most popular and frequently applied Structures known as the 100 Formations.

This is why I have come up with this book: to provide an insight and explain each one of the 100 Formations in detail for you. The average layman may look at a Qi Men Chart and have difficulty deriving anything substantial from it. With this book as a guide, however, readers can instantly seek out the precise information they need. In this modern age, having a clear guide at hand is an advantage no one can deny.

Qi Men Dun Jia is indeed an extraordinary art form, but it does not have to be as complicated as people make it out to be. It is my belief that with dedication, anyone can grasp this metaphysical science and put it to good use in their lives. I feel that it is a great honour for me to reconstruct and simplify this information to make it more easily understandable and share it with those who do not have the opportunity to spend years researching and studying the subject.

Thus, I have devised a specific format in which this book will present its information, to ensure a holistic understanding of the 100 Formations. The reality is that anyone would need many years to fully understand Qi Men Charts, but this book will help you skip the first few steps and focus on the results.

Qi Men is firmly rooted in ancient Chinese history and is a big part of Chinese culture. Many great military minds as well as leaders were recorded to have used it. Its importance to them was profound and its mysticism greatly admired and praised. In this modern age, you can always take the wisdom of Qi Men and apply it in your own life and tailor it based on your needs. There is no need to rigidly adhere to any standards. Qi Men may have had its origins in ancient China, but it has prevailed to this day and thus should be given the same treatment as well as privilege as any other modern tool for decision-making or life-planning.

While no measure of simplified methods will ever adequately explain the elaborate mechanisms of Qi Men, it is my goal to bring you as much clarity as I can so that you may have a better understanding of this ancient art. With this book, you have the opportunity to explore this wisdom for yourself, in your own perspective and based on your own experiences so that it is more applicable to every individual.

I hope you will enjoy using this reference book for your Qi Men analysis. If you have the time, do drop by at my Facebook page (www.facebook.com/JoeyYapFB) and drop me a note. As a teacher and an author, nothing pleases me more than engaging with my students and readers to see how the wonderful workings of Qi Men have changed their lives!

May success find you in all your pursuits as you begin your journey into the world of Qi Men.

Warmest regards,

Joey Yap
June 2014

Author's personal website : www.joeyyap.com
Academy websites : www.masteryacademy.com | www.baziprofiling.com
Joey Yap on Facebook : www.facebook.com/joeyyapFB

INTRODUCTION

Tales of Chinese military prowess has fascinated historians throughout the centuries. In control of vast swathes of land and facing enemy tribes across all borders, Chinese military leaders were forced to defend their country time and again. As they strengthened their defences and amassed powerful armies guided by legendary and revered leaders, the beleaguered nation fought off all-comers.

How they achieved such astonishing victories was due in no small part to a unique forecasting tool, giving them the advantage over the opposing hordes. In accordance with their long-held traditions, the imperial Chinese leaders availed themselves of the comprehensive benefits on offer from their Chinese metaphysical science of forecasting and warfare. With careful planning and thorough study of this ancient discipline, their superlative military tactics were developed.

The science in question was Qi Men Dun Jia.

As time has passed, the reliance on this esoteric method, combined with its frequent use by Chinese leaders due to its unwavering precision, has given it a mystical aura. Today, Qi Men Dun Jia is still regarded with a sense of awe and a fundamental view that it is a divination system which is used to anticipate and predict the outcomes of crucial situations.

While this is true to some extent, it has also given the false impression that Qi Men Dun Jia is inaccessible to all but a privileged few. Yet nothing could be further from the truth.

Qi Men Dun Jia is not only a refined science, it is also adaptable and accessible.

As we explore its uses in this book, we will learn how the use of Qi Men Dun Jia has evolved over the years into the respected forecasting tool it is seen as today.

Before we do this, however, it is essential to gain more of an understanding of Qi Men Dun Jia by examining its main categories.

The Five Areas Of Qi Men Dun Jia

For the purposes of this book, we can divide Qi Men Dun Jia into five (5) principal sections, each of which is outlined below:

1) Qi Men Forecasting

In forecasting, a number of predictive methods are used in order to predict an array of individual actions or circumstances. For this, a Qi Men Chart is typically plotted in the form of a Qi Map. This map can be adapted and applied to a number of situations, ranging from the seemingly trivial, to potentially life-changing events. For example, a Qi Men Chart will offer the user invaluable insight into situations such as a crucial job interview, the likely result of vital business negotiations, the most fortuitous career path and even the most appropriate approach for promotional campaigns. This is in addition to resolving trivial matters, such as helping to recover a lost piece of jewellery.

2) Qi Men Strategic Execution (Date, Time And Activity Selection)

When applying Qi Men, a precise and detailed calculation is required to pinpoint what is referred to as the 'Golden Moment'. This is the exact moment, in conjunction with a precise direction for a specific action, for an individual to ensure the most favourable result for a crucial situation. Legend tells us that iconic Chinese leaders took full advantage of this method in creating their plan of action in military campaigns. Indeed, their battle plans were often derived using only this means. Today, Qi Men Dun Jia is often used by companies launching new products in a competitive market place. It is believed that Qi Men Dun Jia will give organisations the advantage they seek over their competitors.

3) Qi Men Feng Shui

The use of Qi Men Dun Jia is broad and varied. When used with a specific Qi Men Feng Shui method, for example, it is invaluable in undertaking property assessments. The purpose of these appraisals is to provide the residents of the household with vital information on whether their property offers them the Qi required to boost their chances of success. When applying Qi Men Feng Shui, the practitioner can embark on a 'remote viewing' of the property in question. In this way, potential problem areas can be pinpointed and notified to the residents before the property is fully inspected. This way, the incoming Qi source is also identified by the practitioner.

4) Qi Men Destiny Analysis

Destiny Analysis is an exclusive chart which gives the practitioner the ability to assess the 'Soul' destiny or spiritual nature of an individual. This method works by converting the date and time of a person's birth information into the aforementioned chart, referred to as a Qi Men Destiny Chart. The 'Soul' destiny includes an individual's unique spiritual gifts and talents. It also identifies the nature and number of their guardian angels.

5) Spiritual Qi Men: The Mind, Body And Soul Awakening

Within the ancient art of Qi Men, the mind, body and soul of a human are all seen as forms of energy, referred to as Qi. All of these forms can be broken down into fragments allowing an individual to bring about their desired changes in life. Once deconstructed, these energies are plotted onto a chart, referred to as a Qi Men Chart. This unique Chart provides a Qi Men practitioner with the information and insight needed to understand how the Mind (Universal Energy) affects a person's attitude and thoughts. From there, the practitioner may predict how this translates into actions and eventually into day-to-day reality. Under the guidance of this influential chart, a practitioner can enlighten an individual how to control their mind and unique power (Universal Forces). This will give them a comprehensive awareness of their life's purpose as well as their individual vision. The strength and potency of this tool cannot be under-estimated.

The Brief Origins Of Qi Men Dun Jia

Not all readers will be familiar with the evolution or study of Qi Men Dun Jia. For this reason, we have provided further information on the origins of this intriguing art which still captivates and influences society today.

Incredibly, Qi Men Dun Jia can be traced back over 3,000 years through history. As we have seen, it was a crucial tool for Chinese warriors in ancient times and often compared to a game of cosmic chess. The chessboard in this situation is a 'Qi Men Chart' as we will see later in this section.

Here, we have broken down the translation of Qi Men Dun Jia to provide insight into its meaning.

'Qi' 奇 : Qi refers to an essence with an esoteric nature, with nuances of intrigue connected to the universal rules of the cosmos. (It should be noted that this differs from the Chinese word for energy which is Qi 氣).

'Men' 門 : Taken literally, this means 'door' or 'gate'.

'Dun' 遁: This is translated as 'hide' or 'escape to remain hidden'.

'Jia' 甲: This final part of the puzzle alludes to the first of the Ten Heavenly Stems. 'Jia' is also a coded reference to the General or Grand Marshal related to warfare.

When combined, Qi Men Dun Jia may be interpreted as 'Mysterious Doors Hiding Jia' a term which is not only cumbersome but misleading. Today, the more common translation, which is easier to grasp, is *'Mysterious Doors Escaping Technique'*.

Earlier we compared Qi Men Dun Jia to a game of cosmic chess which we will attempt to explain now. Readers familiar with the game will be aware that the overriding goal in chess is not only to protect the King (the centrepiece) but also ensure his progress and ultimate triumph.

With Qi Men, the goal is to either conceal the Jia or reveal its location in the Qi Men Chart. In this context 'Jia' indicates the idea of a Yong Shen 用神 (Useful God) in Qi Men Dun Jia.

As we have seen, the main use of Qi Men Dun Jia was in the forecasting and application of appropriate warfare strategies under the auspices of military leaders in ancient China. Iconic commanders including Jiang Ziya 姜子牙, Zhuge Liang 諸葛亮, Liu Bo Wen 劉伯溫,

Zhang Liang 張良 took full advantage of this metaphysical science. Qi Men Dun Jia not only had a proven track record when it came to securing victory for the Chinese army but allowed imperial Emperors to strengthen their rule across all of their territories.

Furthermore, Qi Men Dun Jia is a vital element of the 'Three Oracles'. Together with Da Liu Ren 大六壬 and Tai Yi Shen Shu 太乙神數, these three metaphysical arts are unrivalled throughout the history of Chinese metaphysics. As such, they are renowned as the legendary Three Oracle Methods of ancient China.

Throughout time, the imperial government – frequently in conjunction with their imperial astrologers – took full advantage of this methodology to forecast future events across an array of areas. These ranged from elements of time to events, people and space. If we are seeking a comparison in today's world, perhaps the essential role of technology in weather forecasts or the capricious stock market are two relevant examples.

Qi Men Dun Jia shares a number of traits with all of the disciplines discovered in Chinese Metaphysics, in addition to the Three Oracles, such as, the Ba Gua 八卦 attributes, the Five Elements 五行, the Heavenly Stems 天干 and Earthly Branches 地支, the He Tu 河圖 and Luo Shu 洛書, the Yin and Yang 陰陽. When compared to these disciplines, however, we can see that it is significantly more advanced. Typically, the standard systems deal only with the concepts of the Trinity of Luck – Heaven, Earth and Man Luck. Qi Men Dun Jia, on the other hand, enjoys an additional dimension, namely the Spirit Luck. This added tier incorporates universal energy, also known as 'spirit realm' as an integral part of its analysis.

As we have noted, Qi Men Dun Jia is now widely accessible to anyone wishing to study its intricate methods, but this was not always the case. In ancient times, its study was the exclusive reserve of the Chinese Emperor and the aristocracy of the day. With its knowledge denied to society at large it quickly became known as 'The Emperor's Exclusive Imperial Knowledge'. Thankfully, for avid students eager to learn about Qi Men Dun Jia, it is not so exclusive today.

With its seemingly infallible accuracy in predicting the outcome of events, Qi Men Dun Jia is the only member of the Three Oracles that remains influential today. Its proven track record of forecasting results of crucial situations has ensured its popularity among society's elite, including business leaders and politicians who apply it to events on both a daily and hourly basis when the need arises.

As the users of Qi Men Dun Jia continue to benefit from its ability, its pre-eminent position in the modern world is secure.

How Does Qi Men Dun Jia Work?

Referred to by its students and practitioners alike as Qi Men, this ancient art utilises a method to calculate the Qi Map relevant to a clearly defined moment in time and space. Traditionally, this technique of Qi Men has always allowed a practitioner to examine the Qi Map in detail. The practitioner can then accurately pinpoint the precise moment which gives an individual the perfect environment and conditions necessary for them to carry out a specific action and attain the result they desire.

In ancient China, Qi Men was invaluable in devising military tactics for generals wishing to understand the precise time and geographical location that would give them an unrivalled advantage and therefore guaranteed triumph over the opposing armies. If we put it in context, this literally saved the lives of countless Chinese troops. Prior to understanding the effect of Qi Men, military leaders often oversaw significant defeats and lost countless lives as a result of poor strategic decisions at vital moments. These might range from weak tactics to a lack of understanding of the terrain in which they were fighting and ineffective direction of their armies. Poor timing also affected their ability to achieve victory.

The structure of Qi Men is straightforward and easy to understand. Qi Men comprises of 1,080 Qi Men Maps, described as 'Qi Men Charts'. Each of these Charts encompasses 8 Directions which are represented by the eight directions seen on a compass. Within each section we find four components which describe the Heaven, Earth, Man and Spiritual influences relevant to that area. In other words, these represent the influences of time, space, events and spiritual elements of a defined event.

As time progressed, Qi Men was transformed from what was in essence a military weapon into the method of Forecasting that we see today (which is a divination of sorts). It is now widely used in predicting the outcomes of significant events and influencing decisions relating to a range of matters. As well as those already mentioned, these include career decisions, business negotiations, marriage, financial situations, finding missing people and even solving crimes.

Furthermore, such is the respect given to Qi Men, noted leaders of industry across Hong Kong and Taiwan take full advantage of its unique and rare abilities. This is often achieved by appointing Qi Men masters as consultancy and investment advisors, especially those with experience in the art of applying Qi Men.

I am often asked what exactly is the secret of Qi Men's success? Without doubt, it is its adaptability and flexibility in comparison with the range of alternative metaphysical disciplines. Furthermore during the Ming Dynasty, the Qi Men system has expanded to encompass applications of Feng Shui and Destiny Analysis which serves only to enhance its appeal. Whether used as a Forecasting, a Date Selection, a Destiny Analysis or a Feng Shui tools the fundamental principles for the use of Qi Men are identical.

For determined students who have taken the time to understand the basics of Qi Men, applying it is then relatively straightforward. In the pages of this book, I have continually attempted to simplify the Forecast application for all students.

To carry out your initial forecast, it is essential to first understand fundamental terms and basic concepts.

After you have familiarised yourself with this information, your next step is to turn to the pages in this book which will enable you to attain the forecast relevant to your specific event.

With the unique combination of Qi Men and the contents of this exclusive book, I am confident you will find it exceptionally straightforward to achieve.

Qi Men Formations – 100 Combinations

Students familiar with the study of Qi Men Dun Jia will know that it is renowned for its unique structures, called the Qi Men Formations 奇門格局.

Numerous structures exist within a Qi Men Chart but in terms of its practical use, the most popular and frequently applied is the 100 Combinations. Even novice students of Qi Men Dun Jia will note the presence of the 100 Combinations in every single Chart today.

These structures comprise of the 10 Heavenly Stems and 10 Earthly Stems, resulting in the 100 Combination Structures. Every single Palace of a Qi Men Dun Jia has both a Heavenly Stem and an Earthly Stem, which leads to the 100 Combination structures.

This book is dedicated to this extraordinary structure and explains each one of the 100 Combinations in detail in one exclusive resource.

As we have seen while exploring the evolution of Qi Men Dun Jia, it is a timeless metaphysical science, whose origins are rooted firmly in the history of ancient China. It is only through this evolution and development that we begin to understand the 100 Combinations.

You will note, for example, that each structure has a different name. This is due to the variety of individual masters who were involved in the development of Qi Men Dun Jia. Each of these revered practitioners understood this structure in their own unique way and through a difference experience.

To enable a straightforward application I have given you the most commonly used structure names throughout the book.

As you work through this book you will note the following format:

- First, you will see the traditional text of each individual combination.

- Next, in the second row you will find the rating which indicates immediately whether or not the structure is an auspicious one.

- The following row is the transliteration of the Chinese text. As students of Chinese will know, it is extremely difficult to provide a literal translation of the text. In my transliteration I have made every effort to provide the closest meaning possible to the original text. Having said that, there is still an abundance of vital information which is not captured by this method. To compensate for that, I have included the actual meaning of the text based on my extensive consulting experience in Qi Men Dun Jia and its practical application based on actual outcomes.

In the study of Qi Men Dun Jia, you will find four types of Charts, labelled Year, Month, Day and Hour respectively. All of these Charts contain the combinations appearing in each of the 9 Palaces.

This can be used in the 5 applications we noted earlier, namely:

- Forecasting

- Strategic Execution

- Feng Shui

- Destiny Analysis

- Mind, Body and Soul Awakening

It should be noted that the original texts were written based on Forecasting, therefore the description will advise the outcome for Forecasting. Students wishing to use this for Strategic Execution are advised to exercise their own individual judgement with some adjustment to reflect the activity under consideration. In this way you will achieve the results you seek.

How to Obtain Your Qi Men Chart for Analysis

You can plot your own Hour Chart using the **Joey Yap's Qi Men Dun Jia Ten Thousand Year Calendar**. In addition, to speed up the chart-plotting process, you can refer to the **Qi Men Dun Jia 540 Yang Structure Charts** and the **Qi Men Dun Jia 540 Yin Structure Charts** for the Hour Chart that has already been plotted for you.

All these books are available at
The Joey Yap Store at **http://store.joeyyap.com**.

How to Use this Book

Step 1
Plot the Hour Chart

The Qi Men analysis in this book is made based on the Qi Men Hour Chart. You must obtain the Hour Chart based on the hour of your reading. You can plot the Hour Chart manually (using the Qi Men Ten Thousand Year Calendar) or find a ready-made Hour Chart in one of the Qi Men 540 Hour Chart reference books mentioned earlier.

Step 2
Determine the Useful God for Analysis

There are four components in a Qi Men Chart: the 10 Stems, 9 Stars, 8 Deities and 8 Doors. As mentioned earlier, you need to plot an Hour Chart based on the Hour of the reading. From there, you need to study the Chart, identify the focus point or the Useful God as the fixed identification for each specific forecast.

Step 3
Analyze the Stem and Stem Interaction

After identifying the focus point in your Chart, get the Stem and Stem combination from this particular section and flip to the right page as you will find the forecast that matches your topic of discourse there.

Read the analysis provided and form your own judgment about the forecast based on your own topic of discourse.

Example 1

Ivan is eyeing on a potential investment deal but is unsure of the outcome. He decides to consult a Qi Men Chart for information to make a better investment decision. In this analysis, he wants to know the outcome of the investment and whether or not it is profitable to proceed. He makes a Qi Men analysis on March 15, 2012 at 7.30 pm.

Step 1
Plot the Hour Chart

The relevant Hour Chart is then obtained from the **Qi Men Dun Jia 540 Yang Structure Charts** book for March 15, 2012 at 7.30 pm.

Here's the Chart obtained by him:

Step 2
Determine the Useful God for Analysis

For money matters, Ivan knows that he needs to look at the Life Door as it represents profits and gains, which is suitable for his analysis. The Life Door is residing in the Southeast sector.

Step 3
Analyze the Stem and Stem Interactions

Next, Ivan studies the Southeast sector of the Qi Men Chart and notices that in that area, the Bing Heavenly Stem and the Wu Earthly Stem are residing there.

Since this is a Bing and Wu Stems combination analysis, he flips to Page 112 to obtain the forecast relating to his endeavour.

Here's the excerpt of his forecast:

天盤 **Heavenly Stem**	地盤 **Earthly Stem**
丙 *Bing* **Yang Fire**	**戊** *Wu* **Yang Earth**

Structure 格局	Flying Bird Fall into Cave 飛鳥跌穴
Rating 吉凶	Auspicious 吉
Classic Verse 十干剋應歌訣	飛鳥跌穴丙加戊，百事可行通天路
Transliteration 字譯	Where the Bing meets with Wu, it is known as the Flying Bird Fall into Cave formation. It is a highly auspicious formation indicating that life will progress smoothly.
Description 解說	Unexpected good fortunes will become abundant and good news is on its way. When coupled with concerted personal initiative and effort, the good fortunes from this formation will will dissolve any present quagmires and put one's life perfectly on track. The path is straight and clear and there are no obstacles to stop anyone from reaching for what the self will dream for.

For more specific outcome on his investment endeavour, he also checks the interactions between the Stem and Stem with the Door in the same Palace.

休 *Xiu* **Rest**	They say two heads are better than one. There is a person you know, or who you may meet, who shares your ambition, vision and drive. He/she is the key that will unlock your full potential and you should make the best of your relationship with this person by communicating your ambitions, goals and even sorry with them.. Think like a brave leader. Cultivate team spirit and do what you can to enhance morale in those around you and move boldly towards prosperity because what you desire can only be obtained with the help of others.
生 *Sheng* **Life**	Good tidings and good news is on the way. With a little more effort, you could turn the good into the great and really reach for the stars. Your problems will dissolve and the path ahead of you is clear. All you need to do is find that extra 10% within yourself and keep doing what is right and what is needed to be done. Success awaits you if you can push yourself just a little further. All the other elements are in place right now so stay on track
傷 *Shang* **Harm**	You will be blessed with above average luck as the Nobleman will be constantly present wherever you choose to go. This will help you get noticed as your progression along your chosen path in life with be smooth, steady and stable. Just be persistent and not be complacent at all times. Keep your eye on the main prize! Remember to avoid gossip or speculation as what goes around, comes around. Do what is right and needed to be done, not what is convenient right now.

From the forecasts obtained, Ivan is able to make a better decision. He knows that positive outcome can be expected from this investment activity. This is a very positive investment opportunity and Ivan will earn the desired gains from it.

Example 2

Anna's mother has been bedridden and her conditions seem to worsen even after a series of treatment. Anna wants to know whether this doctor is competent and has the right skill set to cure her mother's condition. She makes a forecast on February 6, 2014 at 3.30 pm.

Step 1
Plot the Hour Chart

The relevant Hour Chart is then obtained from the **Qi Men Dun Jia 540 Yang Structure Charts** book for February 6, 2014 at 3.30 pm.

Here's the Chart obtained by her:

Step 2
Determine the Useful God for Analysis

For health matters, Anna knows that she needs to check the Heavenly Heart as it represents the doctor or medical personnel giving the treatment, which is suitable for her analysis. The Heavenly Heart Deity is residing in the Southeast sector.

Step 3
Analyze the Stem and Stem Interactions

Next, Anna studies the Southeast sector of the Qi Men Chart and notices that in that area, the Wu Heavenly Stem and the Bing Earthly Stem are residing there.

Since this is a Wu and Bing Stems combination analysis, she flips to Page 170 to obtain the forecast relating to her endeavour.

Here's the excerpt of her forecast:

天盤 **Heavenly Stem**	地盤 **Earthly Stem**
戊 *Wu* **Yang Earth**	丙 *Bing* **Yang Fire**

Structure 格局	Green Dragon Returns 青龍返首
Rating 吉凶	Auspicious 吉
Classic Verse 十干剋應歌訣	青龍返首戊加丙，謀事多吉利，敗因迫墓刑
Transliteration 字譯	Where the Wu meets with Bing, it is known as the Green Dragon Returns formation. It denotes auspicious plans that end with severe punishment.
Description 解說	This formation portends positive outcomes and success in one's endeavors. There will be massive success for all plans implemented. Careers will flourish and business will gain in profits. Individuals who make plans at this time will see them advance just as they planned. However, if the formation goes through Grave or comes into collision with Striking Punishment, the results may turn out contrary to what was expected.

For more specific outcome on the health outlook, she also checks the interactions between the Stem and Stem with the Door in the same Palace.

休 *Xiu* **Rest**	You have probably gotten used to enjoying a stream of prosperity and living the good life. Don't worry because nothing is going to change drastically – thanks to your ongoing favourable luck. Whether you realize it or not, you have many loyal friends who would jump at the chance to help you out. So, if you need an extra pair of hands for help, don't hesitate to ask. Accepting help or gestures of goodwill from others also makes them happy.
生 *Sheng* **Life**	You are fortunate. There are many people who love and care for you. All you have to do is to accept these gifts from other graciously. Gratitude is very important and you will have Noble people and mentors always to support you. This kind of support is often all that is needed for true happiness. Whether the situation is good or bad, you will always land on your feet and enjoy long standing wealth, good relationships and a good reputation. Have some faith in yourself and don't worry. Whatever dreams you have in mind, just go for it.
傷 *Shang* **Harm**	An unlucky sign indeed. Not only do the things you desire just don't seem to come together in a way that benefits you but the situation is beyond your control. Even those who promised you their help is not able to deliver their promise and your dreams are unlikely to come true in the hostile circumstance anyways. Because of your tendencies to act before you think, you are unlikely to make the right decisions. You need to take time to gather the complete info and see the full picture before making decisions. Especially if it relates to money or investments. Do not make your decisions based on only just rumours.

Positive outlook can be expected for her mother's health conditions based on the two forecasts obtained. From this, she can tell that the doctor is capable of curing her mother. Given enough time and patience, a full recovery can be expected.

Example 3

Jessie wants to change her job. She was offered a good position by her friend who is working in another company. Jessie wants to know her career outlook if she accepted this offer. She makes her forecast on September 5, 2014 at 1.30 am.

Step 1
Plot the Hour Chart

The relevant Hour Chart is then obtained from the **Qi Men Dun Jia 540 Yin Structure Charts** book for September 5, 2014 at 1.30 am.

Here's the Chart obtained by her:

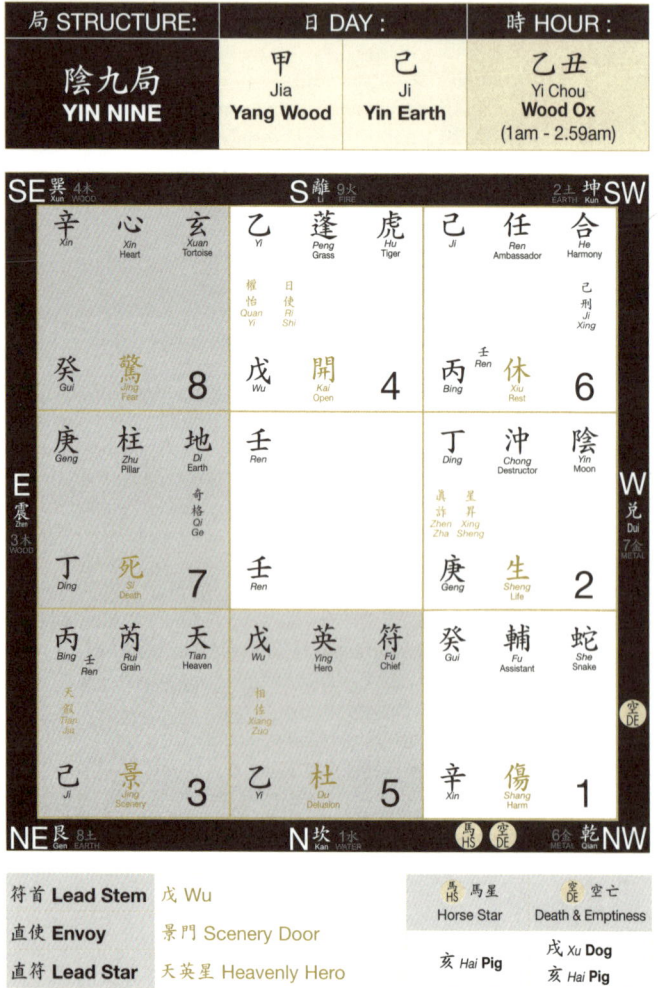

28 Qi Men Dun Jia The 100 Formations

Step 2
Determine the Useful God for Analysis

For professional matters, Jessie knows that she needs to check the Open Door as it represents career outlook, which is suitable for her analysis. The Open Door is residing in the South sector.

Step 3
Analyze the Stem and Stem Interactions

Next, Jessie studies the South sector of the Qi Men Chart and notices that in that area, the Yi Heavenly Stem and the Wu Earthly Stem are residing there. She also finds that the Hour Stem Palace is producing her Self Palace (Day Stem).

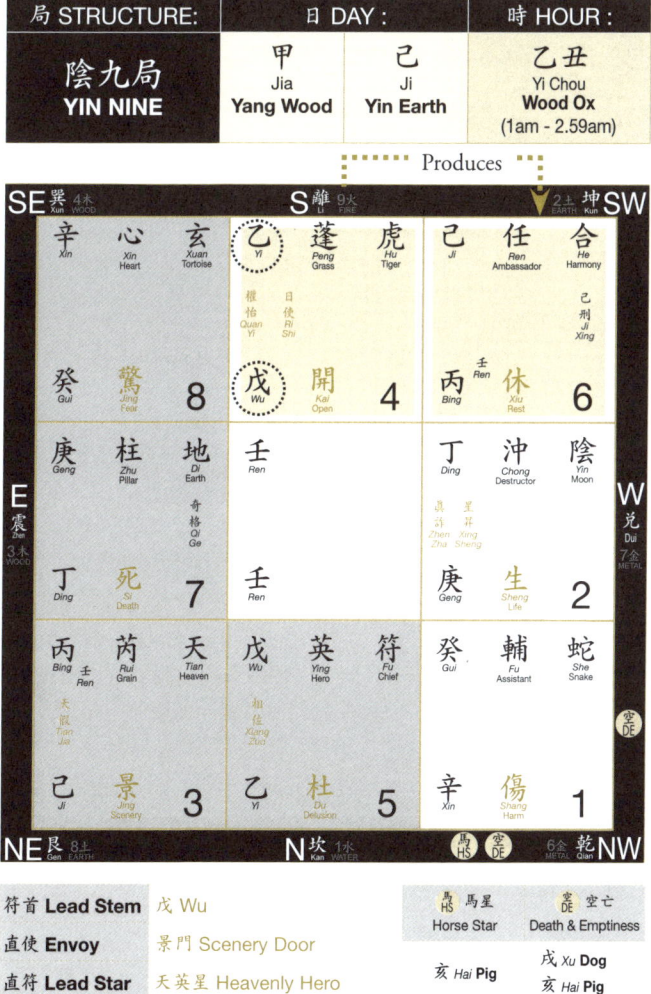

Since this is a Yi and Wu Stems combination analysis, she flips to Page 80 to obtain the forecast relating to her endeavour.

Here's the excerpt of her forecast:

天盤 Heavenly Stem	地盤 Earthly Stem
乙 *Yi* **Yin Wood**	戊 *Wu* **Yang Earth**

Structure 格局	Noble Enters Heavenly Door 奇入天門
Rating 吉凶	Moderate 半吉
Classic Verse 十干剋應歌訣	奇入天門 乙加戊，陰人事利，兇迫門無助
Transliteration 字譯	Where the Yi meets with Wu, it is known as the Noble Enters Heavenly Door formation. It denotes smooth execution of matters that requires discretion. The inauspicious Door indicates helplessness.
Description 解說	The Noble Enters Heavenly Door is an excellent formation for a person who wants to make elaborate schemes and stealth plans. A lot of people will be willing to offer monetary assistance but will do this secretively. The configuration is also excellent for those seeking enlightenment and other spiritual achievements. For individuals seeking to do some deep meditation and self-reflection, this configuration offers very ideal conditions. Although it favors the female, with the presence of Auspicious Qi Men Door, plans should be managed and completed with relative ease.

For more specific outcome on her career outlook, she also checks the interactions between the Stem and Stem with the Door in the same Palace.

死 *Si* **Death**	You will have no Nobleman luck. Without people around to encourage you in the first place or to congratulate you when you succeed – things will become a lot harder. You must rely entirely on your own strengths to stay motivated. You may owe people money. The only hope of things becoming better lies in your willingness to make the necessary changes because you aren't in a winning situation right now. You will need to systematize your work and learn how to control your finances properly. It is imperative to not dwell in unfruitful relationship matters.
驚 *Jing* **Fear**	Even though you may seem to get what you desire, but the troubles and burdens of success will take its tow on you. Be aware of some of the potential pitfalls and stay on track. Even if you have extra money, don't use your wealth to try and gain people's affection. You should also invest in and build genuine relationships with others in order to move ahead. A little sincerity will go a long way. Avoid participating in gossips or spreading rumors.
開 *Kai* **Open**	You are blessed and many others will be eager to help you. There are good mentors and friends out there. You must have a sense of gratitude for the help you get in life. Fame and fortune is on the cards for you as well. You will find yourself in the right place at the right time. You will also enjoy many successes in life. Don't forget that there will be others who are less fortunate. You can increase your luck by offering a helping hand and enriching others. Always start with the people who are close to you and this will keep the good things coming.

Since Hour Stem (denotes outcome of her analysis) produces the Day Stem (represents Self), Jessie can expect smooth proceedings and auspicious outlook in her new career. Good prospects can be expected for her new job role based on the two forecasts obtained.

QI MEN DUN JIA
THE
100 FORMATIONS

甲

Jia
Yang Wood

	Heavenly Stem		Earthly Stem
	甲 *Jia* **Yang Wood**		甲 *Jia* **Yang Wood**

Structure 格局	Forest Formation 雙木成林
Rating 吉凶	Moderate 半吉
Classic Verse 十干剋應歌訣	雙木成林甲加甲，伏吟閉塞靜守察。
Transliteration 字譯	Where the Jia meets with Jia, it is known as the Forest Formation. Known as a Fu Yin formation, it denotes blockage and obstruction.
Description 解說	Proactive individuals will shuffle through various challenges. It works well for the host and a visitor to create a favorable approach. The hands will do what one's heart asks them to do. One's leadership potential will be at an all-time peak. The enhanced leadership will result in tremendous success and will lead to much happiness. It only works for those who are active in searching for a solution though. The presence of a negative Star and Door will symbolize arrogant hostility with a sense of refusal, thus potentially creating a real risk in the field.

The 8 Doors Analysis:

The following evaluates the effects of **Jia** 甲 and **Jia** 甲 with each Door.

休 *Xiu* **Rest**	You do not have to worry about any issues in your life. Sudden fluctuations in the fortune of your family's social matters will not occur, and this is because this combination assures that your family will maintain a solid reputation in the community. This is favourable to both the host as well as the guest and everything will fare well in all your social endeavours. Rest assured that your guests will be in good hands are your leadership abilities increase under this combination. That being said, this combination does favour the active more than the passive. As long as you are actively engaged in your community and in all manner of social situations, fortune will be in your favour and all will fare well for you.
生 *Sheng* **Life**	Prosperity and good fortune will be christened to you under this combination. Your social prominence in your community and possibly on a larger scale as well will continue to grow and benefit greatly, bringing good reputation to your name. This combination is highly auspicious as it indicates that you are a go-getter who will be able to achieve whatever your heart desires. In the case of social situations, your fortune will be further elevated and as long as you are actively pursue what you want, you can be assured to always be able to achieve success.
傷 *Shang* **Harm**	Many difficulties will come and bring chaos to your life at this time as this happens to be a rather inauspicious configuration. You and members of your family may experience issues with gaining the trust of your peers, colleagues, loved ones, or elders. This could very well lead to a permanent damage of your social reputation. That being said, this configuration does allow for the chance of redemption. As long as you are active in working hard to maintain your place in your community, it is possible that you might be able to surpass your trials. However, with this negative door present, stubborn and inflexibility is also in place, indicating that you will have a very difficult time even if you tried to rise above your challenges.
杜 *Du* **Delusion**	Instability may plague your social life as this configuration is an indicator of difficulty and strife. Unfortunately, it is like that you will be put through many trials and it will be truly be a test of your will as you struggle to fight against it. The good news is: it is possible that the problems you encounter are very minimal in nature and do not have prolonged effect. If you are personally able to harness your leadership ability and be hardworking in meeting your challenges, it is very possible that all will fare well in the end.

奇門遁甲十干格局篇

Jia

	景 *Jing* **Scenery**	Changes are going to occur in your social life that will help you rise up through the social ladder of society. Great prominence in social status will ensue as this combination works to bring you more and more opportunities to achieve popularity in your community and gain the trust of others. This is most auspicious for you as it indicates that you will finally be able to achieve what your heart desires and without great difficulty. Your leadership will shine through at this point and it will bring you great success in all your social endeavours.
	死 *Si* **Death**	The Death Door may bring about great suffering to you at this time. This will cause you to have a severely weakened spirit and thus negatively impact your social life. In your physical interactions with your community, it is likely that a physical attack will occur and cause harm to your personal wellbeing. It may be the result of a power tussle, and this combination indicates an increase in stubbornness and inflexibility. You will have to go through countless obstacles, and there is virtually no hope for you to escape these trying circumstances.
	驚 *Jing* **Fear**	You will have to deal with a shaky social reputation, as this combination brings about difficulty to the maintenance of your social standing in society. You are going to have to deal with people in your life individually regarding many problems, and if you do not deal with them properly, you will only aggravate the situation and cement your negative social status. Try to tone down your stubbornness and inflexibility when dealing with these people, otherwise your bad luck with overtake the situation and drive you further into the ground. This combination is inauspicious because it indicates bad fortune.
	開 *Kai* **Open**	You will be blessed with good fortune and increased luck in your endeavours. This luck will boost your place in the social world and you will finally get the chance to use your leadership activities to bring about a change in the lives of others. Great rewards await you and you will have the opportunity of fraternising with a great many successful and influential people. As long as you hold steady to your current path and do not sway from righteousness, everything will fare well for you.

天盤 **Heavenly Stem**	地盤 **Earthly Stem**
甲 *Jia* **Yang Wood**	乙 *Yi* **Yin Wood**

Structure 格局	Green Dragon Combines Spirit 青龍合靈
Rating 吉凶	Moderate 半吉
Classic Verse 十干剋應歌訣	青龍合靈甲加乙，人事隨門斷凶吉
Transliteration 字譯	Where the Jia meets with Yi, it is known as the Green Dragon Combines Spirit formation. This is auspicious but denotes a possible occurrence of adversity with human-error caused circumstances. The Door will determine the final (positive or negative) outcome.
Description 解說	This is a unique mixture as it symbolizes meticulousness and resourcefulness in the use of available resources and the people one trusts in. It indicates a lot of positive energy and a great deal of strength. One will gain an abundance of strength during this time and will continue to maintain it. In spite of this, the Door is inauspicious and there is a likelihood that the energies that come from the door will become twice as inauspicious as they once were.

The 8 Doors Analysis:

The following evaluates the effects of **Jia** 甲 and **Yi** 乙 with each Door.

	休 *Xiu* **Rest**	Your reputation and credibility as a person will continue to be firm and secure for as long as this combination is in place. This is because this configuration ensures a steady and constant social life that is free from any sudden and unwanted fluctuations. Positive energy will permeate in your life and this will give you motivation to let go of problems of the past. You have the opportunity now to look ahead to the future and enjoy life as you are being rewarded for how you have persisted in the past against challenges.
	生 *Sheng* **Life**	Expect nothing but good fortune for you during this auspicious time. You will continue to grow from strength to strength and become more positive about life. This will help you with your social prominence as you become an important member of your community. New opportunities will arise and help you towards bigger pursuits. You will need planning and foresight to achieve success, and you will be helped in this aspect by good advisers and sincere friends. Your path ahead is very bright and you can expect a good outcome in the long run.
	傷 *Shang* **Harm**	This combination is extremely undesirable and will bring a negative social impact on your family. You will be viewed by people in your life in unfavourable light and be considered to be social pariahs. Permanent damage to your social life will ensue. You will try to appear as calm and unaffected as possible, but the truth is you are experiencing unthinkable inner turmoil. This is worsened by your perpetual bad luck. The only thing you can do is try to look at yourself in a better luck and not listen to what others say about you. If you do not do this for yourself, your path towards hopelessness will be as inevitable as your bad fortune.
	杜 *Du* **Delusion**	Socially, you will experience many ups and downs. These trials will directly challenge your reputation and credibility as a person. Your decisions do not seem to ever end in good result. You have a vision for how you want things to work out, but for some reason you never seem to be able to get what you want. Everything is out of your control, which is an indicator of bad luck in your life right now. It is probably best for you to just let things happen and go with the flow, as this configuration is inauspicious for you and little to nothing can be done about it.

景
Jing
Scenery

You will be surrounded by positive energy and this motivates you to want to do more for your community. This will help you experience growth in you social status that will be spurred on by good energy and fortune. Your wisdom is using resources will elevate your position in your community and you will encounter much success in all your endeavours, as everyone you know supports you and trusts you greatly. They will regard you highly as a respectable person of impeccable reputation, and this is likely to be an impression that sticks for a long time.

死
Si
Death

Great suffering will come upon you during this time. You will not have any spirit to challenge these circumstances and may even become physically weak. You are completely demoralised overall and do not stand a chance against this negative fate. It is likely that the situation in your everyday life will deteriorate very quickly and all chances of harmony will be jeopardised. Relationships between spouses are especially at risk and it will be very difficult for you to move on. However, if you do not do anything about moving on, you will be stuck in the past forever and a better tomorrow will not arrive.

驚
Jing
Fear

You will have many conflicts with people in your life and you will face many trials in trying to reconcile with your community. This configuration is inauspicious for you, signifying sudden and unavoidable mishaps occurring to you that will bring your reputation down and tarnish your image. You are doomed to fail at most things you attempt in life, especially your career. It is simply a case of bad fortune, and there nothing you can do to change it. It is advisable that you avoid all drastic changes in your life, from career to relationships, to avoid negative implications that can have irreversible effects on your psyche and image.

開
Kai
Open

Good fortune will bless you and with this on your side, you will thrive in your social environment and continue to experience life-changing personal growth. Great improvements in your life will begin to happen at this point, and you must harness all the positive energy you can to make it happen, otherwise the opportunity will slip away for good. Good tidings and good news are on their way and your previous problems will all soon dissolve. The path ahead of you has been paved nicely for you and all you have to do is follow your heart, for this is a most favourable configuration that will bring you great luck.

奇門遁甲十干格局篇

甲
Jia

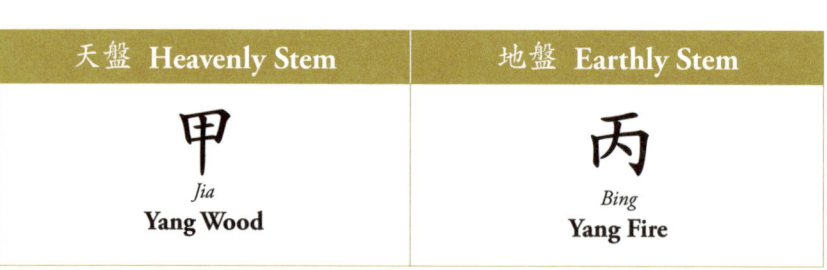

天盤 **Heavenly Stem**	地盤 **Earthly Stem**
甲 *Jia* **Yang Wood**	**丙** *Bing* **Yang Fire**

Structure 格局	Green Dragon Returns 青龍返首
Rating 吉凶	Auspicious 吉
Classic Verse 十干剋應歌訣	青龍返首甲加丙，吉多兇因迫墓刑
Transliteration 字譯	Where the Jia meets with Bing, it is known as the Green Dragon Returns formation. This is highly auspicious but the effect may be reduced with presence punishment and/or if this combination enters Graveyard.
Description 解說	This configuration is highly fascinating. It is symbolic of good results for all sorts of actions and can adjust negative situations to become good ones. Obstacles will become opportunities and one's enemies will become his or her greatest friends. However, in case the combination falls on shelters it will indicate Entering Grave 入墓 or Striking Punishment. This formation can be quite unfortunate. It can be interpreted to mean that plans will backfire and any help will be overly delayed.

The 8 Doors Analysis:

The following evaluates the effects of **Jia** 甲 and **Bing** 丙 with each Door.

休 *Xiu* **Rest**	You can be assured of utmost security in all your endeavours and this will contribute to your reputation being guaranteed at all times. This will be a very calm and harmonious period in your life, where all is smooth sailing without any bumps. You have great fortune at your side and this helps you to achieve whatever your heart desires. At this point in your life, you are most likely to get ahead of your competitors or opponents, so now is the best time to start planning out how to do so! It is likely that you will encounter someone you can trust who will become a mentor of sorts to use. Use this opportunity to get the most out of his advice in how to approach your career and social life.
生 *Sheng* **Life**	Prosperity is in your hands with the good fortune that this favourable configuration brings. Your social prominence will continue growing and your influence multiplying. It is likely that you will develop the ability of turning your enemies into friends and even assets in your daily life. In addition to this, you probably already have a stream of loyal friends willing to jump at the chance of assisting you in anything you wish. Keep these friends close to your heart and always remember their good will, for they are the sort of friends who will be there for you no matter what. Accept their help willingly and without worry, because allowing them to help you will only make them happier.
傷 *Shang* **Harm**	This is an extremely unfavourable configuration and it is regrettable that bad fortune will shape much of your fate during this time. Your image will be permanently tarnished by the negative events that occur during this time when your fortune is at its lowest point. No matter how you try to reverse your situation, it is likely that your plans constantly backfire and no help comes to you. You are plagued by constant dilemmas and are unable to make important decisions in your life, bringing your overall progress to an unbeatable standstill. Opportunities will keep passing you by as you watch helplessly, too hesitant to grab them because of your continuing bad luck.
杜 *Du* **Delusion**	You will be hampered in all your endeavours by shaky circumstances and be thrown into a never-ending circle of chaos. All you do is worry about what is going to happen next but you do not have the direction to know how to proceed from there and right your situation. All you can do is worry and let anxiety take over your life. You find it difficult to trust those around you and are unsure of how they can assist you in this tough time. It is important that you take some time to truly self-reflect, otherwise you will not be able to pull yourself out of this hole.

奇門遁甲十干格局篇

Jia

景 *Jing* **Scenery**	Personal development and social growth is something you are likely to experience at this rather fortunate time. The conditions have been balanced out for you and it seems like the ideal time to start harnessing some of your potential and climb the social ladder. Those you admire will very willingly offer advice and support in all your endeavours. This will make you very happy but you must remember to focus and keep your head in the game. Slacking will not bring you any good fortune and you must continue to work hard at bringer yourself higher in society.
死 *Si* **Death**	This combination is an extremely undesirable one and it is very likely that you will suffer greatly under these circumstances. You may experience physical assault at the hands of someone who is trying to bring harm to you. You encounter obstacles and difficulty in everything you try to do and luck is clearly not on your side. Your personal growth is hampered by this and you are unsure of where you stand in your community. It may be wise to start getting involved in charity work to help make up for all the misfortune you are experiencing. It will make you feel better about yourself and give you a sense of purpose.
驚 *Jing* **Fear**	Personal conflicts with others are a feature of this configuration. You will have to know how to properly deal with these problems without further jeopardising your reputation in the community. If you end up losing something, you can never recover it again. This kind of irreversible damage to your person is highly undesirable and you must do everything in your power to be as calm and collected as possible always. You will be disheartened time and time again by the way things keep falling out of place and so it is important for you to keep trying to look at the brighter side of things, lest you completely lose hope in yourself.
開 *Kai* **Open**	This is a time of great fortune for you. At this point, it is wise for you to seize this once in a lifetime opportunity and do as many good deeds as possible to secure your reputation in your community. This is a period of unprecedented opportunities for you. They come all at once and you have so many options to choose from. Prosperity is in your hands and if you act on your desires, you will attain everything you want. You will be able to turn any obstacle into an opportunity and use it against misfortune.

天盤 **Heavenly Stem**	地盤 **Earthly Stem**
甲 *Jia* **Yang Wood**	丁 *Ding* **Yin Fire**

Structure 格局	Wood Fire Brilliance Formation 木火通明
Rating 吉凶	Auspicious 吉
Classic Verse 十干剋應歌訣	青龍耀明甲加丁，謁見貴人名利行，迫墓招惹是非應。
Transliteration 字譯	Where the Jia meets with Ding, it is known as the Wood Fire Brilliance formation. This denotes a visit from a Noble person and the opportunities to achieve heightened fame and wealth. Where there are negative Doors or if the combination enters Grave, beware of troubles ahead.
Description 解說	The Wood Fire Brilliance Formation can be interpreted to mean that one will meet and receive assistance from very noble people. This is the most opportune time to ask for the help that one has always desired. The combination also portends good outcomes in one's career and academia pursuits. Success in the academics and a career will be followed by fame. This is the best configuration for one to immerse themselves in studies and research. However, if the Formation falls on Grave 墓 location, all the positive benefits mentioned above will be rendered null.

The 8 Doors Analysis:

The following evaluates the effects of **Jia** 甲 and **Ding** 丁 with each Door.

休 *Xiu* **Rest**	You will be in a good state at this time with nothing to worry about. In addition to being secure in all your endeavours, you are also prone to receiving help from others who are experts in whatever field you are having trouble with. Even if you do have slight problems, you have nothing to worry about because as long as you find the right mentor, you will be in good hands. This mentor will help you through whatever obstacles in life and his advice will greatly benefit you forever. This mentor will help you develop new skills and abilities and improve at them until you become a better, newer person.
生 *Sheng* **Life**	This configuration will bring you excellence in everything you do and become a person who is greatly respected in the community for your brilliance and prosperity. Whether it be related to career, academics, or the pursuit of fame, you will successful under this most favourable configuration. You have a very bright future as all the right people are able to notice your talents. Do not be afraid to flaunt what makes you special. Once you have caught the attention of those who matter, you will be propelled up the ranks in life and land in a secure spot of upstanding reputation. Happiness and success is just around the corner for you.
傷 *Shang* **Harm**	You may never recover from the lasting negative effects of this configuration. It is regrettable, but you will not be able to do anything to match up against this horrid case of bad fortune. At this point in your life, most of your friends will seem to desert you and you will at a lost as to how you are supposed to deal with your situation. You keep trying to seek help from people you thought would step in, but unfortunately they seem to turn their backs on you. You must rely on yourself now and figure out a way to get back on your feet without needing the assistance of others. If you do not do this, you will only wallow in constant despair and suffering with no hope of resurfacing.
杜 *Du* **Delusion**	Huge obstacles will emerge in your life and you will feel small and helpless against them. But all is not lost. As long as you are able to think of smart ways to circumvent the problem, you can be safe for a while. This configuration is still considered unfavourable so you will eventually have to face the negative effects, but the good news is you can prepare yourself for whatever it is. All you need to do is remain as calm as possible and always use your rationale and reasoning against misfortune. If seeking help from others will help to comfort you, then it is something you must do in order to keep yourself level-headed and fit to take on your challenges.

46 Qi Men Dun Jia - The 100 Formations

景 *Jing* **Scenery**	This configuration signifies an upcoming change in your life where you might finally have the chance to prove yourself to those who have always doubted you. In both your working and academic life, you will experience immense improvement that will finally place you among the best in your circle. You should use this opportunity to establish close relationships with important members of your society so that when the time comes, you can rely on their expert assistance. At this time in your life, you will realise your potential to lead, and whatever you do from here on out will mark a different path in your life that is headed towards success and happiness.	奇門遁甲十干格局篇
死 *Si* **Death**	You will start to lose sight of who you are, and your goals seem unreachable and distant. Under this configuration, your goals will become a blur and you will be plunged into darkness. Solitude will envelop you and even as you try to do good things with your life, a dark force will keep pushing you back in. You will lose something you consider very dear and this will lead to possible depression. You must remember all the good times before this to avoid this happening. Keep fond memories close to your heart and dwell on those memories when the going gets tough. If you are able to hold out for long enough, you can avoid being irreparably damaged by these circumstances.	甲 Jia
驚 *Jing* **Fear**	You will not be able to keep good relationships with people close to you. Falling outs will occur and this will affect your home life, work life, and academic life. You will not be able to focus on daily activities or long term goals. It is advisable that you let it go and move on. The people that you come into conflict with may not be worth keeping if losing them only makes you so upset. You can try looking for new friends and seeing where that takes you. If you dwell too long and too often on the people that you have lost, you will only be compelled to do something rash and further damage your reputation.	
開 *Kai* **Open**	This is a most favourable configuration that will bring you great happiness in your everyday life. Good fortune will help you in all you daily activities and boost you forward in any long term goals you are chasing. You will have the courage to ask for assistance and be lucky enough to receive the exact help you are looking for. With all this in place, you will secure a position as a formidable member of society and have a reputation for being prosperous and generous. If you are hardworking enough, it is possible for this pattern of great fortune to continue for some time.	

奇門遁甲十干格局篇

Jia

天盤 **Heavenly Stem**	地盤 **Earthly Stem**
甲 *Jia* **Yang Wood**	戊 *Wu* **Yang Earth**

Structure 格局	Shinning Green Dragon Formation 青龍明耀
Rating 吉凶	Moderate 半吉
Classic Verse 十干剋應歌訣	-
Transliteration 字譯	This formation denotes the meeting of two dragons. The first is Jia and the second is Wu, which is sometimes also known as the Lead Stem Jia. It is a highly favorable formation where all endeavors are favorable and good fortune is at hand.
Description 解說	During the Shining Green Dragon Formation, talent and expertise will be awarded. The combination is also a sign that one is headed for a great leadership role. One will have lots of charisma, influence and the potential to gain more followers. All the resources required to accomplish this will be readily available to the individual. However, if this formation happens to get into the Emptiness or Graveyard, there is a high possibility that these pursuits will be unsuccessful. Lonesomeness will result and will be accompanied by a lack of support from all quarters.

The 8 Doors Analysis:

The following evaluates the effects of **Jia** 甲 and **Wu** 戊 with each Door.

休 *Xiu* **Rest**	This configuration indicates that as a result of your good leadership, you will gain many followers and become a person of unchallenged respectability. Your influence will range far and wide and your reputation will be secure for years to come. It may take some time to happen, but your journey will be a peaceful and easy one. Take a moment to reflect on all the hard work you spent into getting this far in life. Let it be a constant reminder to you that nothing comes easily without diligence and a little bit of luck, as it is important that you not let your success get to your head, lest you become too cocky for your own good.
生 *Sheng* **Life**	Your talents will finally be recognised and put to good use, bringing you up in society and giving you the reputation you need to secure your social status. You will prove yourself to all who doubted you and they will now become your followers. Your social influence is so strong that people are now coming to you to seek advice. Bear in mind that whatever you say to them will have a lasting profound effect on all their life decisions. It should be your goal to help them be as successful as you are. One day, you will rewarded again for the help you have given them, and they will be living testaments to your generosity and skills.
傷 *Shang* **Harm**	Bad luck will plague you at this time in your life and unfortunately, you will not receive any moral support from those you thought to be your friends. In a way, this will help you to weed out people you initially thought were genuine. This is quite possibly the only positive aspect of this configuration. You will spend your days worrying and being paranoid about what other ill is going to befall you and you will not have time to deal with any of the immediate challenges you currently face. Because you neglect your immediate problems, you reap the effects immediately and this greatly weakens your spirit.
杜 *Du* **Delusion**	You will be unsuccessful in all your pursuits, particularly that of social status. You will try very hard to get a place in society as someone respectable, but you will always be turned down or shunned. You can try to let this goal rest for a while first to let tensions calm down and pick it up again at a later time. Use your rest time to re-evaluate how you approach problems in life. Chances are, you are far too confrontational for your own good. You need to exercise discretion and learn to control your temper. Even if you are not a temperamental person, it is likely that you have some repressed emotions that contribute to your constant failure in life.

奇門遁甲十干格局篇

甲 Jia

景 *Jing* **Scenery**	Leadership is one of your finer qualities and now is the time for it to finally shine. Previously, it was overshadowed by more irrelevant talents due to your own mismanagement of your resources, but under this configuration, you will have the wisdom of letting your best trait show. The charisma you are able to demonstrate draws many people to you and they will admire you for your confidence and vision. It is important that you do not let this trait come off as arrogance, for you want your talent to be sustainable instead of a flash in the pan.	
死 *Si* **Death**	Utter loneliness will consume you. Your friends and family are nowhere to be found, and you will suffer from the solitude you have been condemned to. You have no support to face your challenges, and this crippling isolation makes you question everything you have ever known about yourself. You no longer see any opportunity in improvement, and instead resign to letting misfortune take its toll. The best you can do is stick to your guns and be courageous in this dark time. Even though constant failure is sure to bring you down, you must remember that there is always a way out, and it is best to be patient and wait.	
驚 *Jing* **Fear**	During this time, your relationships will suffer and you will lose support from those you trust. That being said, not everything is doomed, as you have the chance to show your potential alone. Let this be a lesson that you cannot always depend on others to pull you through tough times. Sometimes, you are the only person who can do anything for yourself. While you will suffer deeply for your losses, you can still turn fate around by keeping your mind focused on your goals. If you want your reputation to remain intact, it is good for you to proceed with your plans and not allow any of your external conflicts affect the way you make decisions.	
開 *Kai* **Open**	You are a great leader of immeasurable charisma and your natural wit and charm draws people to you like moths to a flame. You are a captivating person of vast influence and your social status is marked by great personal achievement and personal relationships with society's best. Resources and help is always at your fingertips because you are connected to all the right industries and networks. Try to keep a level head and prepare for the future where unseen circumstances may try to keep you down. Your success must be sustainable and you need to be careful about how arrogant you are, lest you turn away true friends.	

天盤 **Heavenly Stem**	地盤 **Earthly Stem**
甲 *Jia* **Yang Wood**	己 *Ji* **Yin Earth**

Structure 格局	Nobleman Enters Prison 貴人入獄
Rating 吉凶	Inauspicious 凶
Classic Verse 十干剋應歌訣	貴人入獄甲加己，公私百事全不吉
Transliteration 字譯	Where the Jia meets with Ji, it is known as the Nobleman Enters Prison formation. It denotes that all work and private endeavours are unfavourable.
Description 解說	During this formation, there will be an evident lack of assistance from one's superiors and mentors. This configuration will not augur well with anyone's goals. Those who might attempt to assist will be faced by un-mitigable difficulties and challenges. Any plans and engagements one might have planned during this formation might come to naught. Additionally, any backup plans that one sets up will backfire irredeemably. One should expect difficulties in certain projects. Superiors will give misleading commands that will aggravate the situation and amplify the negative streak.

The 8 Doors Analysis:

The following evaluates the effects of **Jia** 甲 and **Ji** 己 with each Door.

休 *Xiu* **Rest**	It seems that you have missed the boat for your chance at success. It is not every day that one can be exposed to so many exciting new opportunities but sadly, you did not have enough luck to catch such opportunities. You may have the talents needed to move forward, but without the opportunities, you end up just being average in all your endeavours. If you want to move forward, you need to start gaining more experience and preparing for the future, where it is likely that more opportunities will come your way. If you prepare enough, when that time finally comes, you will be not miss it again and instead be able to harness your full potential.
生 *Sheng* **Life**	You have been putting in a lot of effort and sincerity to get ahead in your life, but sadly those around you do not appreciate you gestures and instead find ways to do things behind your back. Through this experience, you realise that you have been associating with a lot of petty people with low character. Luckily, a few people as sincere as yourself are able to see through the hullabaloo surrounding these traitors. These genuine people ally themselves with you and you are able to become great friends with them. With their help, you can slowly learn to ignore the people who betray you, but most importantly you learn how to choose your friends.
傷 *Shang* **Harm**	This configuration foresees that you will be threatened by an individual and spend your days afraid that he is going to harm you. You won't have any support from those you respect. This will contribute to feelings of aloneness, and you end up thinking that the whole world is against you. Even if you do find people who are willing to support you and help you through this tough time, it is likely that they will only meet with unfavourable circumstances as a result of helping you. You are like a harbinger of misfortune at this time and most people want to avoid you. At this point, you are going to feel like you have nowhere to go and no one to go to.
杜 *Du* **Delusion**	Your endeavours are not going to go through as planned. You will have spent the last few weeks thinking that all is well, but with this configuration in place, things will suddenly grind to a halt and you will not be able to continue with your goals. Do not expect success in any task you undertake. It is better to be cynical from the start than to have your hopes crushed mercilessly. This way, you can maintain your pragmatism and plan smarter for the future. Prepare for failure and be careful to not let your emotions get the better for you.

景 *Jing* **Scenery**	Promises made to you in the past will be broken. As a result, you will find it difficult to trust those around you and especially your superiors, who do not seem to be able to give proper instructions or guidance. Unexpected setbacks will keep occurring to hamper you from rising above the occasion. You trust those who only want to use you and this only further suppresses your abilities to be the best you can be. These people only weaken your spirit and drain you of your motivation, so it is best for you to avoid them at all costs, especially if they are your colleagues or if they are traitors simply masquerading as friends.	
死 *Si* **Death**	A severe lack of motivation and connection with the world around you will bring you great unhappiness at this time. You are feeling isolated and nothing seems to be able to snap you out of your trance-like discontentment with life. You will not be able to succeed in anything in your life. Your general lacking of spiritual wellbeing makes it difficult for you to rise against the petty challenges that keep trying to take you down. You have no choice but to assume defeat and give up. Do not let this difficult situation push you over the edge and cause you to succumb to knee-jerk reactions that result in rash decisions. These rash decisions will only make things worse for you and they give others a bad impression of your personality.	
驚 *Jing* **Fear**	It seems that many people are suddenly holding grudges against you and for that reason, many things do not go your way. You come across roadblocks that are mostly social in nature and this makes you paranoid to meet new people. You cannot catch a break and you end up developing ill feelings towards everyone in general. However, the fact is sometimes things just cannot change. Try you best to not make hasty decisions or be affected by those around you who seem to be intentionally trying to take you down. Take a deep breath before responding and show them that you are better than they are.	
開 *Kai* **Open**	Despite your natural talents and rather smooth-sailing life, you still stumble across problems at this time due to the fact that this configuration indicates that superiors who are incompetent will greatly affect you. As they are your superiors, you have no choice but to listen to them and respect their opinion even though you find their words to be highly suspect. You are unable to trust them because you know better, but it is advisable that you not confront them and just go with the flow. They are after all, of a higher ranking than you are, and if you constantly disrespect them, you are only making things more difficult for yourself.	

奇門遁甲十干格局篇

甲 Jia

天盤 **Heavenly Stem**	地盤 **Earthly Stem**
甲 *Jia* **Yang Wood**	庚 *Geng* **Yang Metal**

Structure 格局	Leader Flying Palace 值符飛宮
Rating 吉凶	Inauspicious 凶
Classic Verse 十干剋應歌訣	值符飛宮甲加庚，吉事不吉凶更增，莫問財病人地更
Transliteration 字譯	Where the Jia meets with Geng, it is known as the Leader Flying Palace formation. This diminishes any positive events. When forecasting wealth and health, the outcome will be undesirable.
Description 解說	With the Leader Flying Palace Configuration, events will take a turn for the worse. Auspicious matters will become elusive at the last minute and continue to crumble into pieces. As the situation grows worse, one will start feeling helpless. The power tussles experienced during this period will make one to lose authority and inherent rights. Rivals will appear to gain strength and momentum. Challenges are springing up from the most unimaginable quarters. The feelings of fear and anxiety become amplified and anything that was auspicious is suddenly rigged with doubts and hesitation.

The 8 Doors Analysis:

The following evaluates the effects of **Jia** 甲 and **Geng** 庚 with each Door.

休 *Xiu* **Rest**	Your rivals all seem to gain up on you and challengers emerge everywhere trying to take from you what is yours. Do not be too wary. While they are formidable opponents, you should not lose your cool because it is the same as admitting defeat. Naturally, you feel anxious about this, and it seems like you are unable to do anything about this problem. But always remember that it is not your brain alone that gives you success, it is also your spirit. Surround yourself with well-meaning people and draw inspiration off them. Challenge your opponents respectfully and give them a good fight, and do not let minor failure take you down.
生 *Sheng* **Life**	Up to this point, it seems that things are all going well for you. That being said, things start to become murkier and you begin losing your confidence. Your luck is unstable under this configuration, and you may have to go through an indefinite waiting period before you begin regaining your insight into yourself and your goals. This will not be a smooth journey for you and you will feel like giving up the mission entirely a few times. But you need to remember that with life rewards those who are patient and perseverant. If you can exercise these virtues sufficiently, it is likely that you will eventually get out of your murky spot.
傷 *Shang* **Harm**	Your situation in life becomes so bad that it seems like you have hit rock bottom. You genuinely believe the worst has come and that your entire life was just a nosedive into this pit of failure. The world seems to be closing in you, leaving you unable to catch your breath as you scramble to pick up the pieces. Overwhelmed by absolute defeat, you resign all your efforts as you cannot possibly believe that anything good can come out of your work. Nothing seems auspicious anymore, and all your good fortune has been spent. Now is the time for you to reap all your bad fortune.
杜 *Du* **Delusion**	All your endeavours will fail and you will be unable to correct the situation, no matter how you try. The fact is that fortune is just not in your favour at this point. You may think that sheer hard work and genuine intentions will help, but it is naïve to think that can match up against bad fortune. No matter what you do, unexpected glitches just keep occurring that drag you down. Tireless, you will try and try again but this is dangerous because you will overexert yourself and end up putting yourself in bad physical condition. It is not worth it to do so much and get so little in return, especially when you are doomed to fail anyway.

景
Jing
Scenery

You have to be very careful about your rivals as they are gaining power and will soon topple you. Up till now, you have been shining in your role and showcasing all your abilities. The arrival of your true opponents will set you back and turn the tables on you. Helplessness will cloud your judgment at this point but it is important to remember that everyone has their ups and downs. There is no such thing as eternal happiness of success. Everyone needs to fight for their position in life and if you remember this long enough, you will learn to see these obstacles as stepping stones and learning steps.

死
Si
Death

At this trying time, you are alone to face your troubles and it seems like others do not really care about your strife. The feelings of fear and anxiety that consume will overwhelm you and you feel utter helplessness. Nothing is auspicious for you from this point onwards and you cannot even begin to work out how you want to tackle your problems. You do not have clear vision of how you want your future to look like and all seems lost to you. You face a difficult road full of bumps and twists and it will prove to be a difficult drive. If you do make full use of your emotional faculties, you may just break down and cause irreparable damage to yourself.

驚
Jing
Fear

You are at a foggy stand when it comes to your relationships. No one is keeping you updated about any progresses and you feel lost and ignored. Whether or not people are intentionally ignoring you is not clear, but the fact is you do not feel appreciated or empowered. You are left at a standstill, wondering what your place is in life. People do not seem to recognise you for all that you have done for them and their lack of appreciation brings you crippling self-consciousness. Your confidence suffers a heavy blow and you find engaging in new relationships to be difficult.

開
Kai
Open

This configuration is not too auspicious nor is it inauspicious. Right now, your energy levels are low even though you have the potential to shine. You feel like you are missing something but you do not have the motivation or diligence to look for that missing piece. You need to remember that the answers will never be readily available for you. You must exercise patience and will before you can find what you are looking for. Once you find what you are missing, you can then move on with life and start trying your hand at success. Slowly but surely, you will eventually get what you want, but only if you are hardworking enough.

天盤 **Heavenly Stem**	地盤 **Earthly Stem**
甲 *Jia* **Yang Wood**	辛 *Xin* **Yin Metal**

Structure 格局	Green Dragon Broken Feet 青龍折足
Rating 吉凶	Inauspicious 凶
Classic Verse 十干剋應歌訣	青龍折足甲加辛，吉門生助謀事進，兇門折足須小心
Transliteration 字譯	Where the Jia meets with Xin, it is known as the Green Dragon Broken Feet formation. Presence of an auspicious Door is helpful for strategizing and planning. Presence of an inauspicious Door means be wary of potential disaster.
Description 解説	There is a palpable danger during this formation. The formation portends an internal problem that is slowly but surely eroding away the resources and polluting the thoughts of other people. From another perspective, the formation signalizes delineating one from his/her support and foundation. This period will be characterized by stagnant plans and internal turmoil. Only the presence of the Auspicious Qi Men Doors will protect an individual from getting into fierce confrontation with one's enemies. The presence of negative Doors will lead one to incur heavy loses, causalities and lose fortunes and vitality. Injuries around the feet may also occur.

The 8 Doors Analysis:

The following evaluates the effects of **Jia** 甲 and **Xin** 辛 with each Door.

休 *Xiu* **Rest**	Your place in society is already rather secure, but you should not be too overconfident about your fortunes. It is likely that you may overestimate your grasp of your resources and end up overusing or overspending. This will give you a bad reputation as a person who takes things for granted and you do not want to jeopardise your position in life at all. Therefore, it is essential to be prudent and thrifty whenever you can. Other than this little glitch, it is possible for you to continue with good fortunes and prosperity as long as you are constantly aware of potential problems and dangers. Do not lose sight of reality.
生 *Sheng* **Life**	Good fortune has it that you will be relatively well taken care of during this time. Opportunities open up for you and there is the possibility of self-improvement and advancement through society. You only need to take care that when you are climbing the social ladder, to not climb too fast. If you do that, you risk slipping and exposing yourself to some dangers that lurk below. Keep at a steady pace and rely on the constant support from friends and family to keep you up. If you take things slowly, success is guaranteed. If you try to speed through the processes, you are likely to meet with unexpected challenges that bring you down.
傷 *Shang* **Harm**	Hidden danger lurks around the corner and will try to ambush you at any point when you are most vulnerable. Beware of physical assault from other parties and keep a weather eye on all suspicious activity around you. This will contribute to your overall paranoia, but if you do not exercise caution, there is a high chance of you getting harmed badly. This is a dark time in your life because it seems like the very foundation of your support system has been robbed from you and you are left alone to deal with these dangers. Avoid anything that you are uncomfortable with, lest something horrific happens to you.
杜 *Du* **Delusion**	Internal problems will cause you great suffering. Lack of support will further worsen the situation and plunge you into near-depression. Your progress in life will be brought to a standstill and you will come a point where you can barely function in daily life. At this point, you are probably used to being alone in your life, but be aware that this is possibly the worst that has ever happened to you. Do not take it lightly and be reminded that it could possibly consume you to the point of no return.

景 *Jing* **Scenery**	You need to be wary of hidden dangers and be on the lookout for anyone potentially trying to take advantage of you. You are at a point in your life where opportunities are being made available to you and you do not want to lose your chance to excel in life and move forward in society. If you are not careful, you could lose everything thanks to a few malicious events. If you stay focused and sharp you will be able to grasp your opportunities properly and use them to the best of your advantage to get somewhere better in life. Never let your guard down and try to always assess a situation for dangers before stepping into it.	
死 *Si* **Death**	Loss of fortune and vitality will come to haunt you at this time and slowly but surely, eat away at all your resources and contaminate every aspect of your personal life. It seems that your problems stem from the fact that no one trusts you. If you have been completely honest with your peers then it may just be a case of bad fortune. But if you have not been honest in all your dealings, then it is likely that the universe is turning the tables on you and you have no power to change what it going to happen to you now. You have to accept the things that happen to you as penance.	
驚 *Jing* **Fear**	The very foundations of your relationships are being threatened. Shaky as they already were, now they are in risk of being completely obliterated. If you do not hurry and take care of your relationships, you may lose some valuable people in your life forever. Much of your own internal drama has contributed to how others perceive you, so if you do not deal with your own personal problems first, then you cannot deal with your relationships. This configuration indicates that there is a possibility your internal hardships are only going to get worse, so if you do not deal with them now, you will be forever condemned to having lost people close to you.	
開 *Kai* **Open**	Under the good fortune that this configuration brings, you do not have to worry about coming across any direct dangers. You are relatively safe under this configuration, with a significant amount of fortune on your side. This fortune will help you establish new relationships and hone new talents, and success is not impossible for you if you really work for it. However, do take care to not take things for granted and always remember that the factor of chance could very well change the way things turn out for you. For the most part, your fortunes are positive, but if become too reckless for your own good, you may start to experience a loss of resources or trust from others.	

奇門遁甲十干格局篇

甲 Jia

天盤 **Heavenly Stem**	地盤 **Earthly Stem**
甲 *Jia* **Yang Wood**	壬 *Ren* **Yang Water**

Structure 格局	Green Dragon Enters Heavenly Prison 青龍入天牢
Rating 吉凶	Inauspicious 凶
Classic Verse 十干剋應歌訣	龍入天牢甲加壬，陰陽之事皆不問
Transliteration 字譯	Where the Jia meets with Ren, it is known as the Dragon Enters Heavenly Prison formation. It is unfavourable to ask about Yin or Yang matters.
Description 解說	This configuration indicates heightened miscommunication and misconstructions of one's meanings. The configuration is especially not good for any romance-related functions. One's good intentions will be misconstrued. Communication and relationships will suffer a major blow while obstacles and stunted progress will spring up from everywhere. The spirit will be weak and one will have no zeal to fight with. However, a scenario may present itself where this configuration meets with an Auspicious Door. This scenario is traditionally known as 青龍入水, Green Dragon Entering Water. One may find their way by getting into this prime. By getting into this prime, the situation turns from bad to good and one is able to make progress in their endeavors.

The 8 Doors Analysis:

The following evaluates the effects of **Jia** 甲 and **Ren** 壬 with each Door.

休 *Xiu* **Rest**	You are extremely fortunate in you academic pursuits at this point and have the ability to outwit and outscore all your rivals. This cements your reputation as one of the most formidable minds in your institution and socially, your circle of friends will grow as they realise the value is being acquainted with you. You will be well known for your brilliance and at the end of it all, it will bring great fortune to you. You will reap the rewards of your diligence and intelligence with both material prosperity and social recognition.
生 *Sheng* **Life**	Prosperity and good fortune will be yours under this combination. Your social prominence in your community will grow and benefit those around you. Your reputation will be at its peak at this point. This combination is highly auspicious as you will be able to achieve whatever you put your head to. Socially, your status will be elevated and you will experience the most fame you have ever felt in your life. Do not let it get to your head, but instead remember the faces of every person who supported you. In the near future, you may need to go back to them for help.
傷 *Shang* **Harm**	Many unusual setbacks will take you by surprise at this time and it will be a real challenge for you to figure out how to overcome them. If you are not careful with your emotions, you may suffer from depression. While it is possible that prosperity will come to you under this configuration, the chances of you meeting an unfavourable situation are higher. You may very well be exposed to some of the strangest challenges you have ever encountered in your life. Because of this, you will not know how to adequately deal with this problem and you will be stuck for the most part, unable to move forward and chase other opportunities.
杜 *Du* **Delusion**	Mental health is of absolute importance under this configuration because it makes a person prone to depression and mental break downs. If you can keep yourself happy and healthy most of the time, this might be avoided, but if you just slip a little, you may plunge yourself into a deep, dark pool of suffering. You will be confused most of the time as to what you are supposed to do with your life, but most importantly, you will feel absolutely dejected about this confusion. Try to remember that confusion is normal whenever someone is faced with a problem. You are not expected to be a superhero with no problems. Tackle the issue at your own pace so that you do not cause more harm to yourself.

奇門遁甲十干格局篇

甲
Jia

景 *Jing* **Scenery**		A great many opportunities await you and you now have the chance to showcase your true abilities and impress everyone. Once you have done this, it will be easy for you to garner both prosperity and fame. These two things will bring you great happiness and elevate your position in society significantly. Since it has always been a lifelong dream for you to be at the top of the social ladder, do not hesitate to take these opportunities. You may just cause yourself indescribable pain by forgoing these opportunities.
死 *Si* **Death**		You will suffer under this configuration with little consolation from your friends or family to make you feel better about yourself. You will be held back on every aspect of your life and be unable to move forward to pursue brighter paths due to unusual obstacles hampering your personal growth. You will be very confused as to how to deal with your problems that you will not be able to pull yourself out of crippling anxiety and fear, dwelling instead in the inevitability of your failure. Your constant concern with how others perceive you will make you sadder and more susceptible to depression.
驚 *Jing* **Fear**		Unpleasant affairs will mar your relationships with those close to you and you will not be able to wrap your head around living a happy life. You will be too concerned with your current situation and be unable to harness any of your potential to pay attention to projects that need your help. Communication between you and your peers will be poor and this will cause you to feel alone and unsupported in your endeavours. True, you may lack support, but do not let yourself slip into despair too easily as you become prone to depression or other mental issues.
開 *Kai* **Open**		Wisdom and good leadership will come to you at this time and you will be able to outwit everyone who doubted you. Use these blessings to instil formidability in yourself and make your rivals will be afraid of you. Once you have achieved this, prosperity will come to you effortlessly because the truth is, you possess the natural talent that it takes to succeed in life. All you need to do is use your leadership to bring about a change in the course of your life and you will be rewarded generously. Good fortune is on your side now, so you should definitely seize this opportunity to try everything you have ever wanted to try, because you can be guaranteed to succeed!

天盤 **Heavenly Stem**	地盤 **Earthly Stem**
甲 *Jia* **Yang Wood**	**癸** *Gui* **Yin Water**

Structure 格局	Green Dragon Elegant Seal 青龍華蓋
Rating 吉凶	Moderate 半吉
Classic Verse 十干剋應歌訣	青龍華蓋甲加癸，吉門招吉凶門悔
Transliteration 字譯	Where the Jia meets with Gui, it is known as the Green Dragon Elegant Seal formation. With an auspicious Door, (this formation) attracts auspicious events while the inauspicious Door causes regret.
Description 解説	This configuration is excellent for bringing about achievements in academia. It denotes an increased capability to outsmart one's competitors. One's leadership skills and talent will be on its sharpest acumen and any projects that one undertakes will bear positive results. Auspicious Doors present during this formation will bring increased fame, monetary rewards and good fortunes. The presence of inauspicious doors could led to some unexpected setbacks and contribute to stagnated growth and progress. Inauspicious doors may also signify mental blocks and depression.

The 8 Doors Analysis:

The following evaluates the effects of **Jia** 甲 and **Gui** 癸 with each Door.

休 *Xiu* **Rest**	Good fortune is abounding for you at this time of your life and you are experience vitality in everything you do. You feel like as if all your problems in the past have been swept away by this new wave of good opportunities and widespread support from your friends and family. Take this chance to invest time and energy in every pursuit you have ever wanted to go for, no matter how whimsical. Do not be afraid of being judged, because if you look happy and are passionate about what you are doing, people will not judge you badly but will instead learn to admire you for your courage and passion.
生 *Sheng* **Life**	The prosperity you have been seeking will finally come to you now. Your patience and hard work have finally paid off – proof that all good things come to those who work for them. If you were lazy in the past, then you should not be surprised if your blessings seem rather small. But chances are that you are the kind of person who likes to see things through to the end and always make sure that you are on top of your tasks. Your diligence is the main thing that is bringing you fruits now. Relax and enjoy your rewards because you have earned them. Keep up the good work and be a source of inspiration to others.
傷 *Shang* **Harm**	For some reason, things just do not seem to be going your way. Try as you may, nothing works out for you. You will be expecting a good outcome out of many of your pursuits, but instead you will get either bad outcomes or subpar results. The fault is not with you. You are a sociable person and a hard worker, but bad fortune is just plaguing you at this time. Do not be too discouraged and always try to remember that your time for reward will come soon. It may not be anytime now, but because you were diligent and upstanding in the past, you will certainly be paid back for your goodness. Persevere and do not lose hope.
杜 *Du* **Delusion**	An unprecedented attack onto your emotional health with come at this point. All will have been well in your life, but all of a sudden, someone you trusted will show their true colours and break your spirit. Despite this unforgivable betrayal, everything else in your life is going smoothly. Your career is seeing growth and your reputation as a leader is cemented. But you will not be able to concentrate on these successes and celebrate, because emotionally you will be somewhere else. This trial will prove to be far too distracting for you to handle, and if you do not cope with it well, you may see the best moments of your life just pass you by.

景 *Jing* **Scenery**	Finally, the chance for you to showcase your abilities and impress is finally here. After endless waiting, you will finally be recognised for your talents and passion and an opportunity of great value will come to you. Take this opportunity as you are not a person of generally good luck, and no other opportunity will come. Despite the fact that you may have other commitments at this time, try to remember that this is what you have been working for your whole life and to turn your back on such an opportunity will be a complete waste of your life. Choose wisely so that you do not regret your decision.	
死 *Si* **Death**	Isolation and alienation will come to you at this point, and you will be deserted by everyone you thought you could have had faith in. Do not blame them for leaving you because they too are having problems of their own. You need to buck up and try to solve this issue on your own without having to pull anyone in and giving them additional problems. True, you will be utterly lost and confused, but it is better for you to suffer on your own than for you to bring suffering to others as well. You cannot be selfish now. In fact, selflessness may even help you make up for all your bad fortune.	
驚 *Jing* **Fear**	You find it difficult to tell the truth to others and because of this, they never know what you really feel. You keep trying to convey the message but in different and indirect ways and this leads to much miscommunication. It is a little manipulative of you to do this. Why not just do the upstanding thing and say it like it is? You may fear how people react to you but if you do not say your piece soon, you will continue to be taken advantage of and people will continue to assume that you are fine with being treated that way. Either stand up for yourself, or find another friend to stand up for you if you find it far too difficult.	
開 *Kai* **Open**	New talents will come to you that will help you become a better person. You may not realise it, but this is a reward for all the good things you have done in the past. Continue to carry out these good deeds and use your newfound talents to make yourself an even more effective giver. Charities are meant to make people feel better, whether you are the giver or the receiver. Involve yourself with this community more often and you will find that your levels of positivity skyrocket every time you go there.	

乙

Yi
Yin Wood

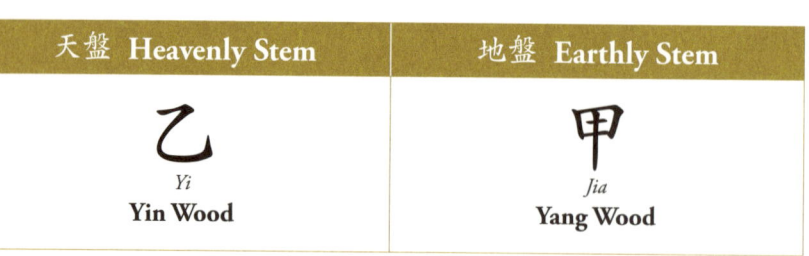

天盤 **Heavenly Stem**	地盤 **Earthly Stem**
乙 *Yi* **Yin Wood**	甲 *Jia* **Yang Wood**

Structure 格局	Maxes Yin Supress Yang 利陰害陽
Rating 吉凶	Moderate 半吉
Classic Verse 十干剋應歌訣	利陰害陽乙加甲，利陰害陽細辨察，門兇門迫人財伐
Transliteration 字譯	Where the Yi meets with Jia, it is known as the Maxes Yin Suppress Yang formation. It indicates that the auspicious Yin and inauspicious Yang should be observed carefully. The inauspicious and compelled Door will decrease the wealth.
Description 解說	This formation is also called Roots Attacking Jia 藤蘿擊甲. The formation signifies the concept of being misused by people. It can also be decrypted as the enemy taking advantage of one's capabilities or a lack thereof. During the formation, there will be a heightened feeling of betrayal. The most talented employee will be replaced by his competitor and one will generally lose a place from dirty tricks applied by competitors. This formation will rain down harm and injury via one's closest friends. The presence of Auspicious Doors may calm down the atrocities of the formation leading to a complete failure

The 8 Doors Analysis:
The following evaluates the effects of **Yi** 乙 and **Jia** 甲 with each Door.

休 *Xiu* **Rest**	You have a rare and uniquely beneficial skill to see things in black and white, good or bad, right or wrong. This helps you sort the better decisions from the ones that are ill-advised. You can also recognize the right people when you see them. You know how to surround yourself with the best kind of people. Do not be afraid to be honest and do what is right and not what is convenient. A Nobleman will appear to help you. Everything will be successful and ends well, thus adding brilliance to your present splendor.
生 *Sheng* **Life**	You are independent and you know how to motivate yourself towards success. You will encounter good luck throughout. This would also mean that you have the necessary ingredients to generate success. Just make sure work is prioritized and work on projects and tasks thoroughly. You should finish what you started and remember that perseverance is key. Do not be afraid to ask for help when necessary/needed.
傷 *Shang* **Harm**	This is an inauspicious configuration: a sign of lack of harmony. It denotes being used by others through dirty tactics. The enemy would also take advantage of your weakness. There will be an element of betrayal and your most valuable employee will be taken away by a competitor.
杜 *Du* **Delusion**	This is an inauspicious configuration: a sign of difficulty and strife. You are looking good, but going nowhere. This is how you may feel as you try to carry forward. Something is empty and it doesn't seem right. Unforeseeable crisis, which must be dealt with. If won't it will keep coming back. If you can persevere for long enough, then stability may come around.

景 *Jing* **Scenery**		Nobody likes working hard with no pay off at the very end and you're not the exception to the norm. Your talents or calling will not reveal themselves to you. You are putting all the effort you can but you're experiencing very little gain. Don't be too difficult on yourself because it's not your fault. This is caused by negative/bad luck which is out of your control. Take it easy and the more you try to control something you can't, the worse things can become.
死 *Si* **Death**		It would seem that you will be fighting a lonely and tiresome battle. It's not easy being you and doing things by yourself. Everything will hit you at once and you will have a hard time trying to remain positive. You might put in 110% effort but it doesn't do much good in return. You want to overcome your challenges but your courage is diminishing. You many eventually want to escape and retreat from it all and this may not be a bad idea.
驚 *Jing* **Fear**		This is not a fortunate sign. Disasters and misadventures will occur without warning and there is nothing you can do to avoid them from happening. Your career will suffer from these situations and you may be doomed to fail at many things. This is usually through the fault of your own. This would not be the best time to seek a career or a relationship change.
開 *Kai* **Open**		Even though there may be mistakes happening, you do not need to worry. A turning point of opportunity is just around the corner waiting for you. Setbacks may slow down and halt your progress but each and everyone one of it can be overcome. When opportunity or good fortune arises, you will appreciate it more after encountering and dealing with these difficulties. Before you try to lend a hand to others, you would need to help yourself first. As the saying goes, charity begins at home. Your luck in wealth will turn good and your situation will allow you to do well soon.

天盤 **Heavenly Stem**	地盤 **Earthly Stem**
乙 *Yi* **Yin Wood**	**乙** *Yi* **Yin Wood**

Structure 格局	Day Noble Fu Yin 日奇伏吟
Rating 吉凶	Moderate 半吉
Classic Verse 十干剋應歌訣	日奇伏吟乙加乙，安分守己遠名利
Transliteration 字譯	Where the Yi meets with Yi, it is known as the Day Noble Fu Yin formation. It denotes law-abiding citizens who are far from obtaining fame and wealth.
Description 解說	This is a Fu Yin Configuration. In normal configurations the Yi Noble is an Auspicious Stem but in this case it means that all expected positive outcome may not materialize. The formation indicates stagnated plans and projects and is not a good time to pursue career related endeavors. The prevailing conditions also do not change at the speed that one anticipated. It is better to not take any risky moves during the configuration. Instead, one should remain in a current sphere or comfort zone.

The 8 Doors Analysis:

The following evaluates the effects of **Yi** 乙 and **Yi** 乙 with each Door.

休 *Xiu* **Rest**	This arrangement denotes positivity. You should not be afraid of a little adversity in your luck cycles. With good luck on your side, you should have nothing to fear. Life will be like a drink that at first tastes bitter, but becomes sweet at the end for you. The bad will turn into the good eventually, and all your dreams will come true. Follow the steps and respect the rules. You are very likely to succeed in the end.
生 *Sheng* **Life**	Hardworking and innovative. You have a creative mind and strive to do your best. This is something that will be noticed and rewarded appropriately. The environment around you will be supportive and all you have to do is show up and do your very best. Innovation is the key. Think about what you can do with the existing resources you have. If you fail to focus or innovate, you will achieve negative and only half-baked results. The same strategy may not work for the second time around. Make a change and put in the effort needed so the future will contain everything you deserve.
傷 *Shang* **Harm**	This is an inauspicious configuration. You seem to always be in constant dilemma. You have an important decision to make soon but you are still unclear or unsure about it all. You are oblivious about the details and you have not made up your mind on what will eventually be the next step. Your indecisive nature is the cause of your downfall. If you hesitate for too long, opportunities may pass you by. Pay attention, stay alert and be sure to move forward steadfastly when opportunity knocks on your door. It's only with this methodology, you can make the most of your potential and have absolutely no regrets.
杜 *Du* **Delusion**	Remember that losers are usually people who are afraid of losing. Small issues may seem larger than it is and causes you a great deal of pain. Minor problems may escalate into major issues if you are not too afraid of losing by not wanting to take on the challenges that life has to offer you. Although, you have many friends, when it all comes down to it, they do not seem to be able to help you when you need them too. Sadly, any dreams you have of being famous and obtaining an exorbitant amount of wealth will be unlikely to come true.

景 *Jing* **Scenery**	The good and bad will be experienced together. There may not be any clear sense of a winner or a loser here because for every opportunity, there will be a catch/problem to it. If you can find a mentor, then you will be able to receive the guidance needed to achieve your goals. The key to success lies in your ability to get on your feet, being proactive, and always looking for some form of positive opportunity. You should not wait for positive opportunities to come along as they won't be forthcoming. You should seek out for them always.	
死 *Si* **Death**	This sign is associated with really bad luck all around. The road ahead will be full of bumps, twists and turns, thus making your journey much more difficult than you may anticipate. Your energy level is too low so you would need to be mindful about your health. You are unlikely to have many lucky breaks and even the best of plans may not work out for you. Be prepared for tough times ahead and change the course of your direction in life while you still can.	
驚 *Jing* **Fear**	It is time to take shelter. The weather in your life changes and joyful parts way for sorrow. For every lucky break you may get, you will also have to encounter some bad news. Your career fortunes are about to face a sharp bend as well. What at first may seem like a good chance, can turn out to be nothing more than a trap. So you would need to be cautious. You would also need to cultivate a sense of fortitude and proceed cautiously. You may ask the questions, check the details and fine print carefully. Remain alert so that you don't get caught unexpectedly.	
開 *Kai* **Open**	If you want to be successful, don't allow yourself the luxury of excuses. You need to do the tasks which are important first and not what is convenient. If you do the right thing, then you can plan with a goal in mind so that you may succeed. When you set out to do something, you can be sure that the wind will go the way you want to and help you sail to your desired destination quicker. All you have to do is to have the courage to take the initial step.	

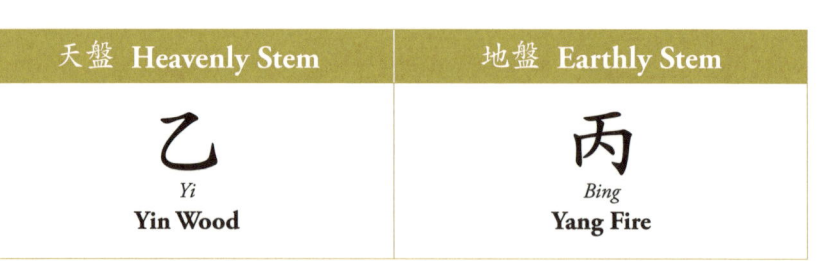

天盤 **Heavenly Stem**	地盤 **Earthly Stem**
乙 *Yi* **Yin Wood**	丙 *Bing* **Yang Fire**

Structure 格局	Noble Crest in Position 奇儀順遂
Rating 吉凶	Auspicious 吉
Classic Verse 十干剋應歌訣	奇儀順遂乙加丙，升官晉職見吉星，夫妻反目見凶星
Transliteration 字譯	Yi and Bing are auspicious Noble Crescents, if met with Noble Star there will be good career prospects and promotions, if met with inauspicious Stars husband and wife will bicker. Yi meeting with Bing is a meeting of two the Nobles of Qi Men. If this combination further meets with Auspicious Stars and Doors, it denotes promotion and career advancement. Where there are instead, Negative Stars and Doors, then it denotes disagreements between husband and wife.
Description 解説	The Noble Crest in Position formation symbolizes rewards for one's efforts and celebratory occasions. It is a very friendly and advantageous configuration that denotes an accomplishment of the success that one has been working towards. Celebrations are expected during this configuration as whatever one has been desiring over time will come to fruition. Problems and challenges will be resolved. The Noble Crest in Position formation is not adversely affected by the presence of Inauspicious Door or Stars. Even if they are around, some disputes may occur but that is the worst of it.

The 8 Doors Analysis:
The following evaluates the effects of **Yi** 乙 and **Bing** 丙 with each Door.

休 *Xiu* **Rest**	You have ambition. You know how high you'd like to climb. This hunger for more is powerful but on its own, it's useless. This is because this combination does not favor huge ambitions. You may lack the true determination necessary to stick with plans and endure hardship long enough to eventually come out on top. Instead of simply dreaming of things for yourself, make sure you also take the time to take things step by step, stay focused on the goal and put in the necessary hard work. Start small, and slowly but surely, you will achieve your gaols. Good time and people management is necessary. Then, victory will finally be yours.
生 *Sheng* **Life**	Making the right decision is a skill whether you are aware of it or not. However, acquiring skill takes time and hence, this combination suggest having a little patience. Don't forget that knowing what to do isn't the same as doing it! Take action only when you are fully ready. You must manage your time and resources intelligently. Achievement, a respectable reputation and results all await you.
傷 *Shang* **Harm**	This is an inauspicious configuration: a sign of difficulty and strife. Good things may turn sour in the long run. Happiness, when attained, may be fleeting and times of good business and prosperity won't persist for too long. Take stock of what you have now or risk losing more in the end. You will find it difficult to bring your dreams to fruition. You may have your work cut out for you more than most!
杜 *Du* **Delusion**	It is best not to request for assistance or receive any unsolicited assistance from others at this point. What seems to good to be true, probably is. This combination suggests that you should take a step back, study and understand your own strengths and weaknesses better before making the next step.

Qi Men Dun Jia - The 100 Formations

	景 *Jing* **Scenery**	The good times don't last forever and they seem to be disappearing in the rear view mirror as you move forward. Justice may not be granted at this time. Worries take the place of a carefree attitude, problems take the place of triumphs, more is lost than is gained. Difficult times ahead filled with doubt, negativity and hardship. Baton down the hatches for the coming storm and stay upbeat. You may find it hard to trust others at this point as many seem unreliable. Best to depend on yourself when it comes to making difficult decisions.
	死 *Si* **Death**	It would seem that everything you do seems wrong. It seems like none of your decisions ever pan out the way you envisioned it. You know how to pick yourself up but then something always seems to come along to knock you back off your feet again. You must stay calm and composed so that you can protect yourself and ride out the storms you find yourself in. Some things are just out of your control for now, so let it be. Control what you still can and cultivate a sense of fortitude. Take a step back for now.
	驚 *Jing* **Fear**	Isolated. Alone. Deserted. Unrecognized. Nobody can fault you for making an attempt at things, where you end up putting in twice or three times as much effort as the next person, but only seeing half the results. In order to achieve your objectives, you need to accept this and continue battling fierce and perhaps unfair resistance to succeed. Yes, things aren't always fair. You are fearful. And your resources seems to deplete. The difficult journey you face right now can build a strong character - if you promise to never give up!
	開 *Kai* **Open**	Luck is on your side and you will enjoy a time of great prosperity, thanks to a nobleman or mentor who is available to help you. Share your fortune with others, proceed wisely and make the most of everything. Small and straightforward steps will lead you to success. Help will be there along the way as and when you need, they will appear.

天盤 **Heavenly Stem**	地盤 **Earthly Stem**
乙 *Yi* **Yin Wood**	丁 *Ding* **Yin Fire**

Structure 格局	Noble Assisting Jade Maiden 奇助玉女
Rating 吉凶	Auspicious 吉
Classic Verse 十干剋應歌訣	奇助玉女乙加丁，最利文考百事興
Transliteration 字譯	Where the Yi meets with Ding, it is known as the Noble Assisting Jade Maiden formation. It denotes that it is beneficial to participate in civil examination and any other endeavours that serve interest.
Description 解說	This configuration is favorable to plans and strategies. One will be able to come up with great ideas and will be very productive. Individuals who make efforts to progress in career and business will get positive results. This configuration is excellent for those looking forward to signing business deals and agreements. Everything will turn out as expected while a Noble Assisting Jade Maiden allows all functions to be executed with care.

奇門遁甲十干格局篇

YI

The 8 Doors Analysis:

The following evaluates the effects of **Yi** 乙 and **Ding** 丁 with each Door.

休 *Xiu* **Rest**	You have great ambitions and will encounter great achievements ahead. You will be able to create a good life for yourself. This is the kind of outlook that everyone wants to have therefore you would need to remember to count your blessings. Whatever you decide to do in life will equate to a successful decision. However ambitious your dreams are, they will eventually come true anyway. All you have to do is do the grunt work and craft a future for yourself because only hard work pays off in the end.
生 *Sheng* **Life**	Many people will have talents they may never get a chance to exploit. But when you are able to capitalize on something, you will usually excel at it with fruitful results. You will be very fortunate as you will meet the right kind of people, at the right place and the right time. Your environment is one that you may use to garner strength from. You will be ahead of the pack and you have what it takes to be on the right path. Success is attainable for you and you will be admired and well-respected.
傷 *Shang* **Harm**	This is an inauspicious configuration. Things start out well but then seem to run off course. You may have the best intentions but somehow you will lack whatever it is that is necessary to convert these things into the outcome you want. You may also be capable of starting your own business but will have the difficulty to get it off the ground. If you are to succeed, you will need to find a Nobleman or mentor to offer you some guidance and advice. You won't be able to achieve the things you want, if you don't enlist the help of others.
杜 *Du* **Delusion**	This is an inauspicious configuration. Don't put yourself in situations that may cause trouble. Focus on your work and respect the rules. Don't bend or break the rules no matter what the situation may be. There is danger ahead that may cause a lot of other problems for you. You can get ahead by being patient and you will need to wait it out before making drastic changes. What is not meant to be yours, will never be yours – do not be overly ambitious.

景 *Jing* **Scenery**	The good times won't last forever and they will seem to disappear in the rear view mirror as you move forward in life. Worries will take over and you will not be able to lead life with a carefree attitude any longer. Problems will take place and more is lost than gained. Difficult times predicted ahead with doubt, negativity and hardship. Be ready for a storm. You may also find it hard to trust others at this point as many will seem unreliable to you. It is probably best to depend on yourself when it comes to making difficult decisions.
死 *Si* **Death**	You did your best but somehow, your best may not be good enough. The outcome of your situation is influenced by a complex mix of factors beyond your control. It is also difficult to get the cooperation of others. Obstruction and hindrance will be present for you. You will lack helpful people in your life and it's always best to choose the path less-traveled.
驚 *Jing* **Fear**	This is not a fortunate sign. Nothing seems to go your way. It's as if life is holding a grudge against you and is holding you back. Troubles predicted ahead, traps occurring, accidents will happen and obstacles will be encountered. Despite your best efforts, you can't break this streak of bad luck. Sometimes, decisions you believe are wise or opportunities you think are good for you will turn out otherwise. The best you can do is to be cautious and stay alert. Question everything. Don't waste your energy cursing things that cannot be changed. There are only two things you can invest right now: time and money. Out of the two, time will be more important for you.
開 *Kai* **Open**	The wind is smooth and the waves are peaceful on your path. The moon will also shine brighter for you. Other people around you may be a little envious of your good fortune. The stars have aligned and given you a clean run at the things you may want. You can expect smooth progress and plenty of small victories leading to an overall success story. Noble people around you will offer their help along your journey. The outcome will be prosperous and happy for you. Make the most out of your good luck and always be grateful for it!

奇門遁甲十干格局篇

YI

天盤 Heavenly Stem	地盤 Earthly Stem
乙 *Yi* **Yin Wood**	戊 *Wu* **Yang Earth**

Structure 格局	Noble Enters Heavenly Door 奇入天門
Rating 吉凶	Moderate 半吉
Classic Verse 十干剋應歌訣	奇入天門 乙加戊，陰人事利，兇迫門無助
Transliteration 字譯	Where the Yi meets with Wu, it is known as the Noble Enters Heavenly Door formation. It denotes smooth execution of matters that requires discretion. The inauspicious Door indicates helplessness.
Description 解説	The Noble Enters Heavenly Door is an excellent formation for a person who wants to make elaborate schemes and stealth plans. A lot of people will be willing to offer monetary assistance but will do this secretively. The configuration is also excellent for those seeking enlightenment and other spiritual achievements. For individuals seeking to do some deep meditation and self-reflection, this configuration offers very ideal conditions. Although it favors the female, with the presence of Auspicious Qi Men Door, plans should be managed and completed with relative ease.

The 8 Doors Analysis:

The following evaluates the effects of **Yi** 乙 and **Wu** 戊 with each Door.

休 *Xiu* **Rest**	It seems like all roads will lead to success for you. Ask yourself what you'd really like to do with your time and where you'd really like to be because most doors will be open for you. Take your pick. Your fortunes are favorable as well. You can expect a smooth path to wealth, prosperity and happiness. Go ahead and begin your journey and you'll surely make it to your destination without too much frustration!
生 *Sheng* **Life**	Your ship sails smoothly on calm waters. You will be able to materialize your heart's desires. Your mentor luck will be good but not everyone will be blessed with this good fortune. You can propel ahead of your rivals and competitors by making the most out of this blessing. As the saying goes, two heads are better than one and with the help of a great mentor, you can come up with better answers. Let them tell you whether your schemes or motives are on the right track.
傷 *Shang* **Harm**	This is an inauspicious configuration and denotes that luck is always changing. When your luck changes, it will be very clear that it has taken a turn for the worse. Mishaps, accidents and bad things may befall you. You will encounter many obstacles all of a sudden. When you're on the path towards prosperity, you should brace yourself to begin hearing bad news routinely. Bad times will appear ahead and you will need to be ready for them.
杜 *Du* **Delusion**	You may have been moving forward for some time now but recently, it might feel like you've gotten stuck in the mud. No matter how much you try to rev it up, you are unable to break free from it. Similarly, it's way too late to back out from your current situation. The key to progression lies in rallying the help from others around you. Take note of the key people around you. Don't be afraid to ask for help when needed. Don't let your pride get in the way and by understanding this, it will help you get back on track quickly.

景 *Jing* **Scenery**	Pride comes before a fall. A sense of aggrandizing attitude won't get you anywhere. The Chinese have a saying, there's always a mountain higher than this one so you would need to recognize the fact that there may be some people who are better than you and take a more modest, humble approach to life. You are not always right, nor are you the best. Being stubborn is not the best way forward. Your situation is a challenging one but if you can be humble and seek the right mentors, you will be able to achieve the right guidance to make it through tough times.
死 *Si* **Death**	You will have no Nobleman luck. Without people around to encourage you in the first place or to congratulate you when you succeed – things will become a lot harder. You must rely entirely on your own strengths to stay motivated. You may owe people money. The only hope of things becoming better lies in your willingness to make the necessary changes because you aren't in a winning situation right now. You will need to systematize your work and learn how to control your finances properly. It is imperative to not dwell in unfruitful relationship matters.
驚 *Jing* **Fear**	Even though you may seem to get what you desire, but the troubles and burdens of success will take its tow on you. Be aware of some of the potential pitfalls and stay on track. Even if you have extra money, don't use your wealth to try and gain people's affection. You should also invest in and build genuine relationships with others in order to move ahead. A little sincerity will go a long way. Avoid participating in gossips or spreading rumors.
開 *Kai* **Open**	You are blessed and many others will be eager to help you. There are good mentors and friends out there. You must have a sense of gratitude for the help you get in life. Fame and fortune is on the cards for you as well. You will find yourself in the right place at the right time. You will also enjoy many successes in life. Don't forget that there will be others who are less fortunate. You can increase your luck by offering a helping hand and enriching others. Always start with the people who are close to you and this will keep the good things coming.

天盤 **Heavenly Stem**	地盤 **Earthly Stem**
乙 *Yi* **Yin Wood**	己 *Ji* **Yin Earth**

Structure 格局	Day Noble Enters Mist 日奇入霧
Rating 吉凶	Moderate 半吉
Classic Verse 十干剋應歌訣	日奇入墓乙加己，門兇事兇被土欺，開門生門可遁地
Transliteration 字譯	Where the Yi meets with Ji, it is known as the Day Noble Enters Mist formation. It denotes that the inauspicious Door is 'cheated' by the Earth. The Open Door and Life Door are hidden or obscured underground.
Description 解説	The Day Noble Enters Mist Configuration represents uncertainty. There is no clear path and a deep darkness looms in one's mind. Everything seems to be stagnated and one may lack faith and confidence in his\her plans. Support from others will be withdrawn, leaving one to feel clueless and more vulnerable. The uncertainty that characterizes this formation can be overcome by remaining calm and still. Ultimately, one will manage to overcome the troublesome with the compliant.

The 8 Doors Analysis:

The following evaluates the effects of **Yi** 乙 and **Ji** 己 with each Door.

休 *Xiu* **Rest**	The road ahead is straight and you're about to pick up some speed on your journey. However, you shouldn't move quickly, just in case something unforeseeable crosses your path. A conservative yet steady pace will be the most beneficial to you. There are no major obstacles along the way but unfortunately, the path that you've chosen is actually a longer route.
生 *Sheng* **Life**	Everyone makes mistakes in life. Don't try to place the blame but control your emotions and focus on the lessons you have learnt instead. Do not expect anything to be handed to you on a silver platter. Complacency will get you nowhere therefore you will need to work hard and work smart. In your case, your success depends entirely on how much you are willing to roll up your sleeves and take on the necessary measures needed. A strong work ethic will enable you to overcome the odds and reach for the stars. If you decide to play it safe, you will stay where you are now but success will be out of your reach.
傷 *Shang* **Harm**	This is an inauspicious configuration and denotes a family which does not operate as a harmonious unit. Spousal and partnership turmoil will be present for you. For now, it would seem that things will be pretty demoralizing for you as well. Don't over-analyze things and blame yourself too quickly. Try to relax and learn to let go in order to move forward for better days ahead. Don't get stuck in the past by hanging on to it, if not your future may look bleak.
杜 *Du* **Delusion**	Everything is stable and secure. With a little bit of handwork, the stone will turn into a diamond and the results will show. If you choose to put in the effort required, you will be able to reach heights that you didn't think you could. Have a little confidence in yourself and take some brave decisions to propel forward. Complacency is your enemy. None of this will come to pass if you sit around and do nothing to cultivate it. Good outcome awaits you – so make your move now!

景 *Jing* **Scenery**	The bad events that are ongoing in your life are about to be over, thus making way for better opportunities ahead. Just like a storm that passes overhead, your problems are about to be nothing more than memories. This sign is associated with above average luck and a future full of hope. Despite the various obstacles in life, you'll be able to achieve your goals after all.	
死 *Si* **Death**	Time only flows in one direction and when it is gone, you can't get it back. Just like the saying, time and tide waits for no man. You may be aware of this but if you fail to seize the opportunity to do so in the past and you may have actually regretted doing so. Not to fear, as you will probably have another chance at success if you seek the right mentor for help. Finding this person is the key to a brighter future for you. This wouldn't be someone you already know. You will need to go out and network to increase the chances of finding this person.	
驚 *Jing* **Fear**	You may feel lost, or you may know what you're searching for but finding that missing piece is like looking for a needle in a haystack. Your energy level is low and you would need to check your health. The answers and solutions don't present themselves easily to you. If you search long and hard enough, you will eventually find the needle that you're looking for. At the end of the day, things will certainly work out for you. It's just a matter of time and patience.	
開 *Kai* **Open**	This sign is associated with very auspicious luck. Everything is in its right place for you and there is a Nobleman or a mentor that will always be able there to guide and help you regardless of your problems, situations, or circumstances. Your health is also vibrant and your energy level is high. Your dreams are all set to come true!	

奇門遁甲十干格局篇

乙
YI

天盤 **Heavenly Stem**	地盤 **Earthly Stem**
乙 *Yi* **Yin Wood**	庚 *Geng* **Yang Metal**

Structure 格局	Day Noble Punishment 日奇被刑
Rating 吉凶	Inauspicious 凶
Classic Verse 十干剋應歌訣	日奇被刑乙加庚，同床異夢產訟爭
Transliteration 字譯	Where the Yi meets with Geng, it is known as the Day Noble Punishment formation. It denotes a separation for couples, and also legal entanglements.
Description 解說	The Day Noble Punishment Formation denotes a lot of negativity, more so in the relationships that one holds dear. Esteemed friendships change into bitter and jealous rivalries. Dispute and un-mitigable animosities rage. Estrangement with one's closest relations occurs. These may lead into expensive lawsuits and lost earnings. Everyone's goal seems to be moving in the opposite direction. It is one of those situations when individuals cannot see each other for who they are.

The 8 Doors Analysis:
The following evaluates the effects of **Yi** 乙 and **Geng** 庚 with each Door.

休 *Xiu* **Rest**	It is finally your turn to be in the spotlight. You will be given the opportunity to demonstrate your talent, skills or knowledge in various situations. So go on and show them what you've got! Reveal your talents and start achieving your dreams. Good fortune doesn't always come so easily so you will need to treasure this time that you've got. Do your best and all your dreams will come into fruition.
生 *Sheng* **Life**	Your situation may look good and appealing on the surface but your fortune is fickle. Wealth and success can disappear as quickly as it comes. Your vision of the future may not likely come true. You must remain cautious and alert.
傷 *Shang* **Harm**	You seem to be missing out on the details therefore it is best you seek an independent third party assessment when it comes to making decisions. If you want to see your ideas succeed, then you can't make this happen on your own when help is required. Otherwise, it would be best for you to temporarily stop your projects or plans and return back to the drawing board to analyze. But for now, you are prone to procrastination and carelessness. This will lead to fruitless endeavors and missed opportunities.
杜 *Du* **Delusion**	Offers you encounter will have a shelf life. Sometimes two of them come along and you may spend too much time deliberating which one to take. You may promise yourself that you'll take a chance eventually – but ask yourself when will that be? Make a decision as soon as possible and respond to the changing circumstances faster and you'll find that you'll be able to get ahead sooner. The window of opportunity is very small. Act swiftly once you have all the facts.

景 *Jing* **Scenery**		It would seem that everything is calm and looking good for you right now. But there is hidden danger lurking around. It is advised that you take extra precaution in your actions and look through every detail carefully. Think twice about a decision you're about to make. Analyze it from different viewpoints/perspectives. Careful planning will stop you from going down the wrong path. This will be a quiet moment to self-reflect and not make big changes or decisions in your life.
死 *Si* **Death**		The things you are looking for are no longer available to you. What you may have lost may never return to you. Learning to let go is the key to a better outcome in life. Your projects, plans and schemes are unlikely to go your way because of obstacles and problems occurring out of your control. All of this can be extremely disheartening and discouraging for you. Hold on to the good memories and learn the valuable lessons needed to move on in a different/better direction.
驚 *Jing* **Fear**		Things are not going smoothly for you and you will be losing sleep because of this. Just remember that nothing remains perpetually good or bad, therefore while it may seem like things do not improve for you, don't be frustrated. If you look at what you've already got, the results will still be acceptable even if they do not meet your optimistic expectations. Stay healthy and mentally alert. Take care of yourself and relaxation is key.
開 *Kai* **Open**		There is hope so don't worry, things will improve for you. Your future will be positive. Opportunities will come along, although not everything will come at once. While there may be some setbacks in your life, don't let it get to you and don't let petty people disrupt your life. Don't get too hung up on the small things that you can't change – everything will turn out right in the end.

天盤 Heavenly Stem	**地盤 Earthly Stem**
乙 *Yi* **Yin Wood**	辛 *Xin* **Yin Metal**

Structure 格局	Green Dragon Escape 青龍逃走
Rating 吉凶	Inauspicious 凶
Classic Verse 十干剋應歌訣	青龍逃走乙加辛，人財兩空奴拐今，六畜傷亡女逃姻，開休生門雲虎聘
Transliteration 字譯	Where the Yi meets with Xin, it is known as the Green Dragon Escape formation. It denotes loss of wealth and love. Females will encounter divorce. There will be death of domestic animals or pets. The Cloud and the Tiger exist at the Rest Door and Life Door.
Description 解説	Green Dragon Escape is characterized by Yi Wood trying to escape from the control and manipulation of Xin Metal. Xin is obviously stronger than the Green Dragon. The formation exemplifies that someone or something stronger is taking advantage of an individual's weak points. One could be faced by foul play in the workplace or suffer abandonment from their supporters or partners. A spouse will walk out of a marriage and a junior employee will resign from their duties. Even the most well-thought out and executed plans will go haywire during this formation and in the unfortunate case where Inauspicious Doors or Stars appear, the formation could have aggravated catastrophic consequences including death and abduction.

The 8 Doors Analysis:

The following evaluates the effects of **Yi** 乙 and **Xin** 辛 with each Door.

休 *Xiu* **Rest**	You may be receiving a lot of criticisms but do not be afraid of them. The only people who are not criticized are those who do not take risks. Although you are troubled and feel weighed down by worries and doubts, you are on the right track. There is still hope for you – you just have to keep your eyes open to see what is in front of you. You may have made a wrong turn and missed a good opportunity but fortunately, there will be other opportunities in store for you. Better times lie ahead for you as well. Focus is power. Your ability to focus on your personal powers and abilities will determine what you will achieve in life. Sacrifices that you have to make will be part of your journey as well. It takes a strong character to keep going forward.
生 *Sheng* **Life**	Your career looks like it is set to be remembered for years to come. You will have a great environment around you with lots of supportive friends and family. The external conditions/factors around you are filled with the necessary resources you may need to move ahead in life. Wealth, prosperity and happiness will all find its way to you without laborious efforts on your part – it seems as though someone up there likes you!
傷 *Shang* **Harm**	It is not enough to just tell people the truth. The information gathered by yourself does not cause transformations/changes. It's tough to make it to the top, especially in your case. You are prone to spending more time day-dreaming and wishing than you are actually getting things done. This makes it very difficult for you to actually achieve anything. You'll need to roll up your sleeves and get to work if you expect anything to change. This sign is associated with a changing situation and signifies changing fortunes - make sure they are the changes for the better!
杜 *Du* **Delusion**	It's all too easy to rush in and do things without first drawing up a thorough plan. If you are aware of this pitfall, then you can get your ideal results with minimum difficulty. You work best when you are working in a systematic manner, so think before you act and breakdown what needs to be done into a series of necessary steps to achieve your goals. Proceed calmly and focus on one step at a time and victory will inevitably be yours.

景 *Jing* **Scenery**	You will have trouble focusing on any one project, idea or goal long enough to achieve its desired results. You will have a lot of ideas, but there will be a lack of focus on your part. Remember, less is more in your case. And if you really want to succeed, you will need to rely on the help of others, especially so if you want to solve your current problems. Don't be afraid to actively seek the help of those around you. When asking for the support of others, it is imperative to remain modest – this will undoubtedly help your cause. Your health may not be as strong as you think and it's advisable to do a medical check-up.	
死 *Si* **Death**	Unfortunately for you, people can't always be trusted. What is said to you may not be what is said when you're not around. Choose your friends wisely and always question yourself whether they're actually your real friends. Likewise, you also need to be careful of your words and the words of others. Be aware of damaging people and those who may backstab you. It's easy for you to be in isolation or in a state of conflict with others due to misunderstandings that may occur.	奇門遁甲十干格局篇 乙 YI
驚 *Jing* **Fear**	Do remember that promises will be broken so be wary and do not waste time trying to reason it out or argue over it. Last minute surprises and twists in events will dampen your spirit. This will ultimately lead to uncertainties in your future endeavors. You should also remember that when at first things may seem like there is a sense of an ending for you but do note that it may also mean the beginning of something new. Be flexible like water and adapt to different situations instead of crying over spilt milk.	
開 *Kai* **Open**	Although life sometimes can feel like a rollercoaster, every up is followed by a down time. You have mixed fortunes and for everything that brings you happiness, you seem to encounter something that will bring you worries as well. You gain and then you lose repeatedly. You can expect problems to be solved if you meet the right mentor therefore you can start by looking for this person immediately. Try and make the most of what you've learnt along the way. Remember to live in the moment and stay joyful.	

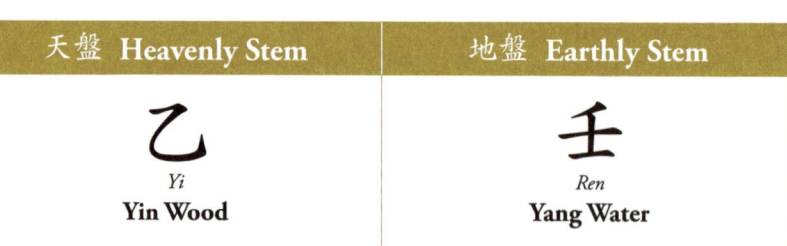

天盤 Heavenly Stem	地盤 Earthly Stem
乙 *Yi* **Yin Wood**	壬 *Ren* **Yang Water**

Structure 格局	Day Noble Enters Earth 日奇入地
Rating 吉凶	Inauspicious 凶
Classic Verse 十干剋應歌訣	奇入天羅乙加壬，尊卑悖亂官非門
Transliteration 字譯	Where the Yi meets with Ren, it is known as the Day Noble Enters Earth formation. It denotes hostile, chaotic and hierarchical relationships.
Description 解說	The Day Noble Enters Earth formation symbolizes resistance. The young will go contrary to the old and employees will go against their employers. The negative karma might portended by this formation could see one get sued in a court of law or get into persistent problems. One's interactions will be filled with venomous jealousy and animosity. During this formation, it is not uncommon for one to lose the support and admiration of those closest to him. To counter this negativity, one needs to stick to protocol and the conventional way of doing things. If the formation is also characterized by Negative Doors, Deities or Stars, the situation will be aggravated.

The 8 Doors Analysis:

The following evaluates the effects of **Yi** 乙 and **Ren** 壬 with each Door.

休 *Xiu* **Rest**	You dream of the impossible. While you may have wonderful ideas, you lack the practical tools and people needed to achieve these dreams. A fairly straightforward chain reaction must take place if a dream of yours is to come true. Unfortunately, you seem to forget that nothing happens without some good old fashioned hardwork. So unless you come up with a more practical strategy, you are likely to spend your time wishing for things rather than seeing them materialize.
生 *Sheng* **Life**	Opportunities that at first seem lucrative turn out to be rotten and problematic with unhappy results for you. Frustration and depression will result from a constant lack of positive outcomes. You will need to work on your relationship with others as well. You must always proceed with caution when you take any action. Expect the worst and plan for it so that you are ready to deal with the problems that may be on its way.
傷 *Shang* **Harm**	This is an inauspicious configuration: a sign of bad luck. The road ahead is bumpy to say the least. You'll need to stay on your toes because there are a lot of obstacles that stand between you being victorious and yourself. Your energy level will be low. This would also mean progress won't be as smooth as you'd like it to be. Factor this into your planning and stay alert at all times. There's no need to think too far ahead in your future and live for now.
杜 *Du* **Delusion**	This is an inauspicious configuration. You'll have plenty of ambition but not enough action. You're unable to make quick decisions; therefore everything seems to be stuck at your level. Others are just waiting for you to get the ball rolling and you will need to make practical decisions, if you want to achieve your goals. If your actions are not aligned with your vision, you'll find it difficult to convince others to follow your dream. You'll also need to start thinking strategically and taking each step into consideration so that you'll move closer to your goals instead of being lost.

景 *Jing* **Scenery**		A bumpy ride will still be a road that has a destination at the end of it. Work will not progress smoothly but you'll always get where you need to be in the end. Learn as many lessons as possible from mishaps and problems and cherish them. This will be a time for learning. These lessons will serve you well in the near future. In addition to that, you'll need to learn to respect yourself before you expect others to respect you. Once you've gained enough wisdom, you'll then reach whatever wealth or relationship goals you seek.
死 *Si* **Death**		Unluckiness. Things you desire just don't seem to gel or come together in a way that benefits you. The situation is beyond your control and those who promised you their help will not be able to deliver to their promise. Your dreams are unlikely to come true due to these hostile circumstances. Because of your tendencies to act before you think, you are unlikely to make the right decisions. You need to take some time to gather the complete information needed and look at the full picture before embarking on these decisions, especially so when it relates to money or investments. Don't base your decisions on hearsay.
驚 *Jing* **Fear**		This is an unfavorable sign in many ways. Despite projecting a calm, composed exterior, feelings of depression, inadequacy and inner rage will be hidden from others. This hidden state combined with repeated external misfortune, makes for broken dreams and slow progression. In terms of wealth, financial losses from misguided investments may occur. You are also prone to gossip which is never productive or beneficial in the long run. There's no need to think too far ahead in your future. You should just try to see more in yourself and look cautiously for the next right and risk-free way forward.
開 *Kai* **Open**		There seems to be a lack of energy in the air for you. Things seem to be stale and stagnant. This may have dampened your appetite to work harder. It will almost seems like you're not making any significant amount of progress on this route. The good news is that everything changes and someone in your upcoming path is going to guide you to the success that you might have missed out on. Pay attention to helping hands around you now and everything will be better once you've been put together with the right person on the job/task.

天盤 Heavenly Stem	地盤 Earthly Stem
乙 *Yi* **Yin Wood**	癸 *Gui* **Yin Water**

Structure 格局	Elegant Seal Meets Star 華蓋逢星
Rating 吉凶	Moderate 半吉
Classic Verse 十干剋應歌訣	華蓋逢星乙加癸，隱遁避厄修無爲
Transliteration 字譯	Where the Yi meets with Gui, it is known as the Elegant Seal Meets Star. It denotes escaping from dangerous situation.
Description 解說	Elegant Seal Meets Star moves into seclusion as a means of allowing someone to be a little more reflective. It creates spiritual beliefs for all the needs one might have. The Yi has a Noble Crescent that represents enhancement, healing and assistance for the self. The Gul has a negative Crescent symbolic of problems and traps. The combination creates the ability to control problems by secluding oneself in order to reflect on one's life. This may be controlled through an added education in order to resolve varying problems as needed.

The 8 Doors Analysis:

The following evaluates the effects of **Yi** 乙 and **Gui** 癸 with each Door.

休 *Xiu* **Rest**	Three things are needed for success in your endeavors: Time, People and Money. You may already have the right people around you but you may need to learn how to ask for help from them. You will also have the financial resources needed or at the very least, you will know how to get access to them. It's going to take you courage but you will be able to find it when the time is right – you just need to believe in yourself. You also need to learn to manage your time wisely. You can achieve anything you set out to do with the right determination and clarity. You need to learn time management skills, as this will lead you to instant greatness and impressive achievements or a list of admirable triumphs.
生 *Sheng* **Life**	In terms of your networking skills, whether you take them for granted or not, they are very good. A lot of people will be mesmerized by you. Your likeability factor is always high and this would equate to a pool of resources (people/friends/family) that you could readily tap into at any time. This support network you have will be integral to your success and will allow you to realize any vision you have with ease, regardless of how ambitious it may be. You should make wise use of this gift!
傷 *Shang* **Harm**	There are a lot of things you'd like to achieve but for some apparent reason, you simply can't muster up the heart and drive to achieve your necessary goals. You seem to have run out of fuel to carry on. Confidence in your own abilities is a primary key. You must rebuild your confidence by taking smaller steps, aiming lower and proving to yourself that you can succeed. When in doubt, just take the next 'right' turn. There's no point thinking too far ahead right now. Don't bite off more than you can chew. Warning: you might find that you can't get your vibe and enthusiam back.
杜 *Du* **Delusion**	This is an inauspicious configuration. You are easily drawn into risky situations. You will also find it difficult to obtain the trust of others and to build a supportive network for yourself. What you need right now is to acquire better leadership skills. Your friends will not follow your suggestions because your suggestions may not be good. Perhaps you are the only one who thinks and feels you are right. If you cannot obtain help from others, you will need to walk this path alone – independently.

景 *Jing* **Scenery**	The situation you are in may be good, but the timing is not right yet. There are still some steps that you would need to take in order for you to reach your goals or full potential. Of course you'll have every reason to be optimistic as your life will only get better from here onwards. Do not expect any kind of free ride though, as there is lack of helpful people in your life. No matter what you plan to achieve, it is likely that you'll have to do this on your own. With perseverance and commitment, fame and fortune will be the result for you. Nurture your talents and don't be afraid to show them off, people will take notice and you'll be rewarded soon.	
死 *Si* **Death**	You will have too many thoughts and too many issues to deal with but whatever you do will seem to get you nowhere. It will almost feel like you're being crushed or trapped thus wasting your time and effort on difficult tasks. This is an extremely unfortunate situation to be in for you and the best thing you can do about it is lay low and be content with what you have for the time being. When times are tough, you will be able to obtain energy from your spirit. Always remember that in spite of all the struggles, it is important to feed your spirit as well as your body.	
驚 *Jing* **Fear**	Even when you can't see the clouds in the sky, the next storm may be brewing. Although things may seem calm and peaceful, you will still need to be alert and ready for the next crisis around the corner. Your path ahead has a hidden sharp turn and it's simply wiser to be well-prepared. You'll need to work very hard and set realistic goals for yourself because your journey is likely to be filled with obstacles and this will make it difficult to achieve the success you desire. The people who promised to help you are now backing out from their word. It is also probably wise for you to be prepared for all this. Be ready for a long marathon in life!	
開 *Kai* **Open**	This sign denotes an almost certain good luck in whichever situation you find yourself in and it will be extremely auspicious for you. You should go ahead and don't be afraid to move forward. You will achieve your goals and become successful. One good thing will lead to another for you and it will have a compounding effect on you. You should also start helping others and reap startling rewards.	

丙

Bing
Yang Fire

天盤 Heavenly Stem	地盤 Earthly Stem
丙 *Bing* **Yang Fire**	甲 *Jia* **Yang Wood**

Structure 格局	Flying Bird Fall into Cave 飛鳥跌穴
Rating 吉凶	Auspicious 吉
Classic Verse 十干剋應歌訣	飛鳥跌穴丙加甲，不勞而獲此中發，迫墓擊刑亦遭伐
Transliteration 字譯	Where the Bing meets with Jia, it is known as the Flying Bird Fall into Cave formation. It denotes a wealth potential that is undeserved. It also indicates possible severe punishment and penalty.
Description 解說	This is one of the more desirable 10 Stem Combinations in Qi Men Dun Jia. Its appearance normally denotes the forthcoming of celebratory events including career advancements and moments of monetary success. One can expect good luck and favorable fortunes through the assistance of a nobleman. This combination indicates that the road ahead will be smooth and that the individual can expect success to come easily no matter what they decide to pursue at that point in time. The presence of auspicious stars will further enhance the positive effects of this wonderful combination while even with the presence of negative stars, the worst one would face is merely some disagreements and logging of heads.

The 8 Doors Analysis:

The following evaluates the effects of **Bing** 丙 and **Jia** 甲 with each Door.

休 *Xiu* **Rest**	The future appears bright as it will present numerous golden opportunities that are ripe for the taking. No matter which path in your life that you choose to go, it will be smooth sailing the moment you take a step towards your chosen path. There are no obstacles as far as you can see and whatever your heart's desire will come true because of good fortune smiling down on you. From there onwards, you can expect the success of building a prosperous and respected reputation to come easily as wealth and an increase of finances will blossom readily for you at any given time. You will receive plenty of help from Helpful People – just ask and you shall receive.
生 *Sheng* **Life**	Your pride can signal your eventual downfall in life if you are not mindful of your actions and behaviour. That is why a self-aggravating attitude will not get you anywhere. There is a Chinese saying that for every mountain present, there will always be another one bigger and higher. So recognize the fact that there will always be people whom are better than you and take the modest and humble approach in life. Remember that you are not always right nor are you the best. Being stubborn is not the best way forward as your life path will always be challenging. Do not fret because help will come in the form of mentions, provided you see them in just time.
傷 *Shang* **Harm**	This sign denotes an optimistic, bright outcome for you right now. Whether you seek wealth, prosperity and the freedom that both of things bring, be wise to remember not to be too complacent and remember instead to appreciate all these for the blessings that they are. And try to appreciate that sometimes imperfections or slight blemishes do not harm.
杜 *Du* **Delusion**	This is an inauspicious sign that denotes that difficulty and strife will plague you throughout your life. All good things may turn sour in the long run, while happiness will eventually drift away. Even business and prosperity won't last long as you will only delude yourself longer if you think otherwise.

奇門遁甲十干格局篇

丙
BING

奇門遁甲十干格局篇

BING

景 *Jing* **Scenery**	The current situations in your life are beyond your control at the moment. Do not be frustrated if you cannot get the desired outcome though as your career outlook is rather unstable at this point and your relationships seem unstable as well. To ride the wave most efficiently, pay close attention to all details and remember to appreciate others around you, especially someone dear to you. Do double check everything before proceeding further.
死 *Si* **Death**	The road is straight and you are about to pick up some speed on your journey but drive cautiously in case something unforeseeable crosses your path. Drive conservatively and steadily and you will reach your destination in due time. Unfortunately, the road you have chosen to drive on is a very long road indeed.
驚 *Jing* **Fear**	Fear of the unknown is what will keep you from breaking new ground and succeeding in life. This is why you follow the edit of easy come, easy go and will never achieve any measurable amount of success in your life. The problem is due to your own belief of your mental limitations as you are constantly stuck in the past and refuse to let go. If you wish to not impede your future, you need to revamp your strategic goals and to keep a low profile this time. If not, you are doomed to failure.
開 *Kai* **Open**	You can always look forward to receiving great news as you continue to reap the benefits of your many successful endeavours. This coupled with your current reputation has earned you fame in your community and most important, has earned you the ultimate goal that everyone is currently seeking – happiness! This is a good sign.

天盤 **Heavenly Stem**	地盤 **Earthly Stem**
丙 *Bing* **Yang Fire**	乙 *Yi* **Yin Wood**

Structure 格局	Bright Sun and Moon 日月並明
Rating 吉凶	Auspicious 吉
Classic Verse 十干剋應歌訣	日月並明丙加乙，公成私就皆爲吉
Transliteration 字譯	Where the Bing meets with Yi, it is known as the Bright Sun and Moon formation. It denotes auspicious public and private affairs.
Description 解說	The combination of the Sun and Moon is a very favorable one. It portends advancement in a career and personal actualization. One will find fulfillment and satisfaction when the fellow chases his or her dreams and vision. Happiness and prosperity comes naturally to the individual whether he or she stays in the present or that person decides to chase one's aspirations. Help from noble people is easily forthcoming. However, despite all the positivity, an individual should refrain from going overboard and remain grateful.

The 8 Doors Analysis:

The following evaluates the effects of **Bing** 丙 and **Yi** 乙 with each Door.

休 *Xiu* **Rest**	A most auspicious sign indeed! You will continue to have good fortunes which will be the envy of many. Thus, it is best to keep a low profile as you will always land on your feet and have things swing in your favour. Your chances of success are very high, so you should strike out and give things a go. Work hard and you will see the results your desire. Don't just sit there. Go out now and make miracles happen!
生 *Sheng* **Life**	Few people have ever had the opportunity to showcase their talents to the world. When those who do, the end results are usually nothing short of amazing. In that sense, you are always fortunate as you are able to meet the right people, at the right time, at the right place. Your environment is one in which you may use your strengths, so you will always stay ahead of the pack. You have got what it takes to get what you want. And when you are in the right place, success is achievable for you and you will be a well respected and admired individual.
傷 *Shang* **Harm**	All that you desire will surely come easily for you. But troubles and burdens of success will also follow suit and eventually take its tow on you. Be aware of the potential pitfalls and stay on track. Even if you have the extra money, do not use your wealth to try and gain people's affections. You would do well in taking the time to build genuine relationships with others in order to get ahead. This means do not participate in gossips or spreading rumors.
杜 *Du* **Delusion**	Unfortunately, your luck is flat out bad. You are the subject of gossip and the center of disputes which you may or may not have instigated. Your relationships with other people are poor and very few people support you. You do not receive any support from others because you do not spend time cultivating trust and reliability in the first place. The solution to your problems lies in the teachings and support of a mentor, so it is better if you can meet this person sooner.

景 *Jing* **Scenery**	Even when you have worked hard in your workplace, you will always find backstabbers and jealous people. You seem to attract a lot of petty people right now and they will want to stick around you for most part of your life. Despite having a Nobleman to help you out, even he/she can do so much for you. This is sometimes the dark nature of your reality as while career success might not be forthcoming for you right now, you will still be able to make plenty of friends especially people who will want to get to know you. There are still many good people out there so get your happiness from this as best as you can	奇門遁甲十干格局篇 丙 **BING**
死 *Si* **Death**	Worry and doubt is constantly weighing on your mind as you continue to think too much. Sadly, you are in this all by yourself and may struggle with feelings of loneliness. Others may not be able to help you right now and even if they tried, they will not fully understand your struggles or your path enough to honestly support you. If you want to make better decisions, it is best that you first determine what your available options are by considering both the short and long-term options before deciding. Pay attention to details and do not make any hasty decisions.	
驚 *Jing* **Fear**	Do not set the bar too high with outrageous pipe dreams because you will only disappoint yourself by choosing goals that are unrealistic. Life will always throw curve balls at you giving you problems and dicey situations that will force you to navigate through as best as you can. In order to be successful, you must always wait for the right opportunity to strike while the iron is hot. Until then, you must be patient. A good leader is always looking for people smarter and more experienced than they are. If you are the smartest one in the room then you are in the wrong room.	
開 *Kai* **Open**	Good fortune will follow you around willingly as you continue to receive more good news as compared to bad news. Your plans will even go off without a hitch as you expect the least resistance when executing them. And you can always count on the enthusiastic support of others. Expect this kind of prosperity to continue for a while as the outcome will be of utmost happiness. Remember that the more you share, the more good returns you will receive.	

天盤 Heavenly Stem	地盤 Earthly Stem
丙 *Bing* **Yang Fire**	丙 *Bing* **Yang Fire**

Structure 格局	Month Noble Rebelling Officer 月奇悖師
Rating 吉凶	Inauspicious 凶
Classic Verse 十干剋應歌訣	月奇悖師丙加丙，文書逼迫耗失並
Transliteration 字譯	Where the Bing meets with Bing, it is known as the Month Noble Rebelling Officer formation. It denotes loss of something important caused by the influence of civil officers.
Description 解說	This formation will bring contract-related lawsuits to one. One will need to keep important legal documents at close reach for such an eventuality. At work, it is be paramount that one handles and stores data carefully. At first, everything goes so smoothly and may lure one to become contented with the way things are. However, the good times do not last for long and problems may strike when one least expects. Being caught without a contingent plan becomes one's undoing.

The 8 Doors Analysis:
The following evaluates the effects of **Bing** 丙 and **Bing** 丙 with each Door.

休 *Xiu* **Rest**	This sign is only associated with those receiving decisions that shape your average outcomes. You can improve your chances of making the right decisions by running them by people that your trust for their unbiased opinion. The truth may hurt, but it is better that your resolve matters before it is too late. You must not be hasty. Making an emotional decision will be bad and there is a possibility that you may lose your current position.
生 *Sheng* **Life**	Most people are not wealthy because of their innate fear of the evils of money. You must not have this fear, as there is nothing evil or wrong about achieving wealth and what's more, it merely magnifies your character. Thus, if you have a good character, your wealth will be magnified more. Unfortunately for you, at this time, this sign indicates that your troubles have just begun. Nobody likes to be told that they are about to be plunge into a time of frustration and hardship but knowing this can help you prepare for it. The wise thing to do now is to proceed cautiously.
傷 *Shang* **Harm**	The things that you are looking for now are no longer there and you may never find them again. It is best to let go of it all. Your projects, plans and schemes are unlikely to pan out because of obstacles and problems beyond your control. All of this can be incredibly disappointing. Just keep the faith and think positively and continue moving on in a different direction.
杜 *Du* **Delusion**	With so many obstructions in the way and a general feeling of despondency, it is no wonder you sometimes feel that date seems to single you out unfairly. With so many bumps in the road for you in the form of mishaps, failures or ill fortune, even sharing your concerns do not bring about anything positive for you. There are some things that are beyond your control. Do not let what you cannot do interfere with what you still can do. Time to switch to plan B if you have one.

奇門遁甲十干格局篇

BING

	景 *Jing* **Scenery**	Some problems cannot be solved and can be unwise to continue pursuing this worrisome issue further.. You might find yourself having to give up on ideas and plans for these reasons, despite every effor,. Learn to let go. Do not hang on to something you know is impossible to obtain. The best thing you can do is to share your feelings with someone. They may not be able to give you a solution but this will lighten the load.
	死 *Si* **Death**	Things start out well but then seem to run off course. You have the best of intentions but somehow you lack whatever it is that is needed to convert these into a desired final outcome,. You might be capable of starting a business for example but you have difficulty getting it off the ground or keeping it from collapsing entirely. If you are to succeed, you will need to find some external guidance.
	驚 *Jing* **Fear**	This sign represents a family who does not function as a family should. This could due to spousal or partnership problems. For noe, it seems pretty demoralizing. Don't over analyse things and blame yourself too quickly. Try to relax and learn to let go if you want to move forward to a better tomorrow instead of getting stuck in the past. If you continue hanging onto the past, the better future will not come.
	開 *Kai* **Open**	One good turn leads to another, as joyous events and favourable occasions are coming to you with the help of Noble people. You will generally find it much easier to achieve a goal – provided you have one set up in the first place, and you can resolve any lingering problems easily this time. There is recognition for your efforts in the end. This is a fortunate sign.

天盤 **Heavenly Stem**	地盤 **Earthly Stem**
丙 *Bing* **Yang Fire**	丁 *Ding* **Yin Fire**

Structure 格局	Month Noble Red Phoenix 月奇朱雀
Rating 吉凶	Auspicious 吉
Classic Verse 十干剋應歌訣	月奇朱雀丙加丁，貴人文利凡安靜，吉門喜慶天遁行
Transliteration 字譯	Where the Bing meets with Ding, it is known as the Month Noble Red Phoenix formation. It denotes that the Nobleman is auspicious to people who are peaceful. Celebrations at the auspicious Door along the Heavenly Dun will be held.
Description 解說	One will get assistance and approval from a noble person. This assistance and approval, which is put in writing, leads to fame, fortunes, success and happiness. One's climb to the top is easy and is littered with a lot of opportunities and breakthroughs in almost everything they set their hearts upon. There are a number of genuine helping hands along the way and goal attainment and self-actualization is quite easy.

BING 丙

The 8 Doors Analysis:

The following evaluates the effects of **Bing** 丙 and **Ding** 丁 with each Door.

休 *Xiu* **Rest**		You are dealt with lucky helping hands in life and this trend is all set to continue for some time. You are fortunate because you are likely to succeed at whatever you attempt. But you can really supercharge your progression in career or in life if you meet a Nobleman or mentor who can give you his/her expert guidance, ideas and inspiration. Look out for this person to maximize your talents in life.
生 *Sheng* **Life**		You are blessed because you will always have people like good mentors and good friends whom are eager to come and help you. Do show gratitude for the help you will receive in life as fame and fortune will be dealt to you in due time. You will also find yourself at the right place at the right time and will enjoy success in life. Do not neglect those less fortunate than you because you can greatly increase your luck by offering a helping hand to them. This karmic blessing will continue on for a long time.
傷 *Shang* **Harm**		A bumpy road is still a road that has a destination at the end of it. Work will not progress smoothly but you will always reach your destination in the end. Learn from mishaps and problems you will face along the road as they are all self-affirming lessons. In addition, learn to respect yourself before you expect others to respect you. Once you have gained enough wisdom, you will reach whatever wealth or relationship goals that you seek,
杜 *Du* **Delusion**		Emotions often get in the way of logic that undermines wise decision-making. Do not let your emotions control your actions. Perhaps you care too much about how others think of you or your ego just gets in the way. Because of this, you are unable to look at the cold facts in realistic and productive way. You are unsure about the future or what to do as you have too many conflicting ideas, concerns and opinions that hinder you from moving forward in any one definitive direction. Clarity is the solution to your problem, be clear about what you want and what you need. When you are clear, you can focus.

景 *Jing* **Scenery**	You will not receive any Nobleman luck this time. Without people around you to encourage you in the first place or to congratulate you when you succeed, things will become a harder for you and you must rely entirely on your own strengths to stay motivated. You may owe people money also and the only hope of things become better, lies in your willingness to make changes because you are not in a winning situation right now. You need to systematize your work and to properly control your finances. And more importantly, do not dwell in unfruitful relationship matters.	
死 *Si* **Death**	Everyone makes mistakes. Do not try to place blame and remember instead to control your emotions and focus on the lessons you have learnt. Don't expect anything to be handed to you on a silver platter as complacency will get you nowhere. Instead, work hard and work smart. In your case, your success depends entirely on how much you are willing to roll up your sleeves and take action. A strong work ethic will allow you to overcome the odds and reach for the stars. If you decide to play safe and stay where you are now, however, then success is going to remain out of reach.	
驚 *Jing* **Fear**	You have trouble focusing on any one idea, project or goal long enough to achieve any measure of success. While you have lots of ideas, you lack focus. Remember, less is best in your case. And if you want to succeed, you will also need to rely on the help of other people, especially if you want to solve your current problems, Don't be afraid to actively seek the help of those around you. But when asking for help, be modest about it as it will help your caus. Your health is also not as strong as you think. Time for a medical check-up.	
開 *Kai* **Open**	You have probably gotten used to enjoying a stream of prosperity and living the good life. Do not worry as nothing is going to change dramatically overnight, thanks to your ongoing favourable luck. Whether you realize it or not, you have many loyal friends who would jump at the chance to help you. So if you need support or an extra pair of hands, don't wait to ask. Accepting help or gestures from others also makes others happy.	

奇門遁甲十干格局篇

丙
BING

天盤 Heavenly Stem	地盤 Earthly Stem
丙 *Bing* **Yang Fire**	戊 *Wu* **Yang Earth**

Structure 格局	Flying Bird Fall into Cave 飛鳥跌穴
Rating 吉凶	Auspicious 吉
Classic Verse 十干剋應歌訣	飛鳥跌穴丙加戊，百事可行通天路
Transliteration 字譯	Where the Bing meets with Wu, it is known as the Flying Bird Fall into Cave formation. It is a highly auspicious formation indicating that life will progress smoothly.
Description 解說	Unexpected good fortunes will become abundant and good news is on its way. When coupled with concerted personal initiative and effort, the good fortunes from this formation will will dissolve any present quagmires and put one's life perfectly on track. The path is straight and clear and there are no obstacles to stop anyone from reaching for what the self will dream for.

The 8 Doors Analysis:
The following evaluates the effects of **Bing** 丙 and **Wu** 戊 with each Door.

休 *Xiu* **Rest**	They say two heads are better than one. There is a person you know, or who you may meet, who shares your ambition, vision and drive. He/she is the key that will unlock your full potential and you should make the best of your relationship with this person by communicating your ambitions, goals and even sorry with them.. Think like a brave leader. Cultivate team spirit and do what you can to enhance morale in those around you and move boldly towards prosperity because what you desire can only be obtained with the help of others.
生 *Sheng* **Life**	Good tidings and good news is on the way. With a little more effort, you could turn the good into the great and really reach for the stars. Your problems will dissolve and the path ahead of you is clear. All you need to do is find that extra 10% within yourself and keep doing what is right and what is needed to be done. Success awaits you if you can push yourself just a little further. All the other elements are in place right now so stay on track
傷 *Shang* **Harm**	You will be blessed with above average luck as the Nobleman will be constantly present wherever you choose to go. This will help you get noticed as your progression along your chosen path in life with be smooth, steady and stable. Just be persistent and not be complacent at all times. Keep your eye on the main prize! Remember to avoid gossip or speculation as what goes around, comes around. Do what is right and needed to be done, not what is convenient right now.
杜 *Du* **Delusion**	The bad events that are ongoing in your life are about to wrap up, making way for better opportunities. Just like a storm that passed overhead, your problems are about to be nothing more than memories. This sign is associated with above average luck and a future full of hope. Despite the many obstacles you have faced, you will finally get to achieve your goals, after all.

奇門遁甲十干格局篇

BING

	景 *Jing* **Scenery**	Kindness is always appreciated by other people. Take this advice to heart. A polite and thoughtful approach to your dealings with others will produce prosperity for you. A Nobleman or mentor in your life will serve as a guide to show you how to turn things around and turn sorrow into joy. Seek out this person as he/she is closer than you think
	死 *Si* **Death**	You seem to be in a state of constant dilemma because you are always confused as to how to make up your mind. You could be just ignorant of the important details of the situation as to how to proceed. This delay will be your downfall. If you hesitate too long, opportunities may stop coming for you. Pay attention when the opportunity arises. This way you can make the most of your potential and have no regrets.
	驚 *Jing* **Fear**	You are a stubborn minded person. This is much is true as when people make perfectly valid suggestions but you ignore them because you did not think of them first. You will find it difficult to concentrate at work and will be plagued by mistakes. The best you can do is to stay quiet and listen more instead of talking all the time. A better plan is needed because the current one is faulty. Consider taking on fewer responsibilities so you can handle each issue more proficiently.
	開 *Kai* **Open**	The dragon soars into the skies and it is clear sign that great fortune will shine on you. For some people, golden opportunities can seem like busses. You can wait a long time for one to come along and then many come at once. You have been waiting patiently and now you can enter a period of unprecedented prosperity – if you are willing to act! So take action and grab the best opportunity that comes your way. Make the most of your bright fortunes as happiness and prosperity awaits you.

天盤 **Heavenly Stem**	地盤 **Earthly Stem**
丙 *Bing* **Yang Fire**	己 *Ji* **Yin Earth**

Structure 格局	Great Rebel Enters Punishment 太悖入刑
Rating 吉凶	Moderate 半吉
Classic Verse 十干剋應歌訣	火悖入刑丙加己，囚人刑杖文不利，吉凶但由門中祈
Transliteration 字譯	Where the Bing meets with Ji, it is known as the Great Rebel Enters Punishment formation. It denotes that the Prisoner and the Rod are both inauspicious. A person can pray for auspiciousness while being warned of disasters at the Doors.
Description 解說	This formation portends bad news, disagreements, disharmony and unending arguments in an individual's life. Things will take a turn for the worse. One is faced with lawsuits. Family breakups and estrangements spring up from everywhere and one lacks the support he or she desires in his or her projects or career. Progress is stunted and there is little approval for almost everything that one does. The only saving grace in this formation is the appearance of Auspicious Qi Men Doors. With their presence, the arguments will dissipate and every mistake will be a disguised blessing.

The 8 Doors Analysis:

The following evaluates the effects of **Bing** 丙 and **Ji** 己 with each Door.

休 *Xiu* **Rest**	Your feelings of insecurity or inadequacy hold you back. Self-improvement is needed as well as a little more self-love. Plan things carefully and do the best work you can for now. If you want to be loved, you must first learn to love yourself. If you want others to love you, you must have confidence to offer your love to them first. If you want the best chance of success, don't aim too high for now. There is no shame in having smaller but more practical goals that you are actually able to achieve.
生 *Sheng* **Life**	Your luck may seem unstable at the moment as things do not go as planned and you end up waiting longer for things to materialize. Patience and hope is important here as all is not lost. Keep moving along in your path and think positively about the journey's end. Remember that if at first you don't succeed, try and try again and you will reach your goal in the end.
傷 *Shang* **Harm**	If you got something to do in your mind, then you should be more confident in your ability to make it happen. What you lack are the true skills needed to succeed in your endeavours. So, what is stopping you from learning the required skill? With careful planning and proper direction, you can achieve your goal and fulfil your ambitions. Simply believing in yourself and setting out to try is the first step towards success in your case.
杜 *Du* **Delusion**	On the surface you look calm, ready and content but it conceals inner turmoil. It only looks good on the outside but inside, your emotions are wracked with fear and worries that hold you back. Lack of information is what caused the fear. Find out more. Learn all you can. See things plainly and ask you whether things are really as bad as they seem. You are more capable than you think. Often, things are not that difficult in reality than you expect, so let go of your inner chaos.

景 *Jing* **Scenery**	Thrashing around, leaping from one decision to the next and never committing to them is a waste of time and energy. The reason you cannot commit to take action is because you are subconsciously busy trying to find an easier way out. Paying too much attention to external influences and being fickle instead of focus-minded will prevent you from fulfilling your goal. Clarity is power – remember this. Priority is next. Do what needs to be done first, and then do what you feel like doing when you have the extra time. Needs supersede wants. And when you don't know what to do yet, relax and wait for the answers to present itself to you.	
死 *Si* **Death**	There are clouds on the horizon and the view ahead is dull and obscured by uncertainty. You may suffer some bullying to some degree at this point. Perhaps this leads to some self-doubt and a lack of the confidence necessary to push forward with your plans. Stop looking for help externally as you will not find any. You are your only solution. Without a strong will and a clear mind for what needs to be done first, you may find it difficult to achieve your ambitions.	
驚 *Jing* **Fear**	This is not a fortunate sign. Disaster and misadventure will occur without warning and there is nothing you can do to avoid them. Your career will suffer and may be doomed to fail often. Though sometimes it is no fault of your own. This is not the best time to seek a career or relationship change.	
開 *Kai* **Open**	Show the people around you that you care and you will discover a whole new world of budding friendship filled with positive rewards. Treat others as you wish to be treated and the karmic blessings will be bestowed on you richly. This good feeling will translate into helping bring your dreams to life at some point down the line.	

奇門遁甲十干格局篇

丙
BING

天盤 **Heavenly Stem**	地盤 **Earthly Stem**
丙 *Bing* **Yang Fire**	庚 *Geng* **Yang Metal**

Structure 格局	Shimmering Enters Great White 熒惑入太白
Rating 吉凶	Inauspicious 凶
Classic Verse 十干剋應歌訣	熒入太白丙加庚，門戶破敗賊耗逢，事業不利兇無成
Transliteration 字譯	Where the Bing meets with Geng, it is known as the Shimmering Enters Great White formation. It denotes potential robbery may occur. It also warns of an unfavourable career outlook.
Description 解說	This is a disparaging formation that portends disintegrated family relationships, loss of personal wealth. Uncertainty and worries will riddle one's mind and negativity seems to have found a field day. The only thing one can do to avoid catastrophic outcomes is avoid making impulsive decisions.

The 8 Doors Analysis:

The following evaluates the effects of **Bing** 丙 and **Geng** 庚 with each Door.

休 *Xiu* **Rest**	You have a rare and uniquely beneficial ability to see things in black and white; good or bad, right or wrong. This helps you sort the better decisions from the ill-advised ones, which ultimately leads to overall success. You can recognize the right people when you see them and avoid the bad apples by surrounding yourself with the best network. Don't be afraid to call a spade, a spade. Do what is right, not what is convenient. Rest assured, a Nobleman will appear at the right time for you.
生 *Sheng* **Life**	You are independent and you know how to motivate yourself. You enjoy good luck in general. This means that you have almost all of the ingredients needed to create a runaway success story for yourself. Just make sure that you focus on your work and do a thorough job of whatever tasks or projects that at hand and will be rewarded with another progression and a reputation that befits you. Finish what you started. Perseverance is the key. Do not be afraid to ask for help when needed.
傷 *Shang* **Harm**	Miscommunication with others will cause difficulties and create conflict. Try not to tread on other people's toes by pushing an action before you have talked things through with them. Your strained dealings with others and the mistakes that arise because of these interactions will eventually lead to a knot in your heart (blame, hatred and guilt). To avoid all of this, minimize confrontations and always run your proposed plans by those around you before you act on them. Proactive attempts to communicate more effectively will mean a brighter future for you.
杜 *Du* **Delusion**	Everything you do seems wrong as it seems like none of your decisions ever pan out the way you hoped. You know how to pick yourself up but then something always seems to knock you back off your feet again. This number indicates bad luck in your life at present. You must stay calm so that you can protect yourself and ride out the storms you find yourself in. Some things are just out of your control right now. Cultivate a sense of fortitude and take a step back for now.

BING 丙

奇門遁甲十干格局篇

奇門遁甲十干格局篇

BING

景 *Jing* **Scenery**	Opportunities don't come around often for everyone and they certainly don't come often enough for you. You have talents but are unable to exploit then. In the place of opportunity, you face adversity. In the long run, you will enjoy success if you keep trying. For now, it is best to be prepared by increasing your professional and work experience. When the time is right, your contributions and talents would be appreciated. If you wait only till then to learn the required skills or gain the necessary experience, you will only achieve a lacklustre outcome. Even in a relationship, one must know how to love in order to be loved back.
死 *Si* **Death**	It is not enough to tell people the truth. Your information alone does not cause transformation. It is tough to make it to the top, especially in your case. You are prone to spending more time day-dreaming and wishing than you are actually getting work done. This makes it difficult for you to actually achieve anything. You will need to roll up your sleeves and get to work if you expect anything to change. This sign is associated with a changing situation and changing fortunes. Make sure they change for the better.
驚 *Jing* **Fear**	Time to take shelter. The weather in your life changes as joy parts way for sorrow. For every lucky break you get, you will have to endure some bad news. Your career fortunes are about to face a sharp bend as what at first may seem like a good chance, can turn out to be nothing more than a trap. Cultivate a sense of fortitude and proceed cautiously. Ask questions and check the details and fine print. Remain alert so that you don't get caught off guard.
開 *Kai* **Open**	Your career looks like it is set to be remembered for many years to come as you have a great environment around you with lots of supportive friends and family. The external conditions around you are filled with resources and you can produce everything you need to get ahead in life. Wealth, prosperity and happiness will all find you without too much laborious effort on your part. It seem as though someone up there likes you.

天盤 **Heavenly Stem**	地盤 **Earthly Stem**
丙 *Bing* **Yang Fire**	辛 *Xin* **Yin Metal**

Structure 格局	Sun Moon Meeting 日月相會
Rating 吉凶	Auspicious 吉
Classic Verse 十干剋應歌訣	月奇遇合丙加辛，謀事能成病不興
Transliteration 字譯	Where the Bing meets with Xin, it is known as the Sun Moon Meeting formation. It denotes successful planning and good health.
Description 解說	This formation signifies favorable results that are emanating from having a sound plan in place. One's reputation is highly regarded after bringing events, enterprise and plans into fruition. What others seek will be readily available to an individual.

In case of illness, one will be placed under the care of a competent doctor who will ensure a fast recovery to back to health. |

The 8 Doors Analysis:

The following evaluates the effects of **Bing** 丙 and **Xin** 辛 with each Door.

休 *Xiu* **Rest**	There will be solutions to your problems, so do not worry, as you will find them soon. This sign is associated with good luck and as long as you persevere, nothing can stop you. Remember to ignore the petty people who try and bring you down, bad mouth you or stand in your way. You do not need their approval to succeed. Keep your energy level high and move ahead swiftly.
生 *Sheng* **Life**	Many people would love to be in your position, with all the benefits your current position in life carries with it. Make the most of what is at your disposal and use the resources that are readily available around you. No matter what you do, you are sure to succeed because of your auspicious luck. Charity and kind deeds will help good fortunes stay with you longer. Help uplift others as the more good you do, the better you will be in life.
傷 *Shang* **Harm**	Your fortunes are fickle like the weather. This means that you cannot count on them to place what you want right into your hands. Your luck is poor and for various reasons, it is unlikely that you can bring your dreams to reality on your own. It's not all doom and gloom, however. If you can enlist the help of great mentors, the chances of you achieving your goals and improve significantly, you need to find better advisors. Not just your friends who may or may not have the necessary skills or knowledge to help you. Look around you and build a team. The key to life is to be happy with or without money because money only magnifies who you really are.
杜 *Du* **Delusion**	Promises will be broken. So don't waste time trying to argue further. There are inconsistencies in how things unfold as last minute twists of events dampen you and your team spirit. This leads to uncertainty about your future so you should remember that what at first may seem like an ending is often a new beginning. Be like water. Be adapting to the situation instead of crying over spilt milk.

景 *Jing* **Scenery**	Family troubles are brewing with lots of bickering and misunderstandings. Your family life is far from harmonious and warm, leading to feelings of depression or lows spirits. By over-thinking, you can get yourself into emotional trouble. Look into ways to bring harmony into your strained relationships and improvements will appear in other areas as a result.	
死 *Si* **Death**	Ambition and talent are not in short supply as far as you are concerned. But when you try and channel these and produce results or progression in your career, you might find that things aren't as easy as you'd like them to be. The Nobleman isn't giving you any help and the people around you are unlikely to give you your big break. Your wealth luck is also shaky at this point. None of this means that you can't achieve what you want to, but simply that you may need to work harder and smarter than others. No one can help you other than yourself right now. It is best to have a reality check on the plans that you have right now.	
驚 *Jing* **Fear**	Isolated. Alone. Deserted. Unrecognized. Nobody can fault you for making an attempt at things, where you end up putting in twice or three times as much effort as the next person, but only seeing half the results. In order to achieve your objectives, you need to accept this and continue battling fierce and perhaps unfair resistance to succeed. Yes, things aren't always fair. The difficult journey you face right now can build a strong character - if you can promise to never give up.	
開 *Kai* **Open**	The key word associated with this sign is "gentleness". If you are kind and gentle and use a soft touch to try and turn the bad into good and make the most out of things, then people will recognize this and are keen to help you. Therefore, control your temper and be nicer to others. With the aid of others, obstacles can be overcome. Keep looking for the silver lining and actively work to maintain a positive attitude to stay on track.	

奇門遁甲十干格局篇

丙
BING

奇門遁甲十干格局篇

BING 丙

天盤 **Heavenly Stem**	地盤 **Earthly Stem**
丙 *Bing* **Yang Fire**	壬 *Ren* **Yang Water**

Structure 格局	Fire Enters Heavenly Web 火入天羅
Rating 吉凶	Inauspicious 凶
Classic Verse 十干剋應歌訣	火入天羅丙加壬，爲客不利是非聞
Transliteration 字譯	Where the Bing meets with Ren, it is known as the Fire Enters Heavenly Web formation. It denotes that the inauspicious guest will stir up trouble.
Description 解說	The two elements of Fire and Water are countering each other. This configuration will result in troublesome quarrels and disputes. One will find him/herself exchanging ferocious words with colleagues or family members. Misunderstandings are unavoidable and most of them might escalate to hostility and a lack of control. The appearance of Inauspicious Doors will escalate the graveness of the formation. One will become the target for lawsuits and enemies of all sorts.

The 8 Doors Analysis:

The following evaluates the effects of **Bing** 丙 and **Ren** 壬 with each Door.

休 *Xiu* **Rest**	You reap what you sow as all your past efforts are finally coming to fruition. Getting here is only the first step. Keeping and maintaining what you got is the next step. Remember that those around you often make or break your chances of success so by maintaining a down-to-earth, earnest and helpful attitude, a bright and fortunate future will continue to be yours.
生 *Sheng* **Life**	You are showered with good fortune and then some. Everything in life is going in your favour. Clearly all your efforts has skyrocketed you to a whole new level, where due recognition, fame and wealth has come within your reach. This certainly gives you a boost of confidence and optimism to go further. Although you can enjoy all the rewards you reaped so far, don't let arrogance get in the way. Don't forget to share your success with those who have helped lift you up where you are now. It is important to stay grounded and surround yourself with people who matters in your life. Always keep that in mind.
傷 *Shang* **Harm**	Do not interfere with other people's affairs. Best to keep your sight only on your matters. Don't ask too many questions about them as it is none of your concern. Instead, find a quiet place so that you can deal with your plans and issues in peace – free from interference. You might find that reflection leads you to change a long standing opinion or change your tactics, especially if your current plan isn't working out. There is not use staying on board a sinking ship, after all.
杜 *Du* **Delusion**	You seem to be missing out on the details. It is best you seek an independent third party opinion. If you want to see your ides succeed, then you cannot make this happen on your own and help is required. Otherwise, it is best you temporarily stop your projects or plans and go back to the drawing board. For now, you are prone to procrastination and carelessness. This leads to fruitless endeavours and wasted opportunities. Recruit the help of other talented people around you and find ways to discipline yourself and remain diligent in your duties.

奇門遁甲十干格局篇

丙
BING

	景 *Jing* **Scenery**	There is a lack of energy in the air as things seem to be rather stale. This may have dampened your appetite to work harder though. It almost seems like you are not making any significant progress on this route but the good news is that everything changes eventually and someone in your upcoming path is going to guide you to the success you have missed out on. Pay attention to the helping hands around you now. Everything will get better once you put the right person on the job.
	死 *Si* **Death**	If you don't have a team of great mentors right now, all is lost. Your luck is not good. It would be nice if things always turned out to be as easy to do as your have imagined. Sadly, your path is not as simple as you think and you will have to deal with more than your fair share of complications with regards to your endeavours. This leaves you stressed, worried and unable to relax. You think you know what is best but your experience and your knowledge in this path is limited and naïve. You must seek the help of trusted and knowledgeable mentors as you may incur great losses when your pursuit fails. Hence when there is still time, seek help.
	驚 *Jing* **Fear**	At home, everything is good but at work, there are many challenges. Progress is not as smooth as you would like it to be. You are destined to continually find yourself in situations you would rather not be in, and end up dealing with problems after problems. Whether you are aware of it or not – or whether you would admit it or not – many of these problems are of your own creation and could have been avoided. Work hard and do things properly and thoroughly to avoid dealing with fallout later on. If you know you aren't supposed to do something, then don't do it. If you play with fire, then you will get burnt.
	開 *Kai* **Open**	Luck is on your side and you will enjoy a time of great prosperity, thanks to a Nobleman or mentor who is available to help you. Your relationships with others at work and in your personal life will thrive and so will your reputation. Share your fortune with others and proceed wisely in making the most out of everything. Like a candle, you can light up your own light. So go now and light more candles because your future seems brighter than ever.

天盤 **Heavenly Stem**	地盤 **Earthly Stem**
丙 *Bing* **Yang Fire**	癸 *Gui* **Yin Water**

Structure 格局	Moon Noble Entering Earth Net 月奇地網
Rating 吉凶	Inauspicious 凶
Classic Verse 十干剋應歌訣	月奇地網丙加癸，奇逢華蓋事暗昧，陰小害事禍累累
Transliteration 字譯	Where the Bing meets with Gui, it is known as the Moon Noble Entering Earth Net formation. It denotes that trouble will occur and it may cause unwelcomed disasters.
Description 解說	Misunderstandings will be at their highest level with an emphasis on written content. One will be accused falsely and traps will be set to bring him or her down. One will need to tread carefully lest he or she falls into the enemy's snare. Incessant conflicts might drain one's energy and one will be wise to avoid getting engaged in the conflicts. His or her energy will be best used elsewhere. Seeking to provide solutions in a clear unbiased manner rather than argue about who is right or wrong will calm the situation.

The 8 Doors Analysis:

The following evaluates the effects of **Bing** 丙 and **Gui** 癸 with each Door.

休 *Xiu* **Rest**	The higher the mountain, the more demanding the climb, the sweeter the view is from the summit once it is reached. Your future is full of hope and positive potential. As you make the difficult climb towards your own personal peak, you will learn many new things and gain new experiences. Sometimes you win, sometimes you learn. Do not worry as you will be happy with inevitable outcome of your efforts. This is the correct direction, so you may continue with total confidence.
生 *Sheng* **Life**	Although the journey may be long, that does not mean it needs to a difficult one. Yours will be peaceful, so even though the destination is far away, you will still enjoy the ride. Take your time and plan things well, and whatever you envision can be done. If you can clearly see it in your mind, you will most likely be able to achieve it. Most importantly, you will be happy long before you reach your goal as the journey to the top will be a wonderful one.
傷 *Shang* **Harm**	On the surface, your situation looks good and appealing but fortune is fickle. This is because there have been stories of lottery winners who have gone from rags to riches to rags again, having blown their lottery winnings. Wealth and success can disappear as quickly as it comes, so your vision of the future may not be likely come true. Therefore, you must be cautions and alert all the time.
杜 *Du* **Delusion**	This sign is associated with bad luck. There is an old saying "look before you leap", which you may have taken too much to heart. It is a good idea to think carefully about things before you do them, but you take this too far and wait too long before making even a simple decision. This can lead to loss of opportunities, and in some worst case scenarios, it can bring damaging and costly errors. When things start to go off the rails, you become impulsive which leads to poor decision-making. Hanging on to too many things in hand, thinking that you are the only one who could do the job well is not the best way forward. Learn to delegate and learn to trust others.

景 *Jing* **Scenery**	Before you can be successful in life, you have to first strive to truly know who you are. Because many people will want you to become something you are not. People think that you can cope with anything, and that everything is going well for you. Only you can know how you are really feeling inside and how much you are struggling in silence. Only you know your true position and your true strength. You are facing up to a bleak future full of challenging situations and constant setbacks. Your efforts do not lead to the results you deserve because you are doing what others want you to do.	
死 *Si* **Death**	Honest people do not do business with dishonest people. Your reputation is your foundation. Have you been totally honest with others and yourself lately? There is nothing wrong with your ideas and your visions are grand but sometimes, all the doors are simply shut. Others don't seem to trust you. You need to build trust with others in order to succeed otherwise no doors will open for you. Making mistakes and learning from them isn't enough to make you successful. You must also admit the mistake, and then learn how to turn that mistake into an advantage. Every time you quit, someone else gets your prize. Every time you make a mistake, you get closer to yours.	
驚 *Jing* **Fear**	This is an unfavourable sign in many ways. Despite projecting a calm, composed image, feelings of depression, inadequacy and doubt rage inside, hidden from others. This inner state combined with repeated external misfortune makes for broken dreams and slow progress. In terms of wealth, financial loss from misguided investments can be expected. You are also prone to gossip which is never productive or beneficial in the long run. There's no need to think too far ahead in your future. Just try and see more in yourself and look cautiously for the next right, risk-free way forward.	
開 *Kai* **Open**	It is one of those times when you have this nagging feeling that things are almost perfect but not quite so. Don't fret too much about it. Perhaps this is a good time to take a step back and reflect or review what you have done so far. There is nothing wrong in re-strategizing your plans before you move further forward. That way, you can ensure smarter moves for better results. Make full use of this time to do so because things are looking bright from here.	

奇門遁甲十干格局篇

BING

丁

Ding
Yin Fire

奇門遁甲十干格局篇

DING

天盤 **Heavenly Stem**	地盤 **Earthly Stem**
丁 *Ding* **Yin Fire**	甲 *Jia* **Yang Wood**

Structure 格局	Green Dragon Salivating The Pearl 青龍吐珠
Rating 吉凶	Auspicious 吉
Classic Verse 十干剋應歌訣	青龍轉光丁加甲，官人升遷常人嘉
Transliteration 字譯	Where the Ding meets with Jia, it is known as the Green Dragon Salivating the Pearl formation. It denotes career promotion and achieving general popularity.
Description 解說	The Green Dragon is salivating for the precious pearl. This is a favorable formation that portends a future full of hope and good things to come. Salary increments and promotions will happen to the individual. Success and authority are just a step away. This formation foreshadows a future bright with achievement. Other people will draw positive inspiration from the individual.

The 8 Doors Analysis:
The following evaluates the effects of **Ding** 丁 and **Jia** 甲 with each Door.

休 *Xiu* **Rest**	Good tidings and good news in terms educational pursuits await you. With only little effort, you could turn being great into a huge star. Your problems will obviously be dissolved and the path ahead of you is very clear. All you need to do is find the extra 10% within yourself to propel forward. Keep doing what you're doing and what needs to be done to succeed. Success awaits you if you push a little further and give your worth the extra mile. All the other elements are in the right place for you to stay on track.
生 *Sheng* **Life**	As this is an extremely auspicious combination, you will encounter fame and fortune. Your varying talents will also depend on your family and the people you know. Everything will remain harmonious for you. Those people who you surround yourself with will deem you as being lucky and utterly blessed. You will be able to enjoy good fortune wherever you go, so make the most out of the fame, wealth and prosperity that you will enjoy. Everything will turn out perfect for you!
傷 *Shang* **Harm**	There is a saying which is commonly heard when things get tough: "No pain, no gain." This could become your new motto in life. The path to greatness isn't always an easy road. Not everyone will have the right guts and glory to walk down this path. All of the difficulties that you may face will be well worth it in the end when you finally emerge as a winner. Stay focused on your track and you will achieve your goals. The troubles ahead can be resolved if you persevere.
杜 *Du* **Delusion**	Everything is stable and secure for you although there may be some scandals which will be resolved later. The stone is about to turn into a diamond with some hard work. Conflicts will go away if the necessary solutions are taken. If you put in the effort needed you will be able to get out of this rut. Have a little confidence in yourself and move ahead. Complacency may be your enemy here and none of this will come to pass if you just let it be. The good will occur if you choose to make a change.

DING 丁

奇門遁甲十干格局篇

DING

景 *Jing* **Scenery**	Remember to finish what you started and you will likely to succeed. What you need right now are two things: the right skills and the right psychology. There will be naysayers and haters who you need to learn to ignore. People around you right now may have the best intentions but they don't see what you see. Learn to use their strengths to your advantage and benefit. If you can do right by the people you meet, your dreams will definitely come true.
死 *Si* **Death**	Some things just can't be resolved for you. It can also be unwise for you to continue pursuing something when it becomes wearisome and tiresome for you. You might also find yourself having to give up on ideas and plans for these reasons despite every effort to try it out. Learn to let go of things as well. Do not hang on to something you know which is hard to obtain. The best thing you can do right now is to share your feelings with others. While they may not be able to help you with solutions, this will at least lighten your burden or load.
驚 *Jing* **Fear**	Even though you seem to get all you desire, the troubles and burdens encountered in light of your success will bring you down. Be aware of potential pitfalls and remain on track towards your path. Even if you have the extra money, don't use your wealth to try to gain the affection, relationship, friendship of others. You should try to invest in genuine relationships and weed out the bad ones to propel ahead. As the saying goes, a little sincerity goes a mighty long way. Avoid participating in gossips and also spreading unnecessary rumors.
開 *Kai* **Open**	Great news is on its way and there will be abundance of opportunities waiting for you. You can also look forward to plenty more, as you enjoy successful events/gatherings and enterprises. Your current reputation is well-regarded as successful by those who you surround yourself with. And most importantly, you will be able to enjoy plenty of the commodity that everyone is ultimately seeking which is happiness. This is obviously an excellent sign for you!

	天盤 **Heavenly Stem**		地盤 **Earthly Stem**
	丁 *Ding* **Yin Fire**		乙 *Yi* **Yin Wood**

Structure 格局	Heavenly Flourish Formation 天運昌氣格
Rating 吉凶	Auspicious 吉
Classic Verse 十干剋應歌訣	天運昌氣格丁加乙，貴人官爵晉升級，常人財帛婚慶喜
Transliteration 字譯	Where the Ding meets with Yi, it is known as the Heavenly Flourish Formation. It is indicative of career promotion, abundance of wealth, and a happy marriage.
Description 解說	With this formation, help and assistance will be available and one is very unlikely to become stuck in their endeavors. Other people will shower him or her with their goodwill and assistance. This level of concern will lead one to true happiness in life. The level of cooperation in this formation is especially impactful in a relationship or marriage. When combined with Man Dun, this formation will be more auspicious! This is the right time for an individual to accomplish whatever plans they might have in mind. Their luck is at its highest peak!

奇門遁甲十干格局篇

DING 丁

The 8 Doors Analysis:

The following evaluates the effects of **Ding** 丁 and **Yi** 乙 with each Door.

	休 *Xiu* **Rest**	You have great ambitions and great achievements. You will also receive and create a good life for yourself. The auspicious stars will shine brightly on your path ahead. This will be the kind of perspective that everyone will want to have – so you would need to count your blessings. Whatever you may decide to do, you will definitely be successful in them. However ambitious your dreams may be, they will in return come true eventually as well. All you have to do is begin your journey. So get to working and be prepared to do the work necessary so that your future will be secured. Remember that everything will pay off in the very end.
	生 *Sheng* **Life**	Your superior talent and versatility will enable you to escalate and scale the ladder to great heights. Other people may think you're blessed but no matter what the situation is, you will have the lead role in the way things go and you will always land on your two feet and come out a winner in the end. This can be attributed to your highly favorable luck as well. Your mentor luck will be outstanding too. Appreciate your fortune and remember to capitalize on it. Life is great for you!
	傷 *Shang* **Harm**	There is always a period of quietness before the storm. During favorable times, you will need to prepare yourself for whatever that will be coming next. Things may look calm to you right now, but the troubles are brewing ahead. Preparation is key and you will need to make sure you check your cash flow now. If you're in a relationship, it is best you ensure your partner is truly happy with you. If not, take action to rectify this before it is too late. When the opportunity occurs, make sure you are ready to open the door and welcome it!
	杜 *Du* **Delusion**	Your feeling of insecurity or inadequacy will ultimately hold you back from realizing your full potential. Self-improvement is necessary and you will also need to appreciate yourself a little more. You will need to plan things carefully and do the best work that you can for now. If you want to be loved, you must first learn to love yourself. If you want others to love you, you must have the confidence to offer your love to them in the very first place. If you want the best chance to succeed in life, don't aim for too high for now. There is no shame from starting at the bottom so be practical and achieve smaller goals first. Remember to always start small in order to go big!

136 Qi Men Dun Jia Strategic Execution

景 *Jing* **Scenery**	Your situation is good but the timing is not right for you now. There are still some necessary steps that you need to take before you reach your goals. Of course, you will have every reason to be optimistic as your life always tend to get better. But don't expect any kind of free ride though, as there are lack of helpful people in your life. Whatever you plan to achieve, it is likely you will have to do it solo through your own commitment and perseverance. Fame and fortune will come to you if you choose to work hard for it. Cultivate and nurture your talents and don't be afraid to show them off. Others around you will take notice and you will then be rewarded.
死 *Si* **Death**	n a variety of situations, it seems like you will continue to face numerous problems. You will be fighting battles on multiple fronts. However, with the emergence of a Noble person, the wind may blow in your favor. You will be able to turn the challenges into stepping stones for your success. But you must be able to learn to control your emotions and direct them towards positivity. Remember to take care of your morale and stay motivated to succeed.
驚 *Jing* **Fear**	Knowing you need to make a change isn't enough. You've also got to also find the guts to do it and put it into action. You'll need to venture out to actively gather the opinion of others through networking purposes. But you'll also need to remember to take note of who you seek advice from by making sure that they are qualified and knowledgeable. Describe your situation, the options you have and see what they would suggest you to do. Analyze it and ask them why. Listen to what they say carefully and don't be afraid to change your mind if their reasoning is not sound to you.
開 *Kai* **Open**	Your Nobleman and mentor luck will be very good and your luck in general will also be the envy of others. You can have whatever you want for yourself whether it may be status, power, wealth or love. It you can offer a helping hand to others and help them succeed to become a better person with your good fortune, it would be deemed advisable for you. Always remember to extend your goodwill and fortune. This will also ensure your path towards success continues to be smooth-sailing for many years to come.

奇門遁甲十干格局篇

DING

天盤 **Heavenly Stem**	地盤 **Earthly Stem**
丁 *Ding* **Yin Fire**	丙 *Bing* **Yang Fire**

Structure 格局	Star Follows Moon Turn 星隨月轉
Rating 吉凶	Auspicious 吉
Classic Verse 十干剋應歌訣	星隨月轉丁加丙，貴人越級高升迎，常人忍讓防不幸
Transliteration 字譯	Where the Ding meets with Bing, it is known as the Star Follows Moon Turn formation. It denotes career promotion, and the possibility of avoiding misfortunes.
Description 解說	This formation is fluorescent with optimism. No matter how hard the tides may billow, an individual will find that they have what it takes to weather them. One will be successful in whichever endeavor he or she sets his or her mind upon. It is the perfect formation for a job promotion and more achievements. However, the appearance of a negative door may portend an abrupt culmination to the success streak. Extreme joy from achievements may also beget sorrow. One may also have to stop the triumphant celebrations in case the negative stars surface. Major losses may occurs since one is ill-prepared to handle minor setbacks.

The 8 Doors Analysis:

The following evaluates the effects of **Ding** 丁 and **Bing** 丙 with each Door.

休 *Xiu* **Rest**	Nobody ever did good work in a rush. You will make many mistakes but don't worry as these mistakes will be lessons for you. The bigger the mistake, the bigger the lesson is for you. Success requires the patience, sacrifice and dedication from you. You will never do anything grand if you are impatient, fickle and too afraid to make any mistakes. Take risks. Your long-term goals require long-term plans and you'll keep failing unless you learn from your mistakes. Come up with a thorough and comprehensive plan and you'll come out a winner at the end. The key towards realizing your full potential is to learn your current lessons well.
生 *Sheng* **Life**	You will get exactly what you put in your life. Unfortunately, being lazy, and half-measured will only produce half the results needed. The problem is, you seem to think that the world owes you something. You expect to have things easy for you. In reality, you didn't contribute enough value to deserve what you want in life. This is why you're not getting enough. If you want it all, you will need to give it everything you've got and not hold back at all. Your own success lies in your hands – so decide how you want to go at it and how hard you're willing to work now!
傷 *Shang* **Harm**	Drama will be part of your life. Drama has its place but the place is not within a team or a family. You must not be the star in the drama. Stay back. Some might say you're your own worst enemy. People will sometimes make helpful suggestions but you are too stubborn to take them on board, simply because you didn't come up with the ideas yourself. You do not see your own mistake and is oblivious to the fact that you could be the cause of the drama in the first place. No matter what you do, it would seem that you've made the wrong choice. It may be best if you keep quiet and let it cool down before making a move in life again.
杜 *Du* **Delusion**	The bad events and occurrences in your life are wrapping up, thus making way for better opportunities ahead. Just like a storm that passes, your problems and troubles are about to be nothing more than distant memories. This sign is associated with above average luck and a future full of hope. Despite various obstacles, you'll finally get to achieve your goals at the end.

奇門遁甲十干格局篇

DING

景 *Jing* **Scenery**		You will be easily drawn into worrying situations. You will also find it extremely difficult to obtain the trust of others and build a supportive network for yourself. What you need right now is to equip yourself with better leadership skills. Your friends won't follow you or your ideas because the ideas you convey are usually bad. It will be only you who would actually think the ideas were good in the first place. If you can't obtain the help from others, you will need to go solo.
死 *Si* **Death**		Things are not going swimmingly as you are losing rest because of this. Remember that nothing remains perpetually good forever and nothing remains perpetually bad forever either. Even though, it may seem like things will never improve from where you are standing – don't be frustrated! If you look at what you've got in life, the results are still acceptable for you even if they do not meet your expectations initially. Stay healthy and adopt an alert mindset. Take care of yourself and remember to relax.
驚 *Jing* **Fear**		You will have plenty of ambition but is probably lacking in the action department. You unable to make quick decisions and therefore everything seems to be stuck at your level. Others are just waiting for you to start to chart your path. You need to make practical decisions if you want to achieve all your goals. If your actions are not aligned with your vision, then you will find it difficult to convince others to follow your dream. You will also need to start thinking strategically and taking each step into consideration so that you're closer towards achieving your goals.
開 *Kai* **Open**		Your career looks like it is set to be remember for many years to come. You will have a great environment around you and lots of supportive friends and family to guide you. The external conditions around you are filled with resources and you can produce anything or everything you need to get ahead in life. Wealth, prosperity and happiness will finds its way to you without a lot of effort so you will need to count your blessings and be thankful for all you've got – don't take for granted of it all!

天盤 **Heavenly Stem**	地盤 **Earthly Stem**
丁 *Ding* **Yin Fire**	丁 *Ding* **Yin Fire**

Structure 格局	Noble Enters Great Yin 奇入太陰
Rating 吉凶	Auspicious 吉
Classic Verse 十干剋應歌訣	奇入太陰丁加丁，文證即至丁奇靈，諸事可爲慎勿驚
Transliteration 字譯	Where the Ding meets with Ding, it is known as the Noble Enters Great Yin formation. It denotes that the Ding Noble is efficacious when the document is submitted. All matters will fall into place when one is vigilant and daring.
Description 解說	Success seems to be prevalent but things may be different from what they seem to be. What appears right now may turn out to be catastrophic later. Cautiousness is advised. The plans that one has will bear fruits. The ride is smooth for those willing to put in some effort. The rewards are generously fair and one is seemingly fortunate. Pride and high-headedness may ruin everything if one is not careful.

DING

The 8 Doors Analysis:

The following evaluates the effects of **Ding** 丁 and **Ding** 丁 with each Door.

	休 *Xiu* **Rest**	You should be so lucky! You're basically showered with good fortune and then some. Everything in your life will be going in your favor. Clearly, all your efforts will have you skyrocketing ahead to successful endeavors where due recognition, fame and wealth will all be within your reach. This will certainly give you a boost to your confidence and your optimism will only take you further. Although you can enjoy all the rewards that you have reaped so far, don't let arrogance get in the way. Always remember to be humble. Humility goes a long way. It is important to stay grounded.
	生 *Sheng* **Life**	Good tidings and good news will be on its way to you. With only minimum effort, you could go from good to great and really reach for your goals. Your problems will dissolve and all you need to do is a little extra and keep doing what is right for you. Your judgments will be correct. Listen to your instincts. You will encounter great success if you push one step further. All the elements will work out for you and you'll be on the right path.
	傷 *Shang* **Harm**	You spend way too much energy and time on trivial or irrelevant matters. You will need to have a little more faith in yourself and your current abilities need to be realized by you as well. You might also feel that you've been fighting a long and losing battle but your competence and capability will get you out of it. A promotion or break at work will happen for you. Soon your stars will align and your path will take a turn for the better – so make sure you're ready for it!
	杜 *Du* **Delusion**	This denotes above average luck for you. The Nobleman will be present wherever you choose to go and you will be noticed. Your progression along your chosen path in life will be smooth, steady and stable provided if you stay persistent and not complacent and persevere at all times. Keep your eyes on the prize! Remember to stay away from gossip or speculation and always tell yourself that what goes around comes around. Also, do what is right and needed to be done, not just what is convenient right now.

景 *Jing* **Scenery**	As far as financial and professional success are concerned, you've got it all figured out and will have nothing to worry about. You can expect good fortune in your pursuits of wealth, power and status. Just make sure you're aware of the people you surround yourself with – clients, colleagues, friends, family and more. Choose your actions and words wisely and make the most of this above average luck with precision and steadfastness.
死 *Si* **Death**	Your fortune will be as fickle as the weather around you. This would mean you can't count on them to place what you want right now in your hands. Your luck is poor and for various reasons, it is highly unlikely that you will bring your dreams into a reality on your own. It's not all bad though, you can enlist the help of great mentors and the chances of you achieving your goals will be able to improve significantly. You will also need to find better advisors in life. Look around you and build a team of yours to help you. The key to life for you is to be happy with or without fortune.
驚 *Jing* **Fear**	Most people are not wealthy because sometimes money denotes evilness. You must not live with this fear in you – there is nothing evil or wrong about being rich. Having money merely magnifies your innate character. If you have a good character, your wealth can help you magnify the good. Unfortunately for you, at this time, the sign indicates that your troubles have only just started. Nobody likes to be told that they are about to plunge into a time of trouble and frustration but knowing this can help you prepare for the worst. The wise thing to do now is to prepare accordingly and proceed in caution!
開 *Kai* **Open**	The condition of things is going your way. You've planned this out for a long time and with a little tweaks along the way – you will be able to see your final work of art be on the display. Your optimistic attitude and good humor will benefit you at all times. Noblemen are always around for you, therefore you would need to make the best and most out of any given situations. You are blessed with good fortunes, advantageous news and appropriate rewards for your work.

奇門遁甲十干格局篇

DING

天盤 **Heavenly Stem**	地盤 **Earthly Stem**
丁 *Ding* **Yin Fire**	戊 *Wu* **Yang Earth**

Structure 格局	Green Dragon Turn Bright 青龍轉光
Rating 吉凶	Auspicious 吉
Classic Verse 十干剋應歌訣	青龍轉光丁加戊，官人升遷常人足
Transliteration 字譯	Where the Ding meets with Wu, it is known as the Green Dragon Turn Bright formation. It denotes an advancement and also the presence of an influential person.
Description 解說	The Green Dragon turns bright. This is a very auspicious configuration that portends great assistance from very Noble people. The assistance offered will make the sailing smooth and effortless. One will get rewards and get recognition for his or her efforts. The ground has been prepared for one's success. By taking their work seriously, individuals will certainly benefit from this auspicious formation and their efforts will not go unrewarded.

The 8 Doors Analysis:

The following evaluates the effects of **Ding** 丁 and **Wu** 戊 with each Door.

休 *Xiu* **Rest**	You won't face any difficulties that you aren't prepared to overcome. You are talented and you know how to use your talent. You reap what you sow and in time, you've set yourself up the benefit from a great harvest as you have a natural tendency to work hard and play hard. In other words, you plant all the right seeds to make it grow and bloom into something great. This sets the stage for continuing improvement because you would be able to make the best out of your situations in life and seem to always think positively. You will always remain victorious.
生 *Sheng* **Life**	You are blessed and the higher power favors you immensely. The higher power will also keep handing you what you need at the right time. All of your dreams will come true and you will carry an attractive aura of positivity, energy and happiness with you. You are set to enjoy a successful and beautiful life ahead. Don't take this for granted because you are truly fortunate. Cultivate a sense of gratitude and share your wealth with others by doing charity work.
傷 *Shang* **Harm**	The road ahead is straight and you're going to be able to pick up some speed along the way. Don't move too quickly as something unforeseeable may cross your path. A conservative, yet steady pace is advised for you. There are no major obstacles along your way but be warned that your path may actually be a longer route.
杜 *Du* **Delusion**	It's all too easy for you to rush in and do things without drawing up a thorough plan at first. If you are aware of this pitfall, then you would get to your desired results with minimal difficulty! You work best when you are working systematically. Therefore, you would need to think before you act and break down what needs to be done to achieve your goals into a series of necessary steps. Proceed calmly and focus on one step at a time and you'll emerge victorious.

丁 DING

Qi Men Dun Jia Strategic Execution

景
Jing
Scenery

Miscommunication with others will cause conflict and difficulties to you. Do try not to offend others by pursuing an action before you consult them. Your strained relationships with others and the mistakes that arise because of these interactions will eventually lead to a knot in your heart which includes situations such as blame, hatred and guilt. To avoid this, minimize confrontations and always run your plans with others around you before you actually act on them. Proactive attempts to communicate more effectively will denote a brighter future for you.

死
Si
Death

The picture doesn't look beautiful for you. Good things seem to fade off in a second and not everyone can enjoy the best of luck. There is always bound to be an unlucky person. From the sequence of events unfolding, you may feel like this person is you. You can also expect to meet more than your fair share of resistance in any matter which you may choose to pursue. This doesn't mean you won't be able to overcome resistance but it does mean that you should probably prepare for it more than you otherwise would. Your turning point requires a lot of effort. Be prepared to work for it!

驚
Jing
Fear

Everyone is bound to make mistakes in life. Don't try to place blame but instead control your emotions and focus on the lessons you have learnt. Don't expect success to be handed to you in a short cut. You'll be needing to work for it so you make sure you enjoy the success you want/deserve. Your entire ability for success, lies in how much you want it and how much you're willing to put in the work for it. Basically, you get the success through the effort you give. Make it a good balance or go the extra mile!

開
Kai
Open

You are dealt with lucky helping hands in life and this trend will set to continue for a while. You are fortunate and likely to succeed at whatever you attempt to do, move forward quicker for a progress in your career or in your life. This would be helpful with encounters with Noblemen. They will be able to provide you with expert guidance, ideas, advice and inspiration that you may need. Be on the look-out for this person to maximize your talents!

天盤 **Heavenly Stem**	地盤 **Earthly Stem**
丁 *Ding* **Yin Fire**	己 *Ji* **Yin Earth**

Structure 格局	Fire Enters Grappling Hook 火入勾陳
Rating 吉凶	Inauspicious 凶
Classic Verse 十干剋應歌訣	火入勾陳丁加己，陰私仇怨婦人起
Transliteration 字譯	Where the Ding meets with Ji, it is known as the Fire Enters Grappling Hook formation. It denotes the occurrence of intolerable situations caused by women.
Description 解說	This formation is total bad news. The conditions are restless and full of turmoil. Deceit and bad luck characterize one's love relationships. One needs to be very careful of treachery and deceit. Trivial issues from petty people are occasioning one a lot of anger and restlessness. One's ambitions will be stagnated by challenges which are out of one's control. Under these unfriendly circumstances, and individual may result to impulsive actions which will only aggravate the situation.

奇門遁甲十干格局篇

DING

The 8 Doors Analysis:

The following evaluates the effects of **Ding** 丁 and **Ji** 己 with each Door.

休 *Xiu* **Rest**	It's one of those times when you have a nagging feeling that things are almost perfect but not quite so. Don't think too much or worry about it. It is perhaps a good time to take a step back and reflect and also review on what you've done in life so far. There's absolutely nothing wrong in re-strategizing your plans before you go on further. Be sure to make smarter moves to fruit better results. Make use of this time to do so because things will look brighter for you from here onwards.
生 *Sheng* **Life**	Something which worries you and keeps you awake at night will actually take a turn to be beneficial for you. This will eventually lead to a happy ending for you. If you can multiply your efforts and correctly capitalize on the opportunities available, fame, wealth and happiness will be on the horizons for you. Work hard and show your potential. Remember to always look at things from a new and optimistic perspective!
傷 *Shang* **Harm**	There will be a lot of barriers which you will encounter. Life may seem unjust for you and sometimes you may feel that fate seem to single you out of the rest. You will also feel like you've been treated unfairly. There seem to be more bumps in the road for you than others. You may have shared these concerns with others around you without any positive results. There are just some things that are beyond your locust of control. Don't let what you can't do interfere with what you still can do. It may be time to switch to Plan B if you have one in mind.
杜 *Du* **Delusion**	With such high expectations of the future, you are bound to be disappointed in the long run. Another problem that you will encounter is spending too much time inside your own head – talking to yourself or imagining what you'd like rather than taking real action on matters. This would also mean that you may have a vision but you are unlikely to succeed in bringing it to life. You are definitely too idealistic and you would need to be more practical to achieve your goals.

景 *Jing* **Scenery**	The road is long and paved with troubles ahead. Don't expect things to be straight-forward for you. In your case, you will simply just need to persevere through difficult circumstances as you encounter them. In the very end, you will achieve triumph and you will also be able to maintain a sense of fortitude. Keep your eyes on the prize when things don't go your way. A leader's role is not only to be a good person but to bring out the best in others.	
死 *Si* **Death**	This sign is associated with bad luck. The road ahead is bumpy to say the least and you will need to be on your toes most of the time. There are bound to be obstacles along the way that may hinder you from achieving victory. Your energy level will also be low and this would mean that your progress wouldn't be as smooth as you'd like it to be. You would need to factor this into planning and stay alert at all times. There's no point getting ahead of yourself and remember to think in the now.	丁 **DING**
驚 *Jing* **Fear**	There are clouds on the horizon and the view ahead is full and obscured with uncertainty. You may suffer some bullying to a certain extent at this point. It is undeniable this would lead to self-doubt and a lack of confidence in you. Stop looking for help externally as you may not find any. You are your only solution so you would need to believe in yourself. Without a strong will and a clear mind for what needs to be done, you may find it very difficult to achieve your ambitions. Remember to build up your confidence and make sure your self-doubts are not hindering you!	
開 *Kai* **Open**	All the resources you need are around you to make things happen. If you don't see this, look harder! It is not lack of resources that will be stopping you; it is the lack of being 'resourceful' that will stop you from finding the right resources. If you have plans in mind but you're not acting on them then you need to be brave or bold and make another move. A fruitful outcome for you is likely to happen if you push for it and you can't expect anything if you didn't try in the first place.	

天盤 **Heavenly Stem**	地盤 **Earthly Stem**
丁 *Ding* **Yin Fire**	**庚** *Geng* **Yang Metal**

Structure 格局	Star Noble Enters Obstacles 星奇受阻
Rating 吉凶	Inauspicious 凶
Classic Verse 十干剋應歌訣	星奇受阻丁加庚，行人必歸訊如哽
Transliteration 字譯	Where the Ding meets with Geng, it is known as the Star Noble Enters Obstacles formation. It denotes that ordinary people will convey negative messages.
Description 解說	This inauspicious formation is also called the Jade Maiden Punishment. Geng, the Deity of Obstruction is blocking the way. Communication and travel will be hindered. One's journey will be blocked and documents they try to send will encounter delays and inconsistencies. The formation is riddled with inconsistencies and obstructions.

The 8 Doors Analysis:

The following evaluates the effects of **Ding** 丁 and **Geng** 庚 with each Door.

休 *Xiu* **Rest**	Your luck is highly unstable at the moment. Things will not come to you as you may have hoped. Everything you want lies in what seem like an indefinite waiting period. It is the best that you get out there and make your own luck. It won't be a smooth journey but with a little patience and perseverance, you can slowly (but surely) move towards your ultimate goal in life. When results don't immediately materialize, that's no reason to get impatient. You have much to learn along the way.
生 *Sheng* **Life**	Good things never last, a cynic might tell you that. In your case, this may be true as your luck will slowly diminish and may run out as well. Anything that has blossomed in your life will wither through time. During periods when nothing good seems to come off your effort, all you can do is keep trying. The key to turning situations like these around lies in humbly asking for help. If your ego is in the way – get rid of it!
傷 *Shang* **Harm**	Your plans need to be put on hold. Your future is filled with dark clouds and uncertainty. This doesn't mean you should give up and it's actually far from it. What it means is that you should continue to work hard and accept that this may be a thankless task at the moment, through no fault of your own.
杜 *Du* **Delusion**	With the strong spirit and a little financial education - you will be unstoppable. All you have to do is train your mind to think like a successful person. If you get excited all too easily, you can fail to spot the small issues, which can grow and escalate into serious problems. Mistakes and sudden incidents can ruin you. Your career fortunes are bad, indicating a hidden crisis in waiting. While this sign is not associated with stability and peace, it isn't all that bad either.

奇門遁甲十干格局篇

丁 DING

奇門遁甲十干格局篇

DING

	景 *Jing* **Scenery**	There will be a lack of energy in the air. Things will seem to be rather stale for you. This may have dampened your appetite to work harder. It almost seems like you are not making any significant progress on this route. The good news is however, is that everything changes and someone in your upcoming journey will guide you to success inevitably. Everything will take a turn for the better once you've been put with the right person on a task.
	死 *Si* **Death**	You will always seem to be in a constant dilemma and you will have an important decision to make soon, but you are still unclear or worst, you are oblivious about the details and you have usually made up your mind on what to do. Being indecisive is the cause of your downfall. If you hesitate for too long, opportunities will pass you by. Someday, the opportunities may stop coming along for you. Pay attention, stay alert and be sure to take a step forward confidently when the opportunity comes along.
	驚 *Jing* **Fear**	Too many thoughts and too many issues to deal with. Whatever you do will seem to get nowhere. It will almost feel like you are being crushed or are being trapped, wasting your time and effort on thankless tasks. This is an unfortunate situation to be in. The best thing you can do is lay low and be content with what you have for the time being. When times are tough, we get our energy from our spirit. We must remember, in all our struggles, to feed our spirit as well as our bodies.
	開 *Kai* **Open**	Opportunities that may seem lucrative at first will turn out to be rotten for you. This will cause unhappy endings for you. Frustration and depression will result from a constant lack of positive outcomes. You will also need to work on your relationship with others. You must always proceed with caution when you take any action. Expect the worst and plan for it so that you are ready to deal with the problems that may be forthcoming.

天盤 **Heavenly Stem**	地盤 **Earthly Stem**
丁 *Ding* **Yin Fire**	**辛** *Xin* **Yin Metal**

Structure 格局	Red Phoenix Enters Prison 朱雀入獄
Rating 吉凶	Inauspicious 凶
Classic Verse 十干剋應歌訣	朱雀入獄丁加辛，罪人釋囚官失今
Transliteration 字譯	Where the Ding meets with Xin, it is known as the Red Phoenix Enters Prison formation. It denotes a released prisoner, and the loss of an official ranking or position.
Description 解說	One's progress is arrested and nothing seems to go as expected. Things may seem very promising at the moment only to turn sour and bitter after a while. This formation portends unhappiness and lead to destruction. No matter the efforts that one puts in, progress and achievements seem to be far in coming. Though some problems could be saved, it almost pointless, time wasting and tedious trying to redeem every single thing that goes wrong. One might have to give up on his or her plans or ideas.

The 8 Doors Analysis:

The following evaluates the effects of **Ding** 丁 and **Xin** 辛 with each Door.

休 *Xiu* **Rest**	The feeling of constantly spinning your wheels without gaining traction makes it very difficult for you to relax and stress builds up along with feelings of self-doubt. Don't even try to argue with others because you're likely to lose. When bad luck strikes, the best you can do is stay positive and accept that some things are totally out of your control. Nothing can go on forever after all, so your bad luck may be gone. Keep an eye on the horizon for positive developments and you'll find some eventually.
生 *Sheng* **Life**	It's tough to be optimistic about the immediate future. Your career path is unclear and it isn't easy to draw any kind of map to chart your path. Your career situation is unclear and it isn't easy to draw any kind of direction from where you are now. There will be resistance from a multitude of sources and progression is rather difficult for you. Despite the hard work that you've done, you may be underappreciated. You can try to get an edge by working smart instead.
傷 *Shang* **Harm**	The things that you are looking for are no longer there. What you may have lost may never return. Learning to let go is key to a better outcome. Your projects, plans, schemes are unlikely to pan out because of obstacles and problems that are beyond your control. All of this can be incredibly disheartening. Keep the good memories, learn the valuable lesson and move on in a different direction in life.
杜 *Du* **Delusion**	The good times will not last forever for you. In fact, they may be disappearing in the rear view mirror as you drive on forward. Worries will take place of a carefree attitude. Problems will also take place of triumphs that you may encounter. Basically, more is lost than gained. There will be difficult times ahead, so you will need to be prepared for that. Stay upbeat and be prepared for an incoming storm. It is best to consult yourself when making extremely difficult decisions in life.

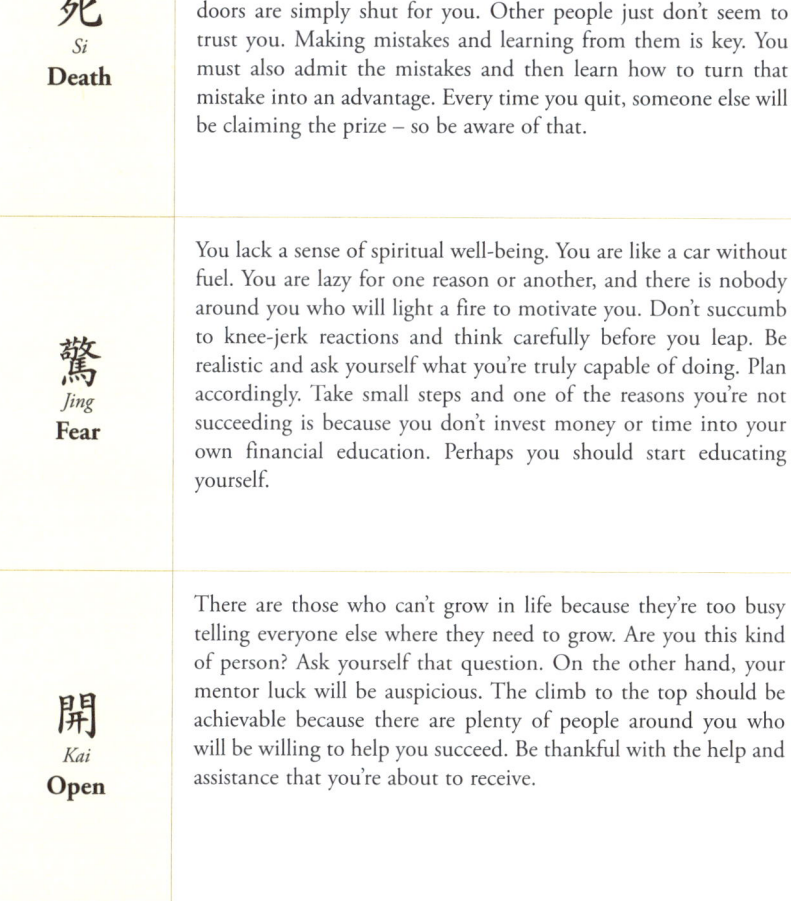

景 *Jing* **Scenery**	Knowing that you need to make a change will not be enough for you. You've got to actively find the guts to do it and go your own way. Be confident with your decisions. In the meantime, also remember to seek advice from others and make sure they're all providing you with sound advice. Evaluate the advice and put in your own beliefs in them and see where it would take you – it will be a collaborative effort.	
死 *Si* **Death**	Always remember that honest people will not do business with dishonest people. Your reputation is your foundation. Have you been totally with others and yourself? There is nothing wrong with your ideas and your visions are grand but sometimes, all the doors are simply shut for you. Other people just don't seem to trust you. Making mistakes and learning from them is key. You must also admit the mistakes and then learn how to turn that mistake into an advantage. Every time you quit, someone else will be claiming the prize – so be aware of that.	
驚 *Jing* **Fear**	You lack a sense of spiritual well-being. You are like a car without fuel. You are lazy for one reason or another, and there is nobody around you who will light a fire to motivate you. Don't succumb to knee-jerk reactions and think carefully before you leap. Be realistic and ask yourself what you're truly capable of doing. Plan accordingly. Take small steps and one of the reasons you're not succeeding is because you don't invest money or time into your own financial education. Perhaps you should start educating yourself.	
開 *Kai* **Open**	There are those who can't grow in life because they're too busy telling everyone else where they need to grow. Are you this kind of person? Ask yourself that question. On the other hand, your mentor luck will be auspicious. The climb to the top should be achievable because there are plenty of people around you who will be willing to help you succeed. Be thankful with the help and assistance that you're about to receive.	

奇門遁甲十干格局篇

J
DING

天盤 **Heavenly Stem**	地盤 **Earthly Stem**
丁 *Ding* **Yin Fire**	壬 *Ren* **Yang Water**

Structure 格局	Five Deities Mutual Combine 五神互合
Rating 吉凶	Auspicious 吉
Classic Verse 十干剋應歌訣	五神互合丁加壬，獄訟公平貴人恩，苟合淫逸密成婚
Transliteration 字譯	Where the Ding meets with Ren, it is known as the Five Deities Mutual Combine formation. It denotes the occurrence of a fair lawsuit and an encounter with a Noble person. There is an errant or secret affair in a relationship.
Description 解說	This formation is metaphorically known as Riding the Dragon Across the Ocean. Ostensibly, every single plan that has been laid down will be successfully executed. The workload will straighten and become clear and there are brilliant rewards waiting ahead. Careers will be strengthened and reputations will increase. Noble persons will come to one's aid at his or her hour of aid and any lawsuits filed against one will be resolved fairly.

The 8 Doors Analysis:

The following evaluates the effects of **Ding** 丁 and **Ren** 壬 with each Door.

休 *Xiu* **Rest**	There is nothing stopping you from making all your wishes come true. It's basically up to you to take your dreams from inception to reality and the only thing that can stop this process is you. A Noble person can be enlisted to help and make your mission easier. You have a bright future ahead, don't worry. If you can envision it, you can achieve it!
生 *Sheng* **Life**	Your ship sails smoothly on calm waters. You will be able to materialize your heart's desires. Your mentor luck will be good and not everyone will be blessed with this, so be ready to count your blessings daily. You can get ahead of your competitors by making the most out of your blessings. With the help of a great mentor, you will definitely make it far. Let those mentors tell you whether your schemes, ideas, or projects are on the right track.
傷 *Shang* **Harm**	It's all too easy to rush in and do things without first drawing up a thorough plan. If you are aware of this pitfall, then you can get your ideal results with minimal difficulty! You work best when you are working in a systematic manner. So think before you act and break down what needs to be done to achieve your goals into a series of necessary steps. Proceed with caution and calmness and take one step at a time.
杜 *Du* **Delusion**	You have a rare and uniquely beneficial ability to see things in black and white, good or bad, right or wrong. This helps you sort the better decisions from ill-advised ones which ultimately leads to overall success. You can recognize the right people when you see them and avoid the bad ones by building a strong network for yourself. Don't be afraid to be honest on all accords. Do what is right and not what is convenient!

奇門遁甲十干格局篇

丁
DING

奇門遁甲十干格局篇

丁 DING

景 *Jing* **Scenery**		It would seem that you've just missed the boat. Opportunities don't come around often for everyone and they certainly don't come often around enough for you. You have talents but are unable to exploit them to your benefit. In the long run, you will achieve success if you keep trying. For now, it is best to get prepared. Increase your professional and work experience as well. When it comes to relationships, must learn to love to achieve love.
死 *Si* **Death**		Some problems can't be solved. In other cases, It can be unwise for you to continue pursuing something when it becomes too wearisome or energy consuming. You might find yourself having to give up on your ideas and plans for these reasons alone. Learn to let things go in the long run. Do not hang on to something you know that is impossible to obtain. The best thing you can do is to lessen your frustration and worry by sharing your worries with someone else. They may not be able to give you a solution but at least someone will hear you out.
驚 *Jing* **Fear**		This sign is associated with bad luck. When the road ahead may be bumpy, you'll need to stay on your toes because there are a lot of obstacles that stand between you and achieving victory. Your energy level will be minimal and this will slow down your progress. You should factor this all into consideration and remain alert at all time. There's no need to think too far ahead in your future.
開 *Kai* **Open**		You should save up your energy, your mojo and your passion for the right moment or opportunity which will be coming soon! You'll know when the right moment arrives and when it does, it will hit you hard. You can look forward to smooth progress and the outcomes you've been hoping for. The outlook is generally favorable for personal and professional endeavors.

天盤 Heavenly Stem	地盤 Earthly Stem
丁 *Ding* **Yin Fire**	癸 *Gui* **Yin Water**

Structure 格局	Red Phoenix Diving Water 朱雀投江
Rating 吉凶	Inauspicious 凶
Classic Verse 十干剋應歌訣	朱雀投江丁加癸，音信沈溺文舌非
Transliteration 字譯	Where the Ding meets with Gui, it is known as the Red Phoenix Diving Water formation. It denotes news or messages that was ignored. It also indicates that one will meet with possible disputes.
Description 解说	Every little thing is going to go wrong. Obstructions block and hinder one's attempts to communicate with his or her peers and an individual's good intentions will be misinterpreted. Gossips about the individual will be spread and there will be little they can do to control the situation. This formation portends strained relationships with other people and diminished support and assistance.

The 8 Doors Analysis:

The following evaluates the effects of **Ding** 丁 and **Gui** 癸 with each Door.

休 *Xiu* **Rest**	You have the ambition required to succeed. You also know how high you'd like to climb. This hunger for more is powerful but on its own – it will be quite useless for you. You lack the necessary determination to stick to plans and endure hardships long enough to eventually come out on top. Instead of simply dreaming of things for yourself, make sure you have time to take things step by step. Stay focused on your goals and put in the hard work needed. Remember time and people management is key!
生 *Sheng* **Life**	Don't give up! After a long struggle on your own to overcome matters, you will find the surge of good luck coming your way. There will be an exorbitant amount of support for you. Helping hands will finally come to your rescue at this point. Be open to it and leave your apprehension aside, as this will help you push through that one last hurdle towards your goal. Remember to show your appreciation and give credit where credit is due.
傷 *Shang* **Harm**	You may be frustrated and lonely. You will work hard but there will be no recognition for you. The good times haven't really arrived but many negative events have already seem to take place for you. This would ultimately cause confusion and frustration in your life. External factors that you can't control will creep in. Do cultivate a strong sense of self and strength in terms of confidence and self-awareness. Maintain a positive attitude and always step back and look at situations from afar.
杜 *Du* **Delusion**	You will be easily influenced or swayed. You could be described as being fickle-minded. You worry if you have made the right choice based on your own abilities. You are slow at doing things and easily exhausted and frustrated. All of this would amount to you feeling underwhelmed. Consider looking for inner strength and confidence to overcome your troubles.

景 *Jing* **Scenery**	It will be tough for you to remain optimistic about your future. Your career path is unclear and you'll feel lost. There will be resistance from a multitude of sources, and the progression will be rather difficult for you. You are an underachiever. You can try to get an edge by choosing the right time to react.	
死 *Si* **Death**	You've stuck to your guns all this while and weathered through the ups and downs. Things have been tough for some time but your courage shone through and now the rewards are due to be claimed. Though things are looking up now, it doesn't mean you can slack off just yet. Keep up with what you're doing – in fact, take it a step further and elevate your game. Implement a good strategy to propel you forward!	
驚 *Jing* **Fear**	You are fighting a lonely battle. It's not easy to do things on your own. Everything will hit you all at once and you'll have a hard time staying firm on your ground. Unfortunately, the odds do not live up to the challenge for your path. Your courage will also be worn out. You will eventually need to escape, vacate or retreat.	
開 *Kai* **Open**	Your career and personal beliefs benefits from good fortune all around. The obstacles and bumpy paths you see before you have been cleared for you by some higher power or people with a certain authority is looking out for you. Remember that you would still need to work hard to achieve prosperity, happiness and success.	

奇門遁甲十干格局篇

丁 DING

戊

Wu
Yang Earth

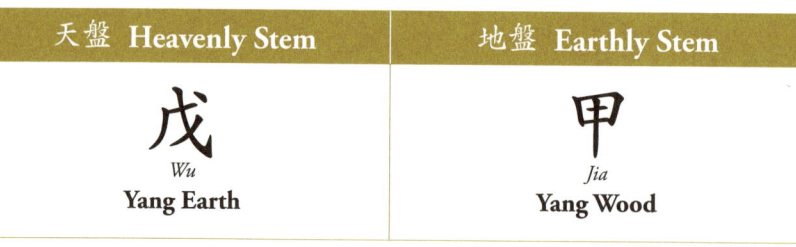

	天盤 **Heavenly Stem**	地盤 **Earthly Stem**
	戊 *Wu* **Yang Earth**	甲 *Jia* **Yang Wood**

Structure 格局	Huge Rock Crushes Wood 巨石壓木
Rating 吉凶	Inauspicious 凶
Classic Verse 十干剋應歌訣	-
Transliteration 字譯	It is a highly unfavorable formation where all endeavors are unfavorable.
Description 解說	There is something blocking advancement and progress. One will be better off remaining calm and not planning any major pursuits. Forging the journey ahead is cumbersome and almost impossible. Too many obstacles litter the road ahead. There are few lucky breaks and times are rough. Passivity will be one's saving grace during this formation.

The 8 Doors Analysis:
The following evaluates the effects of **Wu** 戊 and **Jia** 甲 with each Door.

休 *Xiu* **Rest**	You are dealt with Lucky Helping Hands in life and this trend is all set to continue for some time. You are fortunate as you are likely to succeed at whatever you attempt, but you can really supercharge your progression in career or in life if you meet a Nobleman or Mentor who can give his/her expert guidance, ideas and inspiration. Look out for this person to maximize your talents in life.
生 *Sheng* **Life**	You are blessed and a lot of people are eager to come and help you. There are good mentors and good friends around you. Have gratitude for the help you get in life. Fame and fortune is on the card. You find yourself at the right place at the right time and will enjoy success in life. Do not forget that there are others who are less fortunate. You can greatly increase your luck by offering a helping hand and uplifting others. This will keep the good things coming.
傷 *Shang* **Harm**	Your fortune is unstable and it seems like you don't have the final say in your own destiny as there seem to be too many hurdles in your chosen path. If you clear your mind and look at your situation closely, you will realize that things are not really as bad as they seem. In your case, life really is what you make of it because you will be presented with both the good and bad options. If you decide to take up the challenge, this may be a longer route as you need to work harder, but then this will lead you to eventual success. Bear in mind that if you choose this path, you will walk alone as there will be no external help. But if you choose to give up and give in when faced with adversity, then you can't expect to be rewarded for this choice. The current condition will eventually become worse.
杜 *Du* **Delusion**	Your feeling of insecurity is holding you back. Self-improvement is necessary as well as a little more self-love too. Plan things carefully and do the best work you can for now. If you want to be loved, you must first learn to love yourself. If you want others to love you, you must have the confidence to offer your love to them first. If you want the best chance of success, don't aim too high for now. There is no shame in having smaller but practical goals that you are able to achieve.

奇門遁甲十干格局篇

WU 戊

	景 *Jing* **Scenery**	This isn't a carefree time for you, so you better get your act together and move quickly. Many things worry you and you are doubtful about your plans. Other people will be quick to offer advice if you are willing to share your problems with them. Should you listen to them with an open mind, then new opportunities may present themselves. Sometimes knowing when to abandon a sinking ship is the most important decision of all. When there are no fishes in the current lake. It is time to look for a new location.
	死 *Si* **Death**	Your luck is unstable at the moment as things won't come to you easily as hoped. Everything you want lies in what seem like indefinite waiting period. Is it best that you get out there and make your own luck thought the journey won't be smooth at all. Be patient and carry on towards your ultimate goal for even when your goal does not seem to materialize immediately but you should not give up that easily as there is much to learn along the way.
	驚 *Jing* **Fear**	In the workplace, you put in plenty of hard work and make every effort possible to get ahead, but people still find ways to backstab you and hold you back. You seem to attract a lot of petty people and there is no way to get rid of these petty people. They will stick around for most part of your life. Even when you have a Nobleman to help you out, he/she can only do so much for you. This is sometimes the dark nature of your reality. While success will not come eagerly for you, you will still make plenty of friends who want to know you and help you along the way. There are still plenty of good people out there. Receive your happiness this way.
	開 *Kai* **Open**	You seem to have fortune on your side as you willingly take risks by confronting adversity and triumphing over it. Noble people are quick to give you help, so go ahead and do what you want to, even though the stakes are high and you might fall. But you will never let that happen.

166 Qi Men Dun Jia Strategic Execution

天盤 Heavenly Stem	地盤 Earthly Stem
戊 *Wu* **Yang Earth**	乙 *Yi* **Yin Wood**

Structure 格局	Green Dragon Combines Spirit 青龍合靈
Rating 吉凶	Moderate 半吉
Classic Verse 十干剋應歌訣	青龍和會戊加乙，隨門斷凶忌
Transliteration 字譯	Where the Wu meets with Yi, it is known as the Green Dragon Combines Spirit formation. It denotes that disasters will be experienced. Any auspicious outlook that prevail is determined by the terms of the Doors.
Description 解說	The Qi Men Dun Jia is forming a special combination with the Yi. This formation is highly favorable for one's career advancement and other pursuits. Individuals who invest their money will get strong returns and with the Auspicious Doors being present, the positivity portended by this formation will double. However, a collision with the Inauspicious Doors will lead to reduced benefits from this formation.

The 8 Doors Analysis:

The following evaluates the effects of **Wu** 戊 and **Yi** 乙 with each Door.

休 *Xiu* **Rest**	This sign brings good news for career-focused individuals. Your business and enterprise pursuits are going to benefit from shinning career fortunes and you will enjoy the prosperity and wealth this brings you. Enjoy the freedom that wealth brings you and be thankful for your good fortune.
生 *Sheng* **Life**	Good news is coming soon and you will enjoy the support and love of your friends and family. There is great progress in your life as freedom and respect will follow suit with the growing wealth that you have. You can expect smooth sailing regardless of where you choose to go in life, thanks to your good fortune. There are lots of valuable lessons from your life that you can share with others for the more your share, the better your life will be.
傷 *Shang* **Harm**	Everything is stable and secure. The stone is about to turn into a diamond with a little bit more hard work. If you put in the hard work, then you will reach heights you didn't think you could reach before. Have a little confidence in yourself and make some brave decisions to move ahead. Complacency is your only enemy here as nothing will happen if you just sit still and do nothing. So, get up and start moving.
杜 *Du* **Delusion**	This is an inauspicious sign as it signifies difficulty and strife. Good things may turn sour in the long run and happiness when attained may be fleeting as times of good business and prosperity won't persist for long. Take stock of what you have now or risk losing more in the end. You find it difficult to bring your dreams to reality as your efforts are constantly halted.

景 *Jing* **Scenery**	There is a lack of energy in the air as things become so stale that it may have dampened your appetite to work harder. It seems like you are not making any significant progress on this current route as well. The good news is that everything changes and someone in your upcoming path is going to guide you to the success that you have missed out on. Pay attention to the helping hands around you now. Everything will get better once you put the right person on the job.	
死 *Si* **Death**	You seem to be missing out on the details, so it it is best you seek an independent third party opinion. If you want to see your ideas succeed, then you cannot make this happen on your own and you definitely need outside help, otherwise, temporarily stop your projects or plans and go back to the drawing board. For now, you are prone to procrastination and carelessness and this leads to fruitless endeavours and wasted opportunities. Recruit the help of other talented people around you and find ways to discipline yourself to remain diligent in your duties.	
驚 *Jing* **Fear**	There are tough situations ahead as it could be said that you face a character building opportunity but a bumpy journey ahead. Difficulties and hardships are things that you will get used to dealing with for it seems that you are in it all by yourself and loneliness will be an understatement. There is no one you can depend on for help at the moment. You are your best choice. You can get there one small step at a time but don't be tempted to do anything sudden with dreams of becoming rich overnight, Avoid risks and take the slow, safer route.	
開 *Kai* **Open**	Some luck and great skill are the two main components of success, as any poker player will tell you. Fortunately, your luck is good, so get moving on the actual skill part. For what you want to do – be it in your career, business or even relationship life – you actually need to know how to do it. Master the skills needed and don't waste time procrastinating. Strike when you know luck is on your side. Proceed with confidence and courage and you will surely achieve your goal.	

天盤 **Heavenly Stem**	地盤 **Earthly Stem**
戊 *Wu* **Yang Earth**	**丙** *Bing* **Yang Fire**

Structure 格局	Green Dragon Returns 青龍返首
Rating 吉凶	Auspicious 吉
Classic Verse 十干剋應歌訣	青龍返首戊加丙，謀事多吉利，敗因迫墓刑
Transliteration 字譯	Where the Wu meets with Bing, it is known as the Green Dragon Returns formation. It denotes auspicious plans that end with severe punishment.
Description 解說	This formation portends positive outcomes and success in one's endeavors. There will be massive success for all plans implemented. Careers will flourish and business will gain in profits. Individuals who make plans at this time will see them advance just as they planned. However, if the formation goes through Grave or comes into collision with Striking Punishment, the results may turn out contrary to what was expected.

The 8 Doors Analysis:

The following evaluates the effects of **Wu** 戊 and **Bing** 丙 with each Door.

休 *Xiu* **Rest**	You have probably gotten used to enjoying a stream of prosperity and living the good life. Don't worry because nothing is going to change drastically – thanks to your ongoing favourable luck. Whether you realize it or not, you have many loyal friends who would jump at the chance to help you out. So, if you need an extra pair of hands for help, don't hesitate to ask. Accepting help or gestures of goodwill from others also makes them happy.
生 *Sheng* **Life**	You are fortunate. There are many people who love and care for you. All you have to do is to accept these gifts from other graciously. Gratitude is very important and you will have Noble people and mentors always to support you. This kind of support is often all that is needed for true happiness. Whether the situation is good or bad, you will always land on your feet and enjoy long standing wealth, good relationships and a good reputation. Have some faith in yourself and don't worry. Whatever dreams you have in mind, just go for it.
傷 *Shang* **Harm**	An unlucky sign indeed. Not only do the things you desire just don't seem to come together in a way that benefits you but the situation is beyond your control. Even those who promised you their help is not able to deliver their promise and your dreams are unlikely to come true in the hostile circumstance anyways. Because of your tendencies to act before you think, you are unlikely to make the right decisions. You need to take time to gather the complete info and see the full picture before making decisions. Especially if it relates to money or investments. Do not make your decisions based on only just rumours.
杜 *Du* **Delusion**	Plenty of ambition but not enough action. You are unable to make swift decisions and therefore everything seems to get stuck at your level. Others are just waiting for you to get the ball rolling. You need to make practical solutions if you want to achieve your goals. If your actions are not aligned with your vision, you will find it difficult to convince others to follow your dream. Start thinking strategically in order to get closer to your goal or else, you will go nowhere.

	景 *Jing* **Scenery**	Your luck is good but for some reason you prefer to take a low profile route. Perhaps you have a need to feel safe and take a steady path. Sometimes however, people get ahead by taking calculated risks and stepping out of their comfort zone. Since your luck is favourable, this means that you could be missing out on success and time is passing you by if you do not dare to make a bold move now. Please step out of your comfort zone.
	死 *Si* **Death**	It is not enough to just tell people the truth. Your information alone does not cause transformation. It is tough to make it to the top, especially in your case. You are prone to spending more time day-dreaming and wishing you actually get work done. This makes it difficult for you to actually achieve anything. You will need to roll up your sleeves and get work done if you expect anything to change. This sign is associated with a changing situation and changing fortunes. Make sure they change for the better.
	驚 *Jing* **Fear**	People cannot always be trusted. Unfortunately, what is said to you may not be what is said when you are absent. Choose your friends carefully. Are they truly your friends? Likewise, you also need to mind your words and the words of others, and be aware of damaging backstabbing. It is easy for you to find yourself isolated or in a state of conflict with others due to misunderstandings.
	開 *Kai* **Open**	Sometimes there can be fairy tale endings in real life. This is an auspicious sign. Expect to accomplish what you set out to accomplish and do it pretty quickly and easily too. Besides money matters, your relationship luck is very good too. All good things are coming your way.

天盤 **Heavenly Stem**	地盤 **Earthly Stem**
戊 *Wu* **Yang Earth**	丁 *Ding* **Yin Fire**

Structure 格局	Shining Green Dragon Formation 青龍耀明
Rating 吉凶	Auspicious 吉
Classic Verse 十干剋應歌訣	青龍耀名戊加丁，上貴可見利功名，迫墓乃招是非因。
Transliteration 字譯	Where the Wu meets with Ding, it is known as the Shining Green Dragon formation. It denotes encounters with a superior Nobleman. It is also beneficial to achieve fame and avoid troubles ahead.
Description 解說	This auspicious combination signals that suggest that one will gain favor with his or her superiors. One will establish strong networks and favorable relationships with individuals of high statute. It is the right moment to get fame and reputation. For companies, any efforts done towards branding will be highly fruitful. Perseverance will be needed to see one's dream to the end. However, if this combination happens to come in encounter with the Graveyard, all the positive things it portends will turn to grief and trauma.

奇門遁甲十干格局篇

WU 戊

The 8 Doors Analysis:

The following evaluates the effects of **Wu** 戊 and **Ding** 丁 with each Door.

休 *Xiu* **Rest**	The path is littered with obstacles. But it seems you are able to conquer every obstacle along the way. This will bring enormous satisfaction. Although you have a difficult journey ahead, you also seem to find a way to successfully complete it. You can see the silver lining and find a way to gain from difficult situations. Your fighting spirit is strong. As long as you do not lose this energy in you, you will always set out to achieve what you always set out to do.
生 *Sheng* **Life**	Focus and concentrate. Do not let your mind wander. Stay on target create a strong clear vision of what you want and take decisive steps towards it. Don't waste your time. Show your talents and if you have what it takes yhen pple will sit up n notice. Do not need any support. You get what you need. Your luck is good. Don't be afraid to stand, shine and make the best out of it.
傷 *Shang* **Harm**	This is associated with good luck. They say that you can't have a rainbow without the rain and this saying is especially true in your case. You will need to suffer and endure some hardships in order to enjoy better things later on. Be flexible. Keep putting in the energy and you'll be able to see things through and enjoy prosperity later on. Don't just keep thinking about something, you need to take action too. And every time you think you think you can't do something, someone else thinks they can.
杜 *Du* **Delusion**	On the surface, your situation looks good and appealing but fortune is fickle. There are many stories of lottery winners who have gone from rags to riches to rags again, having blown all their winnings. Wealth and success can disappear as quickly as it comes. Your vision of the future may not be likely to come true. You must be cautious and alert.

景 *Jing* **Scenery**	Think of a marathon runner: independent, self-motivated, hardworking and persistent. These qualities will help them finish the race eventually. Continue cultivating these qualities in yourself and the success you envision isn't far off. Think of how far you have come already and allow this thought to continue as long as it is necessary. It is important to finish what you have started especially if you are pursuing a new knowledge or a new skill. Your success level will increase the moment you increase your personal capacity. (In knowledge, experience or a certain skill).
死 *Si* **Death**	Careful who you get your advice from. You are unfortunately surrounded by lousy advisors. You need to get advice from people who are where you want to be in life. You are in a difficult situation – all by yourself. You work hard but nobody is there to support you or make things easier. A reward of payoff that seems imminent may not come to past will leave you with many regrets, frustration and wondering what went wrong. Don't rely too much on something specific coming together for you because you never know things can change. If you have to deal with an unexpected loss like this, then accept things as they are. In the future, don't put all your eggs into one basket.
驚 *Jing* **Fear**	You work aggressively and diligently to build your future but sadly, your luck cannot change and bad luck appears to follow you around. None of the people around you are willing to help, so your future is one filled with worry. This is because you are looking at the wrong pool of people and have surrounded yourself with mediocre talents. Remember you are only as fast as your slowest teammate. It is best if you either continue working hard on your own or you should simply seek another different horizon.
開 *Kai* **Open**	Happiness is the ultimate goal of many people. Your successful career will bring you satisfaction. Your family and relationship life will be fruitful and you will enjoy a healthy spiritual state. Have a sense of gratitude for the many blessings you receive. This is a very auspicious sign.

奇門遁甲十干格局篇

戊
WU

天盤 Heavenly Stem	地盤 Earthly Stem
戊 *Wu* **Yang Earth**	戊 *Wu* **Yang Earth**

Structure 格局	Fu Yin 伏吟
Rating 吉凶	Inauspicious 凶
Classic Verse 十干剋應歌訣	伏吟戊加戊，諸事難行靜自處
Transliteration 字譯	Where the Wu meets with Wu, it is known as the Fu Yin formation. It denotes that there is difficulty in carrying out endeavours. It also indicates that a person will lead a lonely existence.
Description 解說	This formation is the Fu Yin 伏吟 structure. Everything will come to a standstill. If there will be any progress, it will be very slow and hardly noticeable and no help will be forthcoming. One will be highly rewarded by using this time to cultivate positive thoughts and rejuvenating the spirit other than trying to force things to move. Such passivity will be one's redeeming grace during this formation.

The 8 Doors Analysis:
The following evaluates the effects of **Wu** 戊 and **Wu** 戊 with each Door.

休 *Xiu* **Rest**	Your fortune is unstable and it seems like you don't have the final say in your own destiny. There seems to be too many hurdles in your chosen path. However, if you clear your mind and look at your situation in an unbiased view, your condition is much better than many others. In your case, life really is what you make of it because you will be presented with good and bad options. If you decide to take up the challenge, this may be a longer route as you need to work harder, but then this will lead you to eventual success. Bear in mind if you choose this path, you walk alone. There will be no external help forthcoming. But if you choose to give up and give in when faced with adversity, then you can't expect to be rewarded for this choice. The current condition is expected to be worse.
生 *Sheng* **Life**	A bumpy road is still a road that has a destination at the end of it. Work will not progress smoothly but you will always get to where you need in the end. Learn as many lessons from mishaps and problems as you can and cherish them. This is a time for learning. These lessons will serve you well in the near future. In addition, learn to respect yourself before you expect other people to respect you. Once you gained enough wisdom, you will reach whatever wealth or relationships goals that you seek.
傷 *Shang* **Harm**	The road is straight and you are about to pick up some speed on your journey. Don't move too quickly, however in case something unforeseeable crosses your path. A conservative, yet steady pace would be most prudent. There are no major obstacles along the way. But unfortunately the path you've chosen is actually the longer route.
杜 *Du* **Delusion**	Your luck is always changing and when it changes, it will be very clear that it has changed for the worse – mishaps, accidents and bad things will befall you. Suddenly, you will face many obstacles on the path to prosperity and you should brace yourself to begin hearing bad news often. Bad times ahead, so brace yourself.

奇門遁甲十干格局篇

WU 戊

	景 *Jing* **Scenery**	Tired, doubtful, worried. Whatever you do, you don't seem to win. Looking for the right calling or the right place in life seems to be like looking for a needle in a haystack to you. Bad luck seems to follow you around. The best advice is to stay quiet at all times. Look inwards, not outwards, for solutions.
	死 *Si* **Death**	Luck here is good though one tends to keep a low profile. Take a gamble and step outside in the real world for a chance. Time and tide waits for no man and you should heed this well as your luck is very favourable.
	驚 *Jing* **Fear**	Missed opportunities do not come knocking again once it flies past. However, there is still hope as there is the possibility of a nobleman helping, though he/she may be hard to find that usual. Keep all eyes and ears open and seek this person as they may offer the key to unlocking the doors of opportunities for you.
	開 *Kai* **Open**	Luck is on your side and your future seems to glow brighter than ever before thanks to suppose for a Nobleman and/or Mentor. It is a good time to bask in one's good fortune but do know that I is prudent to spread the happiness to those around you. Doing this will improve your karma and luck tenfold.

天盤 Heavenly Stem	**地盤 Earthly Stem**
戊 *Wu* Yang Earth	己 *Ji* Yin Earth

Structure 格局	Nobleman Enters Prison 貴人入獄
Rating 吉凶	Moderate 半吉
Classic Verse 十干剋應歌訣	貴人入獄戊加己，公私皆不吉。
Transliteration 字譯	Where the Wu meets with Ji, it is known as the Nobleman Enters Prison formation. It denotes that it will be inauspicious to conduct any professional or personal endeavours.
Description 解説	During this formation, things will go haywire. One's helper will no longer be available to help. They are either in prison or far removed from one's predicaments. One has been left without support. This situation is highly precarious to business and careers as they may crumble in the absence of one's support. However, Auspicious Doors may appear, meaning that one may see favorable results at the end.

The 8 Doors Analysis:

The following evaluates the effects of **Wu** 戊 and **Ji** 己 with each Door.

休 *Xiu* **Rest**	Luck and joy will be yours to have. Be aware of the good tidings around you as a Nobleman and/or Mentor will surely be there to guide you towards greater happiness and prosperity. It is wise to continue along this path there will be plenty of food fortune along the way.
生 *Sheng* **Life**	This favourable sign signifies that all past endeavours have proved successful. Let the past go, for the future is sure to be bountiful with plenty of help along the way. One's talents and efforts are easily recognizable and help will be received when asked.
傷 *Shang* **Harm**	Various hurdles in life and work will prove challenging for the individual. Not only is there no internal or external help forthcoming but one will forever walk alone along this path if one so chooses to do so. There will be good and bad options readily available but even when a choice is made, it will still be an unfortunate path to carry on in.
杜 *Du* **Delusion**	Plans will fail miserably as there is a lack of confidence and ambitious-drive present. Any endeavours that have been started will falter in the end as there is lack of support. Seek the help of a Nobleman and/or Mentor before more failures occur.

景 *Jing* **Scenery**	A change for the better is admirable but it is also wise to get the right advice before turning over a new leaf. Only receive advice from qualified individuals before making a decision as there are no U-Turns in this path one will take.	
死 *Si* **Death**	This sign is associated with bad luck as the road ahead will be very bumpy with obstacles in the way. Proper planning and careful consideration is expected before continuing on. If not, then, one may be prone to falling off the edge too soon, too fast.	
驚 *Jing* **Fear**	Fear of the unknown is what is causing the dilemma here. As one is undecided, this causes panic and obstructions in choosing the right answer to one's journey. Take a stand and make a choice or fall behind – that is the only option now.	
開 *Kai* **Open**	In the real world, the smartest people and the ones who are not afraid to make mistakes. A great weight has been lifted off one's shoulders and all good things will bear fruit. Be mindful that one does not give in to pride or arrogance as reaching one's goals may be easy but keeping them is harder.	

奇門遁甲十干格局篇

戊 WU

	天盤 **Heavenly Stem**	地盤 **Earthly Stem**
	戊 *Wu* **Yang Earth**	**庚** *Geng* **Yang Metal**

Structure 格局	Lead Star Flying Palace 值符飛宮
Rating 吉凶	Inauspicious 凶
Classic Verse 十干剋應歌訣	值符飛宮戊加庚，吉難兊更增，莫問財病，易地安身
Transliteration 字譯	Where the Wu meets with Geng, it is known as the Lead Star Flying Palace formation. It denotes that an auspicious outlook is difficult to obtain and disasters will increase. Therefore, this person should not raise questions about health and wealth. Due to illnesses or diseases, this person will need to look for shelter.
Description 解說	This formation denotes derailed plans and aggravating situations. The situations happen so abruptly and are mostly unforeseen. It is like the general in an army being caught, making an already bad situation worse. Enemies will be using every trick in the book to try make matters worse. Even the doctors will not be of much help when one falls ill. This formation could also indicate that one will be shifting positions or moving residence. Nothing will make this situation better, even the appearance of auspicious doors. Things will however take a turn for the worse if the formation happens to encounter the inauspicious doors. Any present or previous efforts at this stage will be in vain.

The 8 Doors Analysis:
The following evaluates the effects of **Wu** 戊 and **Geng** 庚 with each Door.

奇門遁甲十干格局篇

戊
WU

休 *Xiu* **Rest**	It is one of those times when you have a nagging sixth sense that all is not right. Take this as a good sign to take a step back and re-examine your plans before moving forward again. That way, you can be assured of a much smoother road ahead because things are surely looking brighter from here.
生 *Sheng* **Life**	Be 100% committed in whatever you do – be it in work, life or relationships as all your efforts will not go unnoticed. Everything from a well-deserved promotion from your superior among other fortunate things will come in due time. Remember that if you fail to commit, you will fail to achieve. Stay on this track as good outcomes are ahead of you.
傷 *Shang* **Harm**	Plot your journey carefully because there will be obstacles along the way. No matter if you speed or drive cautiously, there will be ongoing issues that challenge you as you go. Although there are not major obstacles in front, it won't be an easy journey for instead of a shortcut, you have actually taken the longer road.
杜 *Du* **Delusion**	Don't trust people so blindly for they will easily backstab you in the back when opportunity arises. Mind how you speak and conduct yourself in front of people for it is easy to be caught in a state of conflict with others due to misunderstandings.

奇門遁甲十干格局篇

WU

	景 *Jing* **Scenery**	Desire and ambition are two different things. While one desires to be wealthy, one lacks the ambition necessary to put in the hard work to achieve this goal. Wanting it all will not generate a five-star wealth when there is hardly any hard work put behind it. Therefore it is wise to live within your means and be prudent in your spending.
	死 *Si* **Death**	Being stubborn in life and work will not win you the support you crave as you continue building an isolated bubble devoid of support and communication around you. This is a no-win situation and will not get you to where you want to go. While you will achieve your goals in the end, it will be a bumpy and twisting journey before you reach your destination.
	驚 *Jing* **Fear**	Promises are meant to be broken, so don't waste your time arguing any further. Last minute changes will dampen your spirit and drive to carry but you must be like the water. Always flowing in any direction and always seeking outlets and destinations.
	開 *Kai* **Open**	Everything seems to be fluctuating for you as your luck and decisions appear to change every day. This means that you cannot really bank on your journey being smooth at all as there is hardly any definitive goal towards reaching your destination. Take each day one day at a time. While there is no need to have every answer in the book, it is wise to know just enough to get by. Seek the advice from helpful Mentors along the way for this.

天盤 **Heavenly Stem**	地盤 **Earthly Stem**
戊 *Wu* **Yang Earth**	辛 *Xin* **Yin Metal**

Structure 格局	Green Dragon Broken Feet 青龍折足
Rating 吉凶	Moderate 半吉
Classic Verse 十干剋應歌訣	青龍折足戊加辛，吉門謀事兇門耗，足疾折傷須小心
Transliteration 字譯	Where the Wu meets with Xin, it is known as the Green Dragon Broken Feet formation. It denotes plans at the auspicious Door and exhaustion at the inauspicious Door, It is indicative that this person might suffer from broken or fractured bones.
Description 解說	This formation portends the collapse of any established structures. It suggests the collapse of a well-knit group and a lack of communication as people are unable to understand one another as well as possible. Promises and contracts will be lost. The Auspicious Door may control the situation and keep it from being worse while establishing an opening. Some setbacks may still be prevalent though. An Inauspicious Door will entail disaster and loss with physical harm.

奇門遁甲十干格局篇

WU 戊

The 8 Doors Analysis:
The following evaluates the effects of **Wu** 戊 and **Xin** 辛 with each Door.

休 *Xiu* **Rest**	All your hard-work and efforts will pay off and you will be rewarded for this. Kindly ignore the naysayers and continue doing what you do. Choose your decisions carefully and think thoroughly before you act. Keep your energy level high and do not lose sight of your goals.
生 *Sheng* **Life**	Your destiny chart is good because despite all any challenges you face, you will surely end up a winner in the end. Do not be afraid of any obstacles in your path as you will easily step over them. All bitter things in your life will become sweeter in the end. Just follow the steps and respect the rules and you are likely to win in the end.
傷 *Shang* **Harm**	Fortunes appear fickle as what looks good and appealing is merely just an illusion as wealth and success can disappear as fast as it appears for you. One must be cautious and alert as the vision of the future may not likely come true.
杜 *Du* **Delusion**	This is an unfavourable sign in many ways for the onset of depression, jealousy, anger and hate will spill like a raging river from all directions. This combined with repeated misfortunes translated in missed dreams and slow progress. Financial loss is also an eminent factor here as things will go sour very fast. Proceed with caution and plan your steps wisely.

景 *Jing* **Scenery**	A bumpy road is still a road regardless of the many potholes along the way. Progress will be slow but one will be able to reach the destination in the end. Learn from all the mistakes along the way and learn to respect yourself before you can expect others to respect you.	
死 *Si* **Death**	This is not a fortunate sign as disaster and misfortunes will occur without warning and there is nothing you can do to stop it. Though most of it is no fault of your own, you will still have to suffer the consequences in the end. Do not change careers or relationships at this time.	
驚 *Jing* **Fear**	Your stubbornness and ignorance will eventually be your downfall in your life and in your career as well. Mistakes will occur more frequently as you are unable to concentrate at work. Perhaps you can consider taking on lesser responsibilities in order to handle each issues more proficiently.	
開 *Kai* **Open**	This sign denotes a bright and optimistic outcome for you right now. Whether you seek fame, freedom and prosperity, they will all come to you in due time. Be patient for all good things will come to those who wait and try to appreciate the fact that there will always be some bad things along the way as well.	

奇門遁甲十干格局篇

天盤 Heavenly Stem	地盤 Earthly Stem
戊 *Wu* **Yang Earth**	壬 *Ren* **Yang Water**

Structure 格局	Dragon Enters Prison 龍入天牢
Rating 吉凶	Inauspicious 凶
Classic Verse 十干剋應歌訣	龍入天牢戊加壬，陰陽之事皆難成
Transliteration 字譯	Where the Wu meets with Ren, it is known as the Dragon Enters Prison formation. It denotes failed Yin and Yang affairs.
Description 解說	The Heavenly Prison 天牢 shows that one's resources have been stolen by the opposition and that there are traps and other forms of trickery at work. There will be a struggle with one's faith and hope can be lost. The presence of Auspicious Doors may allow the problem to be resolved with one's general sense of wisdom.

戊
WU

The 8 Doors Analysis:
The following evaluates the effects of **Wu** 戊 and **Ren** 壬 with each Door.

休 *Xiu* **Rest**	Good news follows you around and you will hear more good than bad news from now on and all your plans will go off without any problems. Expect no resistance when setting out one's goals as there will be plenty of support from others to help one achieve their dreams. Expect this kind of prosperity to continue for a while but do remember that the more you share this happiness, the more good fortune you will receive in the end.
生 *Sheng* **Life**	This is a favourable sign as all past efforts and labours will slowly begin to bear fruit and what may seem impossible will become possible once more. You can count on the people around you as there are many great talents in your circle of influence that can aid you. Just ask for help and you will receive them.
傷 *Shang* **Harm**	Average outcomes are the norm and one should accept such as a fact. One can improve one's chances of making the right decision provided they ask the right person for the right opinion first. The truth may hurt but it is better than knowing that not knowing at all. Making an emotional decision here can prove disastrous as one is in danger of losing one's current position.
杜 *Du* **Delusion**	Things are difficult and your goals seem almost impossible to achieve. This is because you have brave beginnings and weak endings. You start out fast and lose steam in the middle of the journey, hampered down by your own self-doubts. Keep an open mind and always be wary of what kind of advice you tell yourself or from whom you receive it from.

奇門遁甲十干格局篇

戊
WU

奇門遁甲十干格局篇

戊 WU

	景 *Jing* **Scenery**	All good things must come to an end as in your case, as your luck slowly diminishes. The key in turning these situations around is to humbly ask for help and to ask look for the right advisors and mentors who are more intelligent, knowledgeable and wiser than you. Watch for them as they are able to turn your luck around when you need it the most.
	死 *Si* **Death**	Difficulties and challenges are afoot in this instance as you attempt to chase the proverbial success only to fall flat on your back in your haste to be successful. There is the potential to be hurt if you desire things too much and too fast, so it is best to prepare properly in order to weather the new challenges ahead of you.
	驚 *Jing* **Fear**	There are too many thoughts and issues that demand one's attention and there seem to be nowhere to turn too at this point in time. This is an unfortunate situation to be in and the best thing to do now is to lie low and seek spiritual guidance that will boost both the body and soul.
	開 *Kai* **Open**	Progress may appear slow but do not be pessimistic about it as one's luck can quickly change for the better. Luck is always on your side, so always keep an open mind about new opportunities that come your way. Grab all these new opportunities available as they come for these will surely open new doors for you.

天盤 **Heavenly Stem**	地盤 **Earthly Stem**
戊 *Wu* **Yang Earth**	癸 *Gui* **Yin Water**

Structure 格局	Green Dragon Elegant Seal 青龍華蓋
Rating 吉凶	Moderate 半吉
Classic Verse 十干剋應歌訣	青龍華蓋戊癸合，吉門招吉凶門
Transliteration 字譯	Where the Wu meets with Gui, it is known as the Green Dragon Elegant Seal formation. It denotes the auspicious Door attracting auspicious matters, and the inauspicious Door causes regrets.
Description 解説	The Elegant Seal 華蓋 allows for a neutral standing until the Auspicious Door comes into play. It encourages positivity and good will while being useful for students. It creates luck in the art and academic fields. It must work with an Auspicious Door as it will establish a lack of imagination, lethargy and an inability to be motivated if not used right, thus putting one's mind and body at risk of failure.

奇門遁甲十干格局篇

戊 **WU**

The 8 Doors Analysis:

The following evaluates the effects of **Wu** 戊 and **Gui** 癸 with each Door.

休 *Xiu* **Rest**	Mistakes are bound to be made, therefore it is better not to point fingers but to focus instead on the lessons learnt from this. Do not expect things to fall into place as one must be expected to work hard and to work smart. Success here depends on how hard one is willing to work for it. However, if one chose to play it safe, then one will never reach for the stars.
生 *Sheng* **Life**	Luck and good fortune will not last long here and even there will be resistance in all the matters pursued. This is not the end of the world as one should be prepared wholeheartedly for any resistance. All is not lost as there is still hope.
傷 *Shang* **Harm**	Sorrow, pain and frustration will rain heavily on the individual as for every lucky break that they get, bad news will follow suit. Career fortunes will also take a nosedive so it best to remain cautious and develop a strong fortitude before proceeding any further.
杜 *Du* **Delusion**	In order to win in life, one must cultivate both offensive and defensive skills in order to be successful. One must act aggressively, while reacting reactively in all situations for only through better planning and determination can one push forward for a better chance at success. The more one knows the greater control one has over their lives and finances. This is the strategy that they need in order to be successful.

奇門遁甲十干格局篇

戊
WU

景 *Jing* **Scenery**	Individuals are likely to be able to succeed as they are always finishing what they started. What they need to have right now is the right skills and right mental attitude in order to be successful. Ignore all adversities and learn to use the strength of the right people around you in order to achieve your dream.
死 *Si* **Death**	This represent bad luck in the individual's life at present as everything that the person does seems to go wrong. Every time the person gets back on their feet, something else knocks them down again. Cultivate a sense of fortitude by staying calm and compose and know full well than one can always ride out this storm in no time.
驚 *Jing* **Fear**	No matter what the individual does, they will never win. Even when they are close to victory, unpredictable circumstances arises and one's external conditions can change dramatically. Nothing the individual does will ever be recognized or be rewarded for. Therefore, their success is rather limited on this path.
開 *Kai* **Open**	Obstacles and worries may seem to constantly block one's path but it should not be assumed that it is the end of the world. Not only are these just temporary setbacks but there are a million and one ways to overcome these issues. Do not worry too much for it is not the end destination that matters but how one gets there that matters most.

己
Ji
Yin Earth

天盤 **Heavenly Stem**	地盤 **Earthly Stem**
己 *Ji* **Yin Earth**	甲 *Jia* **Yang Wood**

Structure 格局	Dog Meets Green Dragon 犬遇青龍
Rating 吉凶	Moderate 半吉
Classic Verse 十干剋應歌訣	犬遇青龍己加甲，兇門事敗吉轉佳
Transliteration 字譯	Where the Ji meets with Jia, it is known as the Dog Meets Green Dragon formation. It denotes that threatening events will fail, and it will make an eventual turn for the better and become auspicious.
Description 解說	In general, this formation is inauspicious. It indicates that things are not proceeding as smoothly as possible. Due to the formation, the individual may experience many obstacles along the way. He or she may be frustrated by a lack of progress or unproductive steps. Every issue seems to arrive at once and staying afloat admist the problems is difficult. When an auspicious door is present, it indicates that plans will work out ultimately. The favor of superiors will eventually come around.

The 8 Doors Analysis:
The following evaluates the effects of **Ji** 己 and **Jia** 甲 with each Door.

休 *Xiu* **Rest**	The opportunity for you to seize the spotlight and show your true talents has finally come. Gone are the days where you are waiting in the shadows for recognition. Finally, people will ask for you to showcase your abilities. Do not let this opportunity pass you by. Be motivated and go for it – show the world what you can do and wow them with ¬your talents. This may be your only chance as such good fortune does not just show up at your front door with a knock. If you really want to succeed, you must know how to deal with good opportunities and put them to good use. That being said, it is wise for you to take this in stride and not let it get to your head. Treat others with honour and respect and not only will people admire you for your abilities, but also for your modesty.
生 *Sheng* **Life**	You will have strong luck in romance and your love life. The world seems to be spinning on its axis just for you, and life seems to going on with all its nuances just to please you. This will bring you great serenity and peace of mind, and thus you will be able to pursue your love interest with confidence. It is important to remember that when it comes to romance, charisma is important for first impressions. Harness your inner confidence and do not hesitate with your actions. If you are able to show that special someone your confidence and charisma, you have virtually nothing to worry about. Other people may be perhaps a little envious of how well everything is going for you now. Do not worry about them, because even they will have their chances with good fortune one day.
傷 *Shang* **Harm**	A rollercoaster goes up and down, twists and turns, and can be full of scares and unexpected surprises. You will experience the same thing in your life under this configuration. While you may have good days where all goes well and it seems like you have the potential to keep things running smoothly, there will be an equal number of days when things are just not going according to plan. Because of this, you will not have a very clear sense of where you stand in terms of failure and success. Without clarity, you eventually lack focus as well. This means you will have many ideas circulating in your head but you will not know how to pursue any one of them or what you are expected to do with them. Use your energy to work hard for more knowledge to give yourself a clearer sense of what you need to do with your life.
杜 *Du* **Delusion**	Losers are people who are afraid of failure. This is a mantra that you need to keep in mind while pursuing your everyday goals. This is because you will not have good fortune at this time, but life needs to go on. If you hesitate in everything you do because of fear, you are not going to go anywhere in life. Even though this may be a difficult time, you should see it as a learning opportunity to get better at some skills. When a person works under pressure, he inevitably hones some valuable skills that will take him further in life later. Small issues seem to turn into big problems for you and you are too scared to do anything about it. Because of this, it seems unlikely that any of your dreams will come true.

	景 *Jing* **Scenery**	Networking with the right people in the right manner will bring you great success in the future. It is likely that you are unaware of your skills as a social butterfly, but the fact is you can have a lasting positive impression on the people you meet. If you are able to use this talent properly, you will find yourself meeting many influential and helpful people who will prove to be extremely useful contacts in the future. Use the fact that people are easily mesmerised by you to your advantage. Likability is not as easy to achieve as some people make it out to be so do not take your gift for granted. The support network you end up developing will be vital for your future and you should cherish it.
	死 *Si* **Death**	Life seems to be going down a bad path for you now. Your goals will be difficult to achieve and this is probably because you're the kind of person who starts out in your mission excited and motivated, only to use up all your fuel later and not have enough energy to finish what you started. You are the kind of person who is easily motivated, but your problem is staying on the right track and not losing interest. It can be said that you are easily distracted, moving from one thing to another without regard for consequence. Once you have gotten used to this pattern of work, it will be difficult for you to adapt to a better style of working and you will be stuck in this cycle of difficulty for a long time.
	驚 *Jing* **Fear**	What you want most in life in no longer in your grasp. You have lost sight of it forever and it has moved on elsewhere. Once you lose it, you can never attain it again. All this is a result of obstacles and hardships that you have no way of controlling. With this in mind, it is better for you to let go and move on rather than dwell on the thought of what you do not have. This will only bring you more suffering and there is no way for you to improve this situation. If you dwell on it continuously, you will be trapped by the sorrow of it all with no hope of moving forward. Find something else to give your attention to and try not to think about everything that you have lost. At times like this, you need to keep the good memories and focus on them, because it is likely that they will be the only thing keeping you above the surface.
	開 *Kai* **Open**	A good deed will always be rewarded with another in turn. Your good actions in the past will be repaid now at this auspicious time, and you will receive all the goodness the universe has to offer you under this configuration. Joyous occasions and momentous events will be a characteristic of your everyday life now, and you expect pleasantly surprising news to reach your ears very soon. If you have any goals that you want to achieve, fortune is in your favour and you will find it very easy to go through with those goals. If you use this opportunity well, there is a chance you can even absolve age-old or lingering problems. Good news of your upstanding reputation spreads far and wide and this creates a lasting impression of the goodness of your person.

天盤 **Heavenly Stem**	地盤 **Earthly Stem**
己 *Ji* **Yin Earth**	乙 *Yi* **Yin Wood**

Structure 格局	Hidden Grave Deity 墓神不明
Rating 吉凶	Moderate 半吉
Classic Verse 十干剋應歌訣	墓神不明 己加乙，遁跡藏形修道宜，事多暗昧隱居利
Transliteration 字譯	Where the Ji meets with Yi, it is known as the Hidden Grave Deity formation. It denotes that leading a solitary life is appropriate and encourages the practice of Taoism to elude troubles.
Description 解說	The Ji 己 Stem represents the Earth Gate. It is known as the Hidden Grave Deity 墓神不明. The appearance of this formation denotes that keeping a low profile will be beneficial. Otherwise, the individual will experience a sense of hopelessness, fear and doubt. It may be difficult to stay focused on ambitions or goals. Due to this, it would be better to patiently wait for an opportunity instead of forcing an opportunity to develop. Things may appear murky and unclear. Without clarity, it is impossible to act. Hasty actions bring about disasters, so it is generally better to stay secluded or remain in hiding.

The 8 Doors Analysis:

The following evaluates the effects of **Ji** 己 and **Yi** 乙 with each Door.

休 *Xiu* **Rest**	It is easy to allow worry and paranoia to consume oneself when encountered with a difficult problem. But remember that at this time, luck is on your side and unnecessary worry will only result in stress for you. Things are not going to be as bad as they seem for you at this time, mostly because under this auspicious configuration, things will go your way. Before losing your cool, assess the situation for what it really is with a clear mind. Keep your senses sharp and your perspective true and you will find that you overcome these problems without much difficulty in the end. Be cautious with how you react to these situations and do not be too impulsive. This is a good life lesson for you to help you hone better crisis management skills.
生 *Sheng* **Life**	You possess the rare and invaluable ability of seeing things for what they really are. You tend to distinguish things by whether it is good or bad, black or white, or right or wrong. This gives you a very focused approach to life and helps you to very easily sort through what you perceive to be good decisions versus what you perceive to be bad decisions. This clear cut way of doing things sets you apart from everyone else. Because are quick to assess things for what they are, you can immediately tell who is a good person with good intentions and who isn't. This helps you navigate through life very smoothly and avoid everyone who will bring you strife.
傷 *Shang* **Harm**	Fate seems to single you out and make things immensely difficult for you. You think it is unjust that you seem to suffer more compared to everyone else, who lead normal, unassuming lives. It feels like there are more bumps in the road for you, and you have to put in so much more effort to pull through. Sadly, the fact is that you have no control over this and there is nothing you can do about it. That being said, why let what you cannot do take over your life, when there are things that you still can do? It is wise to not give up. Do not sit around and blame fate for your predicament. Get up and go do something that makes you happy. It can at least take your mind off your troubles for a while.
杜 *Du* **Delusion**	You are the kind of person who has a lot of potential but no opportunities. You have great ideas and vision for the future but for some reason you can never bring them to fruition. Other less talented people can somehow find more success in life simply due to chance. This may seem unfair, but sometimes fate just isn't in your favour. If you give it time, things will start to turn around and you will get what you deserve. Do not be disheartened too easily but instead keep at what you are doing. You are doing good work and if you give up now, there will be no chance of you ever succeeding in the future. If you stay true to yourself, chances are eventually someone will realise the great potential you have and reward you for your perseverance.

景 *Jing* **Scenery**	Ambition is one of your most prominent qualities. Everyone knows this about you and notes that you are someone who always knows what you want. The truth is, while you know how high you would like to climb, the climb itself it what really matters. If you only focus on your ambition instead of the hard work it takes to achieve it, you will not progress very far. Do not allow yourself to come to a point in life where you lack the motivation to seek out your ambitions. Do not let your dreams be only dreams, make them realities and then you can secure your happiness for the long run. Try to employ a step by step approach and take things slowly.
死 *Si* **Death**	People around you are making it difficult for you to harness your talents. Even though you are rather ambitious and skilled, the fact that everyone refuses to support you is a huge factor in your eventual failure. It does not always have to be due to their outright refusal; sometimes they are genuinely unable to give you any support at this time. To make matters worse, your personal wealth is suffering at this point and this further demotivates you. This does not mean that you will always encounter absolute failure. You can still achieve what you want, but you are going to have to toil extremely hard for it. Perhaps it is time for you to take a reality check and reassess your goals on whether they are achievable for you at this time.
驚 *Jing* **Fear**	Fairness is never guaranteed in life. Either you have fate on your side, or you do not. Under this configuration, you will encounter many difficulties with personal relationships with other people. Backstabbing will be common at this time and even your close friends cannot be trusted. There are a few that you could possibly trust, but it going to take time for you to figure out who they are. Be careful with how you approach them, for you do not want to make it look like you are only going to them because you have nowhere else to go. They will not feel appreciated as friends. Keep these people close to you and treat them well, and stay away from supposedly close friends who only want to undermine you behind your back.
開 *Kai* **Open**	You are a highly independent person with strong motivation to get things done quickly and properly. In general, you tend to enjoy good luck and prosperity. Things seem to go your way most of the time and you get to easily solve problems and achieve goals. Truly, you have all it takes to be an inspirational and famous success story, as long as you stay focused and make sure you prioritise your work. If you do so, you will be rewarded with everything you ever wanted in terms of success. That being said, do not be too arrogant and presumptuous to think that you are free from problems. If you run into any setbacks, lower your opinion of yourself and ask help from others. Sometimes, these people will be the ones to carry you far.

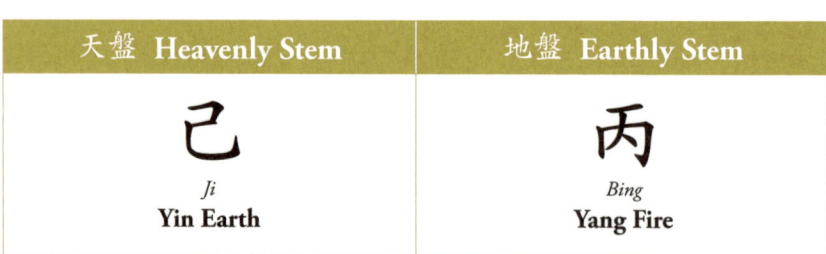

天盤 Heavenly Stem	地盤 Earthly Stem
己 *Ji* **Yin Earth**	丙 *Bing* **Yang Fire**

Structure 格局	Fire Rebelling Earth Door 火悖地戶
Rating 吉凶	Inauspicious 凶
Classic Verse 十干剋應歌訣	火悖地戶己加丙，男冤相害女遭凌
Transliteration 字譯	Where the Ji meets with Bing, it is known as the Fire Rebelling Earth Door formation. It denotes wronged men and victimized women.
Description 解說	This formation indicates that there are positive benefits from fighting fire with fire. It denotes that everything will work out if the individual takes a stand. There may be a range of problems across different settings. The individual may find him/herself fighting a battle across many fronts. It is possible to overcome these challenges by developing strength and staying power. Unfortunately, the formation indicates that this energy and staying power may be lacking. At times, emotions will bring about failures and prevent everything from going smoothly. There may be obstacles and challenges along the path, but there will be no progress without some struggles. He or she should protect their morale and stay motivated on achieving success. When there are negative stars, it denotes the possibility of an illness occurring.

The 8 Doors Analysis:

The following evaluates the effects of **Ji** 己 and **Bing** 丙 with each Door.

休 *Xiu* **Rest**	On the surface, everything looks well to those who are unassuming. But when you go deeper into the problem, suddenly all the issues are made clear and the fact that there is a crisis at hand takes you aback. Therefore you need to be doubly aware during this time of any possible misadventures or potential crises. If you are not cautious, you will end up with a shattered reputation, family problems, and financial issues. It helps to be calm and level-headed. If you approach your problems too impulsively, you will not be able to see the small details that can only be seen with attentive eyes. Give your heart to this issue and you will have no problem distinguishing between facades and realities.
生 *Sheng* **Life**	Life is as fair as it can get. You have chances to succeed and chances to fail. That being said, sometimes you can take charge of fate through your actions. For instance, being hardworking, resilient, and smart will increase your chances of success whereas being lazy, demotivated, and careless will increase your chances of failure. In your case, what will end up helping the most is if you learnt to disregard people who only want to criticise you and make you feel about your attempt at success. Ignore these demotivating comments and channel your energy to your goals instead. Believe in yourself and do what needs to be done because there is no way you can ever please everyone.
傷 *Shang* **Harm**	This is an inauspicious configuration signifying strife and hardship. Even the good things that you have now will eventually be overrun by bad fortune and turn sour. Whatever happiness you do manage to attain will be short-lived and not meaningful. Good fortune will not come to you at this time and the prosperity that you seek is far from attainable. Be grateful for what small pleasures you have now or you may find that once you lose them in the future, you will have absolutely no comfort in life. It will be far more difficult for you to find happiness compared to anyone else.
杜 *Du* **Delusion**	A high likelihood of obstacles and difficulty will hamper your personal growth and make it hard for you to go anywhere in your life. Luck is not on your side and everything you touch seems to fall apart. You have interests in building up your goals but whenever you start to think that it can go anywhere, it seems that leakages occur and you cannot finish your task. A way to counter this bad fortune is by getting more involved in charitable activities to make up for all the bad things that are happening to you. Besides, charitable activities can even serve to bring some joy to you, especially at this time when everything seems to be all doom and glum.

奇門遁甲十干格局篇

JI 己

	景 *Jing* **Scenery**	Things do not pan out the way you want them to. Fortune is just against you at this point, and everything you do seems to be going wrong no matter what you try. Even though you keep a strong head and a positive outlook, when you try and pick yourself up for some reason something comes along and knocks you right back down with little warning. For your part, you should continue to stay calm and collected and take things in stride. Do not overreact or lose your cool or you might potentially jeopardise more things in your life. It is wise to continue to try to be positive, at least until this current wave of bad luck passes over.
	死 *Si* **Death**	The intentions of those close to you are unclear to you now. You feel as if they should be loyal to you because they are your close friends and family, but after thinking about things carefully, you realise that they do not seem as genuine as you hope them to be. You are alone in your path and you are clueless as to how you should proceed. In order to get back on track, you need to collect your thoughts and organise a plan of action in the most precise and calm way you can manage. Do what needs to be done immediately and do not delay the cure, for if you hesitate or take your time, you might possibly damn yourself to sustained bad fortune.
	驚 *Jing* **Fear**	Despite your genuine efforts to succeed, you cannot seem to achieve the same success others seem to be attaining with relatively low effort. You are left confused and angry that such injustice has befallen you. You will come up against fierce resistance in all your attempts at trying to move forward, but you must keep your wits about you and continue striving for your goals. The journey may be full of toil, but if you keep on your path you will ultimately learn an invaluable lesson that you will come in handy in the future when you are yet again faced with such challenges.
	開 *Kai* **Open**	Opportunities have an expiry date. When they come to you, do not spend too much time deliberating how you are going to proceed next or which opportunity you take. Your hesitance will delay the entire process of your progress and for all you know, the opportunities will pass you by. Make your decision based on your gut feeling immediately, because that is most likely what you want most. If you question your desires too long, the opportunity will slip from your fingers and you will go back to where you were before. Take a chance now or you will never have the same luck again.

天盤 **Heavenly Stem**	地盤 **Earthly Stem**
己 *Ji* **Yin Earth**	丁 *Ding* **Yin Fire**

Structure 格局	Red Phoenix Enters Grave 朱雀入墓
Rating 吉凶	Moderate 半吉
Classic Verse 十干剋應歌訣	朱雀入墓己加丁，文書詞訟曲後平
Transliteration 字譯	Where the Ji meets with Ding, it is known as the Red Phoenix Enters Grave formation. It denotes the occurrence of trial or legal cases after wrongful judgments.
Description 解說	This formation shows possible lawsuits, arguments and complaints. Facts may be twisted or the information may be mismanaged. The individual may have a tendency to speak without thinking. This tendency indicates a rise in family troubles and personal disagreements. Due to this, life within the household will seldom be warm or inviting. The individual may suffer from depression or low spirits. He or she has a tendency to over-think basic matters and may spin their wheels needlessly. Things seldom turn out successfully; this leads to depression and low spirits. An auspicious door shows that even the worst events will straighten out in the end.

The 8 Doors Analysis:
The following evaluates the effects of **Ji** 己 and **Ding** 丁 with each Door.

休 *Xiu* **Rest**	Everything appears to be going rather well, but do not be too naïve to assume that they will remain that way forever. Under the surface, turmoil is occurring steadily. It is a hidden danger that seeks to ambush you at a time when you are most unaware and vulnerable. You can take suitable precaution to ensure that you are not taken advantage of. For instance, always think twice about a decision. Do not be impulsive and try to seek advice from those you trust. Their words will reinforce your decisions and make you feel more confident about how to act. Carefully plan everything and try to accept different perspectives about your plans too.
生 *Sheng* **Life**	You are a constant mover. You cannot sit still but instead move from place to place constantly seeking new experiences. This can be good because this shows that you are the kind of person who looks out for your own best interests and will not let anything come in the way of your personal happiness. That being said, this also instils a culture of discontent in your life. The real reason you cannot commit to anything is because you are subconsciously only trying to find the easiest way out. In the end, it is not really about your happiness but more about your convenience. This is dangerous because it closes up a lot of opportunities to yourself and eventually you get used to moving around a lot.
傷 *Shang* **Harm**	While it is a good thing to not let inner turmoil mess with how we project ourselves on the outside, in your case it may be better for you to openly express yourself rather than keep all your feelings of depression and inadequacy to yourself. These feelings will end up suffocating you if you do not know how to let them out. Furthermore, you are lying to yourself if you pretend that nothing is wrong in your life and giving a false impression to close friends and family who trust you to be honest to them. Look at yourself in a more positive way and remember that despite whatever negative things that are said about you, you are still important to your close friends and family. Motivate yourself and keep moving forward with positive messages.
杜 *Du* **Delusion**	Looks can be deceiving. You look like you are in a good place, but you do not realise that you are actually going nowhere. The general atmosphere around every day deludes you into thinking that you're in safe hands when in fact, you are taking things too lightly and causing yourself problems in the future with your lack of serious action. An unforeseeable crisis will soon arise and take you by surprise, and because you are unprepared, you will not know how to deal with it despite the fact that you have the resources and people around you to support you. Even if you try to battle the problem, fortune is just not on your side during this time.

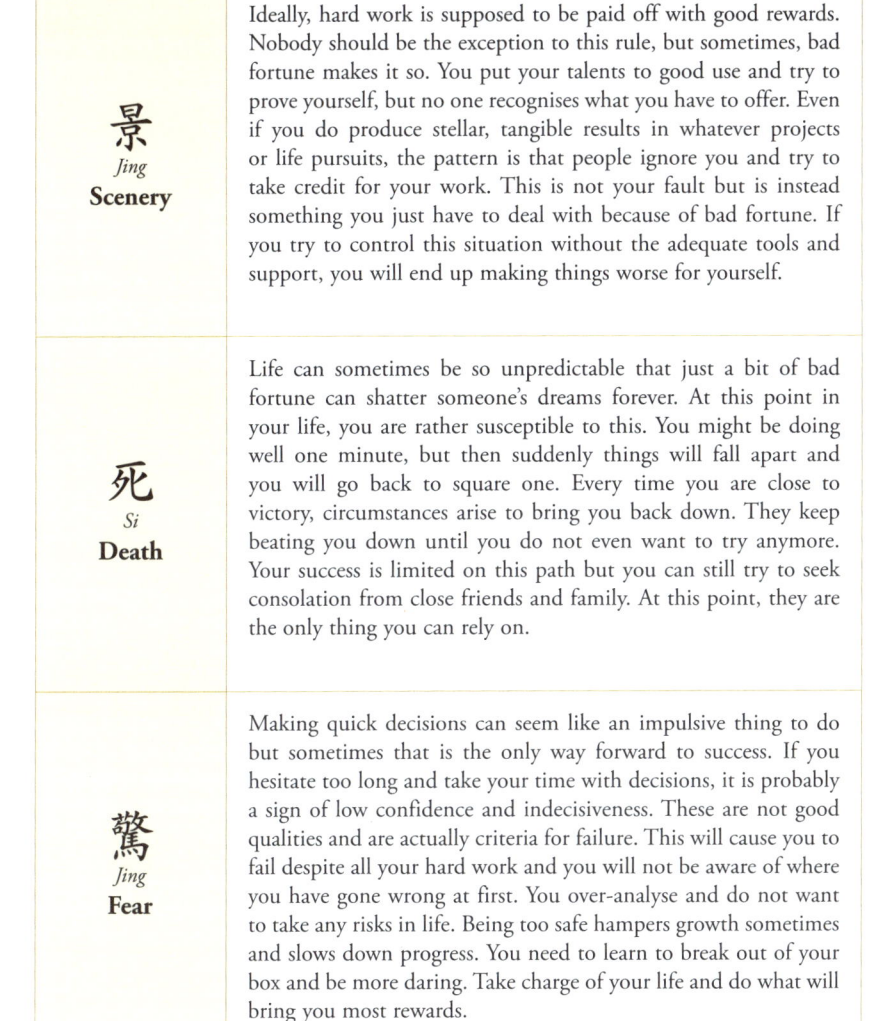

景 *Jing* **Scenery**	Ideally, hard work is supposed to be paid off with good rewards. Nobody should be the exception to this rule, but sometimes, bad fortune makes it so. You put your talents to good use and try to prove yourself, but no one recognises what you have to offer. Even if you do produce stellar, tangible results in whatever projects or life pursuits, the pattern is that people ignore you and try to take credit for your work. This is not your fault but is instead something you just have to deal with because of bad fortune. If you try to control this situation without the adequate tools and support, you will end up making things worse for yourself.
死 *Si* **Death**	Life can sometimes be so unpredictable that just a bit of bad fortune can shatter someone's dreams forever. At this point in your life, you are rather susceptible to this. You might be doing well one minute, but then suddenly things will fall apart and you will go back to square one. Every time you are close to victory, circumstances arise to bring you back down. They keep beating you down until you do not even want to try anymore. Your success is limited on this path but you can still try to seek consolation from close friends and family. At this point, they are the only thing you can rely on.
驚 *Jing* **Fear**	Making quick decisions can seem like an impulsive thing to do but sometimes that is the only way forward to success. If you hesitate too long and take your time with decisions, it is probably a sign of low confidence and indecisiveness. These are not good qualities and are actually criteria for failure. This will cause you to fail despite all your hard work and you will not be aware of where you have gone wrong at first. You over-analyse and do not want to take any risks in life. Being too safe hampers growth sometimes and slows down progress. You need to learn to break out of your box and be more daring. Take charge of your life and do what will bring you most rewards.
開 *Kai* **Open**	Missed opportunities are a normal thing for you at this point. But fear not and do not be discouraged! Sometimes it is necessary for people to miss opportunities before they learn how important they are. You have talents that should be exploited by now but you just have not allowed yourself to take a break and go for an opportunity you really want. You will eventually achieve success if you keep trying, but it may be a long time before you even see the slightest results. The conditions must be perfect for you, but under this configuration, luck may be a little difficult to come by.

天盤 Heavenly Stem	地盤 Earthly Stem
己 *Ji* **Yin Earth**	戊 *Wu* **Yang Earth**

Structure 格局	Dog Meets Green Dragon 犬遇青龍
Rating 吉凶	Moderate 半吉
Classic Verse 十干剋應歌訣	犬遇青龍己加戊，吉門見喜兌柱度
Transliteration 字譯	Where the Ji meets with Wu, it is known as the Dog Meets Green Dragon formation. It denotes happy events at the auspicious Door.
Description 解說	This formation indicates that there is nothing that can stop the individual's dreams from coming true. All that is necessary is to take the goal and bring it into reality. With the influence of the formation, it shows that ambitions can be realized if the individual works toward them. When help is needed, a noble person can be enlisted for extra help. This added help makes any mission easier. Although the future is bright, he or she should avoid any speculative investments. Risky investments will not bring about a favorable outcome.

The 8 Doors Analysis:
The following evaluates the effects of **Ji** 己 and **Wu** 戊 with each Door.

休 *Xiu* **Rest**	Your future is a hopeful one. If you take the opportunity offered to you, a successful family life, career, and healthy lifestyle are yours for the taking. All the doors are opening up for you and you only need to take the step through. Do not be afraid of anything, just take the chance and do what is best for yourself. Always be positive and look forward for opportunities to come your way. This is the best way to attract good fortune. Spread your joy to others and do good deeds for the community to pay back for all the good fortune that you are being blessed with now. Show gratitude, and you will continue to be rewarded.
生 *Sheng* **Life**	Kindness and gentleness will take you far under this configuration. Sometimes a soft approach will bode better for you than a tough approach will. A tough approach will instil fear and obedience, but a soft approach will bring about respect and adoration. Control your temper and be nicer to others, especially those who are helping you or directly working with you or under you. They will recognise your good intentions and remember your goodness to them, which they will repay in kind in the future. You will need their help to overcome obstacles in the future.
傷 *Shang* **Harm**	No help will come to you even though you are in need of assistance desperately. You put a lot of effort into getting things right but because of the severe lack of support you end up not being able to get anything done. The best thing to do is to just not stress out and let things sort themselves out. Use this opportunity to take a well-deserved break and seek out some spiritual harmony. You may not get what you want right now, but if you push it, you will only end up upsetting yourself further. This is a good time to take a step back and avoid any further disappointment in your life.
杜 *Du* **Delusion**	The details of life are passing you by and you are missing out on everything you are supposed to be grasping. You cannot succeed because your ideas are lacking all these important details. Your projects will crumble because they do not have vital pieces to hold them together. Try seeking out a third-party's opinion and be open to whatever criticism they have. Criticism is not meant to make you feel bad about yourself, but rather help you improve yourself so that you can feel better about yourself in the long run. That being said, ensure that the third party you consult is truly independent and has no malicious intent in what he is saying to you. Otherwise, you may just be backtracked even further.

奇門遁甲十干格局篇

JI

景 *Jing* **Scenery**		In the game of poker, players do not only need skill and strategy, they also require luck. This is the same for almost anyone. It is impossible to achieve total success just based on skill and will. One needs luck in order for things to fall into place. Fortunately, this configuration shows that your luck is satisfactory at this point. You should take this opportunity to go ahead with whatever ambitions you are seeking out. Be confident in yourself and play to your strengths. Master the skills required for you to go forward with your pursuits and then the rest will be taken care of by good fortune.
死 *Si* **Death**		Your future is obscured by clouds and you cannot think clearly about how you want to tackle your problems. Others may take this opportunity to cut you down and make you feel bad about yourself. This will lead to severe self-doubt on your part and your confidence will be damaged badly. This bullying will continue for some time until you learn to stand up for yourself and start believing in yourself. Do not let the fact that your future in uncertain meddle with the way you see yourself in the present. If you do not exercise a strong will and be who you are meant to be, you will find it impossible to achieve your ambitions in the future.
驚 *Jing* **Fear**		A character-building opportunity will come to you at this point because your life is going to be very tough now. You will encounter challenges after challenges and you will almost have no rest. That being said, you will somehow get used to these problems and slowly learn to pick yourself up after each trial and face the next one with renewed confidence and better strategies. Keep in mind to be frugal with the kind of action you take against these challenges. Do not be too extravagant or overconfident otherwise you will just end up exhausting yourself. Take it step by step and remember to always rest. If you are not feeling up to the challenge at whatever point in your life, just let it go and rest.
開 *Kai* **Open**		Auspicious luck is yours under this configuration! You will be blessed with good fortune and prosperity and can be rest assured that no significant challenges will come your way. With all these great opportunities coming your way, it is best for you to keep a low profile and level head in order not to attract too much attention to yourself and incur jealousy from others. Aside from that, you are pretty much guaranteed to have a smooth sailing life under this combination. Go all the way and make your dreams come true!

	天盤 **Heavenly Stem**	地盤 **Earthly Stem**
	己 *Ji* **Yin Earth**	己 *Ji* **Yin Earth**

Structure 格局	Earth Door Meets Ghost 地户逢鬼
Rating 吉凶	Inauspicious 凶
Classic Verse 十干剋應歌訣	地户逢鬼己加己，病險謀爲諸兇起
Transliteration 字譯	Where the Ji meets with Ji, it is known as the Earth Door Meets Ghost formation. It denotes that inauspicious events will bring about sickness, endangerment and conspiracy.
Description 解說	This is known as a Fu Yin 伏吟 formation. It denotes that there may be stagnation along the path to a goal. Likewise, obstructions and obstacles are likely to occur. It may take additional soul-searching and ongoing internal anxiety for everything to work out. Overall, the outcome is likely to be unfavorable. He or she may succumb to a disease that they are ill with due to the influence of Ji 己. Extra worries will plague the individual because none of the people around he or she is willing to come to his or her aid when it is needed.

The 8 Doors Analysis:
The following evaluates the effects of **Ji** 己 and **Ji** 己 with each Door.

休 *Xiu* **Rest**	You seem to be in a good place at this point, but do not let minor setbacks destroy your confidence in yourself forever. It can be said that your insecurity has always been there and that it was simply waiting for a trigger to set it back. Do not allow this to happen. Anything can be considered a trigger, and that is why it is so dangerous. If you do not exercise self-confidence, you will lose everything as easily as you gained everything. Other than that, you should be in a good place. You luck is satisfactory at this point, and you only need to take care of your own personal wellbeing and emotions to ensure that the road does get too rocky for you to handle.
生 *Sheng* **Life**	Petty people seem to be attracted to you. Even though you are a rather upstanding person with good morals, people cannot help but want to betray you and make you feel bad about yourself. Backstabbing and accusing is a common feature of the kind of people who like to be around you and pretend that they are your genuine friends. But do not let this discourage you into thinking every single person is out to get you. There is a high likelihood of you meeting a person who will be very good for your success in the long run. Not only is this person sincere, this person is also wise enough to advise you about your life.
傷 *Shang* **Harm**	If you do not have anyone you can rely on for wisdom or advice right now, all is lost. Only with this encouragement from mentors or friends can you pull through this tough period. Fortune is not in your favour right now and you will have a difficult time getting anything done. You will be bombarded with difficult challenges and be expected to be able to deal with them within a short amount of time, which is far more than you can handle what with some personal issues also arising at this time. Before all this goes out of hand, it is wise for you to start searching for your trustworthy mentors so that when the first wave of trials comes, you will be prepared.
杜 *Du* **Delusion**	Life is not being kind to you at this point. You will face many hardships and feel like you are at the end of your road. Do not be too depressed. The first step to recovery is always self-belief. Take some comfort in the fact that even bad things are never permanent. Soon, this will pass and you will be greeted with a new outcome. Bad fortune must occur in order for good fortune to exist. You have to brave the storm for now and stay strong. Do not make any rash decisions that might potentially bring more harm to yourself. The odds are already against you, there is no need to go against yourself.

景 *Jing* **Scenery**	The many challenges and obstacles you face now will leave you exhausted. Your faculties will have all been spent on trying to overcome these trials. Take care to not let your temper get the better of you. If you are less naïve with your emotions, it is likelier for you to be able to cope with your problems better. You often give in to frustration too easily and end up letting your challenges defeat you. Remember that nothing is ever lost as long as you keep trying to do your best. If you truly want to enjoy good fortune, invest some time in gaining real knowledge and practical experience. This will help you have better confidence in your future pursuits.	
死 *Si* **Death**	Bad luck will plague you at this point. You are going to have to stay sharp and keep your wits about you because if you so much as lose sight of reality for a moment, you will be plunged into unbeatable difficulties. There will be many obstacles in your way. Instead of running headfirst into the obstacle in an attempt to push it out of the way or conquer it, trying navigating around it. Your energy level is already low at this point so trying to pick fights and being too ambitious in your problem solving will only lead to more problems. Stay calm and be reasonable in how you face your problems.	奇門遁甲十干格局篇 己 JI
驚 *Jing* **Fear**	Doubts fill your heart and you lack any confidence in yourself. Negative thoughts and woe plague your soul and this stops you from engaging in normal everyday activities. You have only a muted hope as to whether things will work out for you or not. You are fearful of what life has in stake for you and do not feel like you are up to any challenges. It is not surprising you feel this way, as your fortune is bad at this point. Try to avoid impulsive actions. You might be prone to them as you are in a shaky emotional state. Patience and endurance is necessary right now for you to be safe.	
開 *Kai* **Open**	Do not be too eager to please others and focus instead on what makes you happy. You may think that by gaining the favour of others you are securing for yourself a better future, but the truth is trying too hard to accommodate the opinions and preferences of every single person is too exhausting for any human being to handle. Do not worry about other people too much and focus on yourself, for it is time you gave yourself more attention. Do this and you can be assured of success and happiness. When you pay attention your own personal needs, your mind and body will respond positively and you will have a better outlook on life.	

天盤 Heavenly Stem	地盤 Earthly Stem
己 *Ji* **Yin Earth**	庚 *Geng* **Yang Metal**

Structure 格局	Bright Hall Hidden 明堂伏殺
Rating 吉凶	Inauspicious 凶
Classic Verse 十干剋應歌訣	明堂伏殺己加庚，謀害禍來陰星生，官非詞訟客不成
Transliteration 字譯	Where the Ji meets with Geng, it is known as the Bright Hall Hidden formation. It denotes that conspiracy and disaster exists, and the occurrence of the Yin Star. It also denotes unsuccessful litigation.
Description 解說	This formation indicates upcoming legal disputes and arguments. As such, wealth may be lost and one's private life be opened to scrutiny. There will be a need to be careful as there is a possibility of being framed. The best option will be to stay low and not take on any aggressive stance and this includes initiating any lawsuits. Problems will keep surfacing for a while due to the presence of petty people and troublemakers. The best way to counter these issues is to seek the assistance and advice of others during disputes. Otherwise, one will find himself or herself further mired in troubles that not only waste time and effort but also ruin reputations.

The 8 Doors Analysis:
The following evaluates the effects of **Ji** 己 and **Geng** 庚 with each Door.

休 *Xiu* **Rest**	Pride will be your downfall eventually if you are not careful. Self-praise and self-righteousness will only pull you down rather than bring you up like what you expect. Recognise the fact that you are not infallible and that you are not the best person there is out there for whatever it is you are doing. Do not be so naïve as to think that people will just silently accept your behaviour. Soon, someone may speak out and influence everyone to turn their back on you. Your stubbornness will further impede any peace talks with this person, and this may permanently damage your reputation.
生 *Sheng* **Life**	You are currently trying to stay afloat in unstable waters. You cannot control anything and the outcome of your destiny seems to be all over the place. However, if you could only clear your mind and step out of yourself to view your situation with a fresh pair of eyes, then only will you realise that your situation is actually much better compared to others. If you can do this and gain a better perspective about life, you will have an easier time trying to deal with your problems. Always remember that you are not the only person dealing with problems at any one time and that you should always maintain consideration for others even if you are in a horrible spot in your life and do not feel like it.
傷 *Shang* **Harm**	There are many famous sayings that encourage caution before action, but in your case, this advice may be counterproductive. If you take too long to consider anything before making decisions, you will be missing out on opportunities. Learn to trust fate and let it take hold of your life. Do not keep trying to fight reality and design your own outcome. Hardly ever does anyone succeed in getting things their way when fate is against them. The best you can is just go with the flow and make decisions based on your first impression.
杜 *Du* **Delusion**	You do not lack capability, but something seems to be keeping you from going all the way. For instance, you have the skills to start up a project, but for some reason you cannot keep it going or maintain its position in the community. You need a lot of guidance to keep your feet on the ground and ensure your projects do not collapse on themselves. Find someone you trust to be your source on guidance in this matter and keep going back to them for words of advice. You are not going to be able to go all the way yourself and are in dire need of guidance from a mentor.

景 *Jing* **Scenery**

It is unwise to continually pursue something that is obviously far out of your control. Some things cannot be changed and if you think about it, spending more time trying to right something that has already gone so wrong is just going to tire you to the point that you can no longer function normally in everyday life and pay attention to the here and now. Other things require your attention more because they are budding pursuits that need to be developed. Old problems are simply missed opportunities and should not take up too much of your time and energy.

死 *Si* **Death**

Families are supposed to be harmonious units in which there are strong support systems. For you however, this configuration brings the exact opposite. Perhaps you need to reassess the way you deal with your loved ones. If they did something wrong, do not chew them out and expect them to repent immediately. Sometimes human communication requires giving and taking, and if you do not first address some of your own problems and flaws, they are not going to see you as a credible person to instruct them or give them advice. Do not overanalyse their flaws and make them feel bad. Instead, help them to become better people.

驚 *Jing* **Fear**

All the options you are trying to dispel your troubles are not working. You feel pushed into a corner where there is no turning around. But the truth is, you are getting all this now because you are an underachiever. You tolerate being mediocre and because of that, that is all you have ever been all your life. If you continue this way, you will always feel like you are not going anywhere in life. You can try and make things better for yourself by improving your skillset and mind-set and striving to become the best rather than just someone with satisfactory performance in life.

開 *Kai* **Open**

Your fortune seems to be influenced by both extreme luck and extreme unluckiness. You are being pushed in pulled in the completely opposite directions, with copious success in one direction and absolute failure in the other. This may feel very confusing for you but it is best for you to just simply appreciate whatever goodness comes your way and try to very calmly deal with your problems. If you do not allow your successes to take your mind off your failures, you will not be able to pay sufficient attention to the truly important things in life. As long as you are sincere in your attentions, your wave of bad luck will soon lapse until fortune is only pulling you in one direction: towards success.

天盤 **Heavenly Stem**	地盤 **Earthly Stem**
己 *Ji* **Yin Earth**	辛 *Xin* **Yin Metal**

Structure 格局	Spirit Enters Grave 遊魂入墓
Rating 吉凶	Inauspicious 凶
Classic Verse 十干剋應歌訣	遊魂入墓己加辛，陰邪鬼魅須小心
Transliteration 字譯	Where the Ji meets with Xin, it is known as the Spirit Enters Grave formation. It denotes that attention should be paid to evil spirits and ghosts.
Description 解說	When this formation is seen, it is indicative of superficial things, meaning things may appear well on the outside but behind the façade, everything is stagnating. Avarice may cause one to lose sight of the bigger picture. As such, your fortunes will start to dwindle as problems begin to appear by the dozen. These problems will prove to be difficult to solve and will stall your plans. To make matters worse, the more one tries to keep on top of it, the more he or she will suffer.

The 8 Doors Analysis:

The following evaluates the effects of **Ji** 己 and **Xin** 辛 with each Door.

Xiu **Rest**	Both the good and the bad come together. No person can have one without the other. In some ways, they complement each other and keep a person's character in check. You will not have any clear sense of where your life is headed; whether or not something good or bad will come to you. But it is no matter, because in the end, if you are able to find guidance from someone wiser and more experienced than you, you will be able to learn from him. This mentor will have been through exactly you have gone through and he will be able to teach you what to expect and how to react to situations.
Sheng **Life**	With your unrealistically high expectations, it is no wonder that you tend to get disappointed in life. You need to stop being so idealistic and focus instead on what is practical and doable. You too often have your heads in the clouds and are stuck in your head all day. You spend most of time fantasising about what you want your life to be like instead of thinking what you should do to make that happen. This makes you a visionary, and it is a good thing to be a visionary, but what use is a visionary if his visions do not come true? You need to start focusing and exercise more diligence if you ever want to get anywhere.
Shang **Harm**	Stubbornness is one of the worst qualities a person can have and unfortunately, you seem to be proud of your stubbornness. You are in a severe situation right now but you ignore its depth because you think you are in safe hands, oblivious to the troubles that await you. You have a tendency to stay away from other people and reject their offers of help, instead choosing to be alone because you think they will only bring you down. You will never get anywhere with an attitude like this and it is going to be impossible for you to overcome your challenges, especially if you alienated everyone who cares about you.
Du **Delusion**	Your expectations about life are far too high and worse still, your fortune at this point is not good and it is impossible for your expectations to be met. Obstacles that cannot be beaten will come in your way such as financial problems. Take care to not invest in anything too impulsively. Conflicts in your personal life are also prone to happening, particularly if you expect too much of your friends and family. They will have their own personal issues that prevent them from committing to you. All things considered, financial investment is not recommended at this point and you will need to plan your finances carefully.

景 *Jing* **Scenery**	The road to success is paved with bumps and potholes. Do not speed through this road and ignore the signs – you will surely encounter an accident. Do not expect anything to be straightforward. Your road will twist and turn unexpectedly and if you do not watch out, you will miss the turnings and plunge drive off the path completely. Be very careful and do not take anything for granted. It is dangerous for you to assume anything. Always clarify the certainty of something and refrain from making impulsive judgements. Success can come to you as long as you do not jeopardise your journey with unnecessary accidents.
死 *Si* **Death**	Disaster will follow in your wake and there will be no warning when it reaches you. There will be nothing you can do to avoid these catastrophic events. You will suffer because you are constantly being caught unawares by such situations. They come to you at the most undesirable of times, such as when you are just experiencing a surge of positivity in your career. These negative events will turn everything around suddenly and you will not have time to pick yourself up. As a result, you are doomed to fail at many things. At this time, it is best for you not to make any big changes in your life and just remain comfortable with what you have.
驚 *Jing* **Fear**	Stubbornness will not bring you any good, despite the fact that you think it makes you look strong-willed. Being strong-willed is in fact not the same as being stubborn. A stubborn person is someone who would ignore the advice of others for the sake of ego. If you truly want to avoid failure, you must take a step back and be the listener for once. You will have many mistakes in your projects but will be too stubborn to do the right thing about it. The fact is, if you do not put aside your pride and start thinking about the best thing you should for your future, you will be trapped in a perpetual state of denial and failure forever.
開 *Kai* **Open**	Communication is an important tool for success in any person's life. No man is and island and aside from the company that good company brings a person, what is more important is how information in conveyed and received, especially in a career setting. If you are able to master this concept, you will not have a problem getting on with your life. But if you happen to suffer from social inadequacy, all you have to do is hone more self-confidence. You have to first believe in the words you say in order for others to believe in them later. Being convincing and persuasive is not a skill that a person is born with. It takes hard work to develop.

奇門遁甲十干格局篇

己 JI

天盤 Heavenly Stem	地盤 Earthly Stem
己 *Ji* **Yin Earth**	壬 *Ren* **Yang Water**

Structure 格局	Earthly Net High Stretch 地網高張
Rating 吉凶	Inauspicious 凶
Classic Verse 十干剋應歌訣	地網高張己加壬，狡童佚女不守本，傷毀姦情人共憤
Transliteration 字譯	Where the Ji meets with Ren, it is known as the Earthly Net High Stretch formation. It denotes the murder of an adulterous couple, causing resentment all around.
Description 解説	This is a highly inauspicious formation as it denotes scheming, betrayal, adultery, scandals and treachery. One's mental state will be in constant turmoil and he or she will find it difficult to keep a clear mind. As such, one will feel constantly trapped emotionally and be constantly stressed even by the most trivial of problems. A lack of planning and poor strategy further compounds the problem. This is not helped by the fact that there is an indication that either the children or the employees are disloyal and unsupportive.

The 8 Doors Analysis:

The following evaluates the effects of **Ji** 己 and **Ren** 壬 with each Door.

休 *Xiu* **Rest**	It looks like the situation is dark and there is no way out. You are under the assumption that you are going to fail in whatever endeavour it is you are undertaking. Despite all this, the truth is you are actually on the verge of being blessed with a great many rewards. Do not overlook this opportunity and continue with a negative state. Blessings such as these do not come along very often and you miss it because you were too blind to see it, then you will have missed out on a lifetime opportunity. Your success completely depends on your ability to recognise opportunities and what you make of them.
生 *Sheng* **Life**	You generally have a bad case of luck about you, with supposed friends backstabbing you and making you the subject of their vicious rumours. You have poor interpersonal skills and your relationships with other people are not satisfactory. You experience conflicts with them often; conflicts which are only solved through the healing powers of time. That being said, someone will some sympathise with you and realise that you actually have a lot to offer, despite what other people think about you. This person will act as a sort of mentor and provide you with the guidance you need to improve as a person and eventually succeed in life.
傷 *Shang* **Harm**	An important decision is in need of your immediate attention but you are unable to make a quick decision because you feel that you are being bombarded with a dilemma that is too difficult to solve. Ultimately, this indecisiveness will be the cause of your downfall. If you want to be seen as a good leader, you cannot let this indecisiveness mar your reputation and make you come across as the kind of person who cannot make important calls for the team. Opportunities will just pass you by if you do not seize them fast enough. Keep your wits about you and stay on your toes. Try to go with your gut feeling and choose which option you think will have the ultimate best outcome for yourself.
杜 *Du* **Delusion**	Your luck is very unstable at the moment and good things will not come to you as previously hoped. You will be subject to an indefinite waiting period wherein the object of your desire will seem close but still too far. In a way, it is tormenting you that despite how hard you try, there just doesn't seem to be any way that you can get what you want. You will need extraordinary patience and perseverance if you want to pull through this period in your life. Results will not immediately materialise and be the best for you, but do not lose your cool. If you give up and end up having an outburst, you are only going to make things worse for yourself as other people will start seeing you in a negative light.

奇門遁甲十干格局篇

JI

景 *Jing* **Scenery**	The world is full of opportunistic people with no loyalty and ethics. Trust is scarce among many people of this modern age; honest, upstanding people are hard to come by. As for yourself, you are rather naïve because you have not accepted this simple truth about the world. You need to be very clear on who you trust and be stingy with this trust. Do not simply christen any Tom, Dick, or Harry that you see with your valuable trust. They will abuse it and turn on you and by the time you realise what their intentions were the whole time, it will have been too late. There is no shame in being shrewd to protect yourself. It is better than being too innocent and then being taken advantage of.
死 *Si* **Death**	Be very careful who you put your trust in. Your advisors do not have malicious intent, but unfortunately they are just simply not sharp enough to be giving other people life advice. Their words may end up being harmful as they are not experienced or wise enough themselves. Do not get advice from your peers because they are in the exact same spot as you are and not moving anywhere in life. Get advice from people whom you want to emulate. They are the ones you aspire to be like so it is only logical for you to ask for their take on life. They will tell you how to approach problems the way they did.
驚 *Jing* **Fear**	Do not count on good fortune at this time. It is dangerous for you to put your future in the hands of a wobbly fate, thinking that things will pan out for you in the end. Either you take responsibility and act to make things turn in your favour, or you prepare to readily accept an undesirable outcome. If you are too lazy to take action, then you will reap what you sow – which is nothing. If you feel that you are too weak or too inexperienced to do anything about your current state, then you need to immediately seek out someone who has the capability of helping you. It is likely that you are the kind of person who cannot get up on his own. Therefore it is wise for you to think of who you want to be your mentor now.
開 *Kai* **Open**	Things are slowly starting to work out for you and you are gradually moving forward to where you want to be. Success always requires a fair amount of sacrifice before it can be achieved. So if you want to keep this pattern going, you need to constantly work hard. Do not simply hope for the best, but instead put your heart into all that you do and concentrate on your goals. The future is shaping up nicely for you and you do not want to lose this opportunity. Be clear cut with your goals so you can focus your energy on them, and do not be wary of putting in any extra effort. After all, you know deep down in your heart that it is what you need to do.

	Heavenly Stem		Earthly Stem
天盤	己 *Ji* **Yin Earth**	地盤	癸 *Gui* **Yin Water**

Structure 格局	Earthly Punishment Black Tortoise 地刑玄武
Rating 吉凶	Inauspicious 凶
Classic Verse 十干剋應歌訣	地刑玄武己加癸，囚獄詞訟病垂危
Transliteration 字譯	Where the Ji meets with Gui, it is known as the Earthly Punishment Black Tortoise formation. It denotes the occurrence of imprisonment, lawsuits, and critical illness or diseases.
Description 解說	This is an unfavourable formation which indicates failure in one's plans. A lot of people will be clamouring for assistance but yet at the same time, one will receive none from others. Due to this, the individual may feel lost and alone, and every problem will feel like a mountain to climb. Manipulative individuals will attempt to take advantage of the situation for their own gains. There is also an indication as well that health will fail and there is the possibility of legal issues that lead to a jail term.

The 8 Doors Analysis:

The following evaluates the effects of **Ji** 己 and **Gui** 癸 with each Door.

休 *Xiu* **Rest**	You will experience positivity in every aspect of your life. Thank your lucky stars for this development because you were once very unlucky in all your pursuits. This is fantastic news for you but do not be too elated that you lose focus on the real issues at hand. Your struggle now will be to maintain this positivity and figure out ways to stay on top even without good fortune. Start seeking out expert advice from those you can trust. Go to more than three sources for absolute clarity. If you must, take some time off work to relax and clear your mind before going back into the fray. During that time, it is likely that you will have come up with a strategy on how to make your success sustainable.
生 *Sheng* **Life**	Great wealth will come to you and will be at your happiest at this time. Everyone loves money, but not everyone knows what to do with it. In fact, you have been so used to bad prosperity, that now that you have an abundance of wealth, you may start spending it unwisely and cashing in on everything you set your eyes on. Do not buy impulsively but that is the top sure-fire way of losing your money. You may see many things that you have been eyeing to buy for a long time but you need to exercise self-control and tell yourself that the opportunity for you to be wealthy does not come along very often.
傷 *Shang* **Harm**	Fatigue will try to break your spirit during this time but you must not let it win over you. It is understanable that you are so exhausted because you have been toiling away for a long time, trying to find a solution to your problems. Physically, you have become vulnerable to illness and disease. Mentally, you are tired and unable to come up with anymore original ideas. Emotionally, you are drained and do not have time to have any fun or spend any time with people around you. This is dangerous as it can lead to total isolation and eventually a break down. Manage your time well and make room for relaxation and fun, otherwise you will only push yourself over the edge.
杜 *Du* **Delusion**	Relationship issues will greatly affect you now. You are constantly distracted and worried about your relationship. You feel like this is your last chance to establish a truly meaningful romance with someone, but that person does not seem to be putting in the same amount of effort. You are not willing to let this person go because you feel that this person is the one for you. Sadly, the reality is that you cannot be so naïve when it comes to matters of your own heart. If you are not careful with who you give your affections to, you will end up broken forever and a broken heart is one of the most difficult things to repair.

景 *Jing* **Scenery**	The worst of your problems have passed and it is now time for you to relax and take a break. Do not bother to pursue any new goals or successes at this time. This is a time for reflection and planning. If you speed off to get more things done, you will only end up failing again because you did not give yourself time to recuperate and you did not plan properly how you were going to approach your new problems. Take a break, go on vacation, meet up with old friends; do anything that will make you happy and take your mind off your troubles for a while. Only if you take this healing step can you make the next step to success.
死 *Si* **Death**	Your own actions have caused people to think lowly of you. Your friends turn away from you and are confused about the way you have acted. Some even claim that you deliberately betrayed their trust. On your part, this may not be true. Sometimes we end up doing bad things even though we do not have evil intentions. The best thing for you to do now is to stay away from the people you have offended. Given them space and time to think about how they want to deal with you, and in the meantime, you should start planning your grand apology.
驚 *Jing* **Fear**	Too often, you find yourself consumed by the fear of what others think about you. You are afraid to act on anything or voice your own opinions. As a result, even though you are highly talented, you have never shone in your life because you are adverse to attention. This is foolish for you. If you truly want success, how can you let such childish fears hold you back? If necessary, see a therapist or engage in some activities that will help you open up. If you do not fix this problem soon you will forever be confined to be a wallflower.
開 *Kai* **Open**	A stroke of brilliant luck will carry you out of your dark place and push you toward the path to success. Take things in your stride and do not act too impulsive. Oftentimes, people tend to take things for granted and start thinking they are invisible after being blessed with such luck. Instead, you should be humbled and grateful, acting with prudence and respect for others. For every person who is blessed, there is someone who is cursed. Remember this always so you do not become too cocky and forget your place. If you do not act appropriately, your luck may just be taken away from you again to teach you a lesson.

庚
Geng
Yang Metal

天盤 Heavenly Stem	地盤 Earthly Stem
庚 *Geng* **Yang Metal**	甲 *Jia* **Yang Wood**

Structure 格局	Leader Slaying Palace 值符伏宮
Rating 吉凶	Inauspicious 凶
Classic Verse 十干剋應歌訣	值符伏宮庚加甲，多成多敗人地罷
Transliteration 字譯	Where the Geng meets with Jia, it is known as the Leader Slaying Palace formation. It denotes one's success that will turn into failure.
Description 解說	With this formation, the outlook is highly inauspicious. The formation indicates that a seemingly good situation will suddenly transform into a negative situation. The unfavorable combination denotes a probability that financial losses will be incurred. A bankruptcy or monetary dispute is likely. When it comes to career matters, a loss of authority or a demotion is increasingly likely. The individual's employees or inferiors who were once loyal may ultimately betray the individual. Likewise, health matters may take a turn for a once. There is an increased chance that a separation from loved ones or family members will occur.

The 8 Doors Analysis:
The following evaluates the effects of **Geng** 庚 and **Jia** 甲 with each Door.

休 *Xiu* **Rest**	Your destiny chart is good therefore you should not be afraid of a little adversity in your luck cycles. With good luck on your side, there should be nothing to fear from a little challenge. Simple proceed in a calm and collected manner and all success will follow suit,
生 *Sheng* **Life**	This individual is blessed with possessing a hardworking and innovative attitude in their career and life. They will have a creative mind that will be bound to be justly rewarded and recognized in a supportive environment. Focus on the ultimate goal because if it is pursued half-baked, nothing good will come off it. If one eagerly puts in the effort, then the future is going to contain everything that one desires.
傷 *Shang* **Harm**	Challenges and strife will be the bane of this individual's life and this will leave them tired and irritable. To avoid this, they must be less naïve and they need to be conservative and realistic when facing such frustrations. More importantly, they need to gain real skills and be grounded in reality for only when that happens can they truly enjoy success afterwards.
杜 *Du* **Delusion**	Doubts, negative thoughts and worries fill this individual with a nagging feeling that their dreams and ambitions will fail to take flight. Their current bad luck signifies that they are constantly unable to catch a break and will be plagued by ongoing issues every day. To lighten this burden, it is best to take a step back and evaluate the situation before coming to a conclusion.

奇門遁甲十干格局篇

GENG 庚

	景 *Jing* **Scenery**	Letting it go is the key factor here as the individual is constantly besieged by unsolvable problems that are either wearisome or time-consuming. Do not hang onto something that is impossible to obtain as this will only burden oneself down further. Talking to someone may not help solve the problem but it can help lighten the load.
	死 *Si* **Death**	Family strife is abundant in the sign represented here as there is evidence of spousal or partnership troubles at present. Do not overanalyse things nor be quick to accept the blame. Learning to let go is important for the individual here because if they continue to hang onto the past, then the better tomorrow will not come.
	驚 *Jing* **Fear**	Fortune does not smile for the individual for it seems to throw obstacles and setbacks at the individual in an unfair way. Not only are their position unstable right now but they have come to willingly accept this bad luck. Although luck is not on their side, they can still make the best of things by having a better mind-set and trying to make the best of their situation.
	開 *Kai* **Open**	Long standing problems that have plagued you will be resolved, finally clearing the path ahead for you to move on once and for all. You will obtain good wealth luck leading to an increase in income. Listen carefully to the advice you receive from mentors or helpful and then be sure to act on them swiftly. Matters of the heart will also be positive, so do not worry.

天盤 **Heavenly Stem**	地盤 **Earthly Stem**
庚 *Geng* **Yang Metal**	**乙** *Yi* **Yin Wood**

Structure 格局	Great White Meets Star 太白逢星
Rating 吉凶	Moderate 半吉
Classic Verse 十干剋應歌訣	太白逢星庚加乙，進兇退吉合謀宜
Transliteration 字譯	Where the Geng meets with Yi, it is known as the Grave White Meets Star formation. It denotes inauspicious events that lead to aggression. It is auspicious for retreat and collaboration.
Description 解説	With this formation, it is far better to stay active. Remaining passive or waiting for opportunities to occur will not turn out well. The formation denotes that an extreme joy will beget sorrow in the end. As such, it is better to conceal a victory. Advertising success or boasting of conquests will only stir up jealousy among other people. Enemies surround the individual and are watching for an opportunity. Due to this, the individual should conceal their movements. It is better to keep private counsel and not tell anyone about his or her secrets. There is also a possibility that negative thoughts like doubt and worry will plague this individual.

The 8 Doors Analysis:

The following evaluates the effects of **Geng** 庚 and **Yi** 乙 with each Door.

休 *Xiu* **Rest**	Things come and go so fast that the individual is sometimes unable to hold onto what they have before it disappears. It is also difficult for the person to break new ground and succeed. The problem is the individual's mental limitations as they are stuck in the past and are unable to see the future. The person can try again but they must keep a low profile and push forward quietly.
生 *Sheng* **Life**	Better things are coming this way and the individual would be wise to be in this pathway in order to capitalize on it. They have a clear chance to move forward and achieve their goals with minimal resistance therefore they must step forward and get things done immediately. Knowing that they need to make a change to do it is not enough for they will also need to be courageous to do it.
傷 *Shang* **Harm**	A sense of loss and confusion grows stronger for the person as even their own health and energy takes a nosedive. The answers and solutions appear harder to find at times but with persistence, one will eventually find it. Be patient and the solutions will eventually work itself out eventually.
杜 *Du* **Delusion**	This is an inauspicious sign as the individual will find themselves often in a jam without any help whatsoever. No matter what this person does or how hard they try, no good will come out from this and they will feel disappointed and discouraged by all of this.

奇門遁甲十干格局篇

GENG 庚

景 *Jing* **Scenery**	Appearance can be deceiving and none is more so as this person is stricken with bouts of bad fortune all the time. Wealth and success can disappear as quickly as it comes and their vision of the future may not be likely to come true. The individual must learn to be cautious and alert and all times.
死 *Si* **Death**	Your situation is not kind to you. In your career. You may be experiencing rough times. Take comfort in knowing that nothing is really permanent. For now, do not make any brash decisions for the odds are not in your favour.
驚 *Jing* **Fear**	A very unlucky sign indeed as everything that you desire will not come together in a way that benefits you. The situation is dire as even those who had promised to help you previously have now turned their back on you. In these hostile circumstances, your dreams are unlikely to come true and you are unlikely to make the right decision given your desperation to see things thoroughly. Be wise and make sure you see the complete picture before coming to a conclusion, especially when it deals with money and investments.
開 *Kai* **Open**	There is no need to feel jealous or suspicious of others. Just make sure you are doing your part well. In terms of your business and career, growth and development looks set to continue steadily and healthily. This sign indicates that there is hope and that you will be safe from harm, no matter what difficulty arises, Keep doing what you feel is right and everything will play itself out smoothly,

天盤 **Heavenly Stem**	地盤 **Earthly Stem**
庚 *Geng* **Yang Metal**	**丙** *Bing* **Yang Fire**

Structure 格局	Great White Enters Shimmer 太白入熒惑
Rating 吉凶	Inauspicious 凶
Classic Verse 十干剋應歌訣	太白入熒庚加丙，須防盜賊為客贏
Transliteration 字譯	Where the Geng meets with Bing, it is known as the Great White Enters Shimmer formation. It denotes the need to let customers win in a robbery or theft situation.
Description 解說	Political games and mental torture are possible problems for this individual. The formation denotes a rise in torments that relate to the mind, body and soul. Likewise, stress and fear may dominate the individual's mind. He or she may lose emotional stability. There is a potential for the individual to suffer a loss in a career-related project or have a emotion. They may be unknowingly framed for something or harmed. He or she may give orders in the workplace that are not carried out efficiently.

The 8 Doors Analysis:
The following evaluates the effects of **Geng** 庚 and **Bing** 丙 with each Door.

休 *Xiu* **Rest**	You have been through some rough patches of late. Don't falter now if you had persevered through it diligently all this while. Better things are finally coming for you. Continue on with your best efforts and don't let anything sway you from your objective. Keep your head high as you are almost there.
生 *Sheng* **Life**	Nothing really comes for free as nobody will make you successful or have the responsibility to make you happy. You have got to get out there and put in some effort to get what you want. The good news is that good luck is also on your side. Help will be found where help is needed. So do not worry as you will achieve your dreams in due time.
傷 *Shang* **Harm**	Your luck is slowly diminishing and running out as nothing good seems to come of your efforts, despite your efforts. You can turn this situation around by simply asking for help and looking for the right mentor who is skilled and intelligent enough to guide you through this dark period in your life.
杜 *Du* **Delusion**	Promises will be broken, so do not waste your time trying to argue further. These broken promises can cause a dampening of one's spirit and uncertainty about their future. Though they should remember that every ending, there will be a new beginning. So learn how to adapt to any situation thrown at you.

奇門遁甲十干格局篇

GENG

	景 *Jing* **Scenery**	To others, you look like you have an easy life right now, but it is actually very challenging. Not only is your life like a roller-coaster but one wrong move can actually spell disaster. Try not to make too many assumptions as all you can do now is to take on new challenges with a positive attitude and deal with the problem one at a time. Pay attention and watch out for a sudden change of tides or an accident.
	死 *Si* **Death**	Fortune does not smile for you and it seems to throw obstacles and setbacks at in an unfair way. You may feel there is very little options you can take or that your position right now is unstable. Although luck is not on your side, you could still make things better if you had better skills and a better mind-set. Try and do what you can to make the most of what is presented to you.
	驚 *Jing* **Fear**	This is not a fortunate sign as disaster and misadventure occur without warning and there is nothing you can do to avoid them. Your career will suffer from these and you may fail at many things, often though, through no fault of your own. This is not the best time to seek a career or relationship change.
	開 *Kai* **Open**	Kindness is always appreciated by other people, so take this advice to heart. A polite, measure, thoughtful approach to your dealings with others will produce prosperity and wealth for you. A nobleman or a mentor in your life will serve as guide, who can show you how to turn things around and turn sorrow into joy. Seek out this person as he/she is closer than you think.

天盤 **Heavenly Stem**	地盤 **Earthly Stem**
庚 *Geng* **Yang Metal**	丁 *Ding* **Yin Fire**

Structure 格局	White Pavilion of Deceit 亭亭之格
Rating 吉凶	Moderate 半吉
Classic Verse 十干剋應歌訣	亭亭之格庚加丁，官非爭訟私匿情，門吉有救守無驚
Transliteration 字譯	Where the Geng meets with Ding, it is known as the White Pavilion of Deceit formation. It denotes evidences concealed before a trial. If this combination meets with the auspicious Doors, it denotes hope without fear.
Description 解說	There are drastic changes afoot in the individual's life. They may suddenly have changed circumstances or new developments. Not all of these changes will be position. There is a possibility for explosive disputes, arguments and obstacles. Challenges and legal battles may occur along the way. Personally, he or she may be surrounded by secret obsessions and drama. At times, he or she may feel like they have lost their direction in life. Although he or she may make some gains, he or she is likely to lose these gains in the end. This is partially due to the fact that there is no one around to help them gain their bearings. Without the help of supportive people, he or she will feel that every struggle is twice as hard as it actually is. Due to this situation, it may seem like everything is geared to work against the individual and progress is difficult. When an auspicious door is present, it provides an unexpected opportunity. This new opportunity can help the individual to escape from their problems and can be a source of positive change.

奇門遁甲十干格局篇

庚
GENG

奇門遁甲十干格局篇

GENG 庚

The 8 Doors Analysis:
The following evaluates the effects of **Geng** 庚 and **Ding** 丁 with each Door.

休 *Xiu* **Rest**	Save up your energy and your passion for the right moment or opportunity, which is coming soon. You will know when the right moment arrives and when it does, hit hard. You can look forward to smooth progress and the outcome you have been hoping for. The outlook is favourable for personal and professional endeavours.
生 *Sheng* **Life**	It takes time and effort to do anything worthwhile, and if you have not found success yet, then it isn't an excuse to throw in the towel just yet. This number indicates that success depends on your ability to stay dedicated and positive about the future. Keep going and your dreams will come true in time.
傷 *Shang* **Harm**	Careful planning will help stop you from going down a different path for there are hidden danger that you could not see. It is advised that you take extra precaution in your actions and look through every detail. This is a quiet time and it may not be the best time to make big changes or make big calls either.
杜 *Du* **Delusion**	You have lost your sense of direction and may not know how to find your way back to the path. What you do know is how to worry about your future instead. Breaking free from your bad luck will involve some serious self-questioning and some clear rational thought about what you are doing now and what you should be doing instead. Remember – do what needs to be done first.

奇門遁甲十干格局篇

庚
GENG

景 *Jing* **Scenery**	Offers have a shelf life and sometimes two of the get along and you may spend too much deliberating which one to take. Make decisions quickly and respond to the changing circumstances faster and you will find that you get ahead faster. The window of opportunity is very small, so act swiftly once you get all the facts.
死 *Si* **Death**	Nobody can fault you for making an attempt at things where you end up putting in twice or three times as much effort as the next person, but only seeing half the results. In order to achieve your objectives, you need to accept this and continue fighting in order to succeed. Things aren't always fair but this journey can help you build a strong character – if you promise to never give up.
驚 *Jing* **Fear**	You are looking good but going nowhere. This how you may feel as you try and move forward. Something is empty and it doesn't seem right as unforeseeable crisis, which must be dealt with, keep arising. If you can battle on for long enough, however, then stability will come around. In the short term, success is something that does not come easily.
開 *Kai* **Open**	You spend too way too much energy on trivial or irrelevant matters. Have a little faith in yourself and your current abilities as self-doubt does not help anyone. You might feel that you have been fighting a losing battle but your competence and capabilities will get noticed soon, and you'll get your promotion or break when this happens. Soon your goals will suddenly be within your grasp as your situation is about to take a turn for the better, so be prepared.

Qi Men Dun Jia Strategic Execution 239

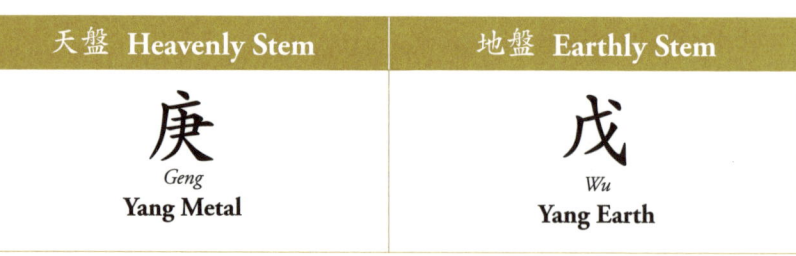

天盤 Heavenly Stem	地盤 Earthly Stem
庚 *Geng* **Yang Metal**	**戊** *Wu* **Yang Earth**

Structure 格局	Sitting Palace Structure 天乙伏宮
Rating 吉凶	Inauspicious 凶
Classic Verse 十干剋應歌訣	天乙伏宮庚加戊，謀爲大凶數
Transliteration 字譯	Where the Geng meets with Wu, it is known as the Sitting Palace Structure formation. It denotes it will be inauspicious for most activities.
Description 解說	There are obstructions and hindrances in the path ahead. Individuals may find that bureaucratic red tape slows progress toward any goal. Due to the formation, he or she is likely to fail dramatically before they can ultimately succeed. Likewise, this situation shows that matters will worsen before they get better. Once the worst has passed, a change of fortunes and improvement will occur. In general, it will seem like events and circumstances will not go to plan. Since his or her expectations will go awry, it is beneficial to have a contingency plan.

The 8 Doors Analysis:
The following evaluates the effects of **Geng** 庚 and **Wu** 戊 with each Door.

休 *Xiu* **Rest**	The key word associated with this sign is "gentleness". If you are kind and gentle and use a soft touch to try and turn the bad into good, then others will recognize this and are keen to help you. With the aid of others, obstacles can be overcome. Keep looking for the silver lining and actively work to maintain a positive attitude to stay on track.
生 *Sheng* **Life**	At first, progress does not go smoothly and your goals can seem like they are a million miles away. It may be tempting to give up on them, but if you go the distance and stay committed, then your perseverance will pay off as you reach success at the end. Keep working hard and things will become easier for you, leading to the happy ending you deserve.
傷 *Shang* **Harm**	The situation is beyond your control. Do not be frustrated if you cannot get the desired outcome. Your career outlook is rather unstable at this point and your relationship prospects seem unchangeable. Protect yourself by paying close attention to the details. Remember that you have always been taking someone dear for granted and must learn to appreciate others. Double check everything before your proceed.
杜 *Du* **Delusion**	You are looking good but going nowhere. This is how you may feel as you try and move forward. Something always does not feel right but if you can be strong enough to fight this issue, then stability will come eventually. In the short term, success is something that does not come easily.

奇門遁甲十干格局篇

庚
GENG

奇門遁甲十干格局篇

GENG

	景 *Jing* **Scenery**	Nobody likes working hard with no pay-off – you are no exception. Sadly no one wants their talents and efforts to go unappreciated. Don't kick yourself over it because it isn't your fault, just your negative luck. So just take it easy as the more you try to control something you can't, the worse things can be.
	死 *Si* **Death**	Doubts and negative thoughts feature prominently in your soul and heart today. For now, you have only a faint hope that your ambitions and dreams will come to be fulfilled but there is still that nagging fear in you. Your current luck is bad which means that you rarely catch the breaks that could bring you closer to your dreams. Resist t the urge to be impulsive for the right time will come when it presents itself.
	驚 *Jing* **Fear**	Things start out well but then seem to run off course for you. Although you have the best intentions, you somehow lack the necessary skills to turn these intentions into a positive outcome. If you wish to succeed, you will need to find a Nobleman or Mentor to give you some guidance as you cannot do this alone.
	開 *Kai* **Open**	The path is littered with obstacles but it seems you are to conquer every obstacle along the way. This brings an enormous sense of satisfaction for you because even when you have a difficult journey ahead, you will always find a way to successfully complete it. Your fighting spirit is strong and as long as you do not lose that spirit or energy, you will most likely succeed in everything that you do.

天盤 **Heavenly Stem**	地盤 **Earthly Stem**
庚 *Geng* **Yang Metal**	己 *Ji* **Yin Earth**

Structure 格局	Punishment Structure 刑格
Rating 吉凶	Inauspicious 凶
Classic Verse 十干剋應歌訣	刑格庚加己，官訟牢獄兇不利
Transliteration 字譯	Where the Geng meets with Ji, it is known as the Punishment Structure formation. It denotes the occurrence of a lawsuit that could lead to imprisonment.
Description 解說	This combination indicates a rise in disharmony. Due to this, he or she may experience frequent lawsuits and arguments. Among loved ones, family disputes and debauchery are likely. Additionally, the combination indicates problems with overindulging in intoxication. This could indicate excesses in sex, drugs and alcohol. Overindulgence in anything will lead to undesirable outcomes. When it comes to relationships of any type, this combination is exceptionally undesirable. He or she may have a desire to achieve better things and grab life by the throat. When it is time to put these desires into action, the individual may lack the motivation to achieve it. In addition, he or she may develop a short temper and irritable outlook that makes even the simplest of problems to difficult to solve.

The 8 Doors Analysis:

The following evaluates the effects of **Geng** 庚 and **Ji** 己 with each Door.

	休 *Xiu* **Rest**	Although you have nothing more than average luck, that doesn't mean that you can't look forward to some great times ahead. Even if you have to work extra hard, what matters most is that you get to achieve your finale goals in the end. Learn whatever important life lessons you can learn from your current situation and keep your chin up because all the hardships that you are facing now will seem nothing more than distant memories in the end.
	生 *Sheng* **Life**	Even though you seem to get what you desire, but the troubles and burdens of success will take its toll on you. Be aware of some of the potential pitfalls and stay on track. Even if you have the extra money, don't use your wealth to try and gain people's affection. Instead, invest in and build genuine relationships with others in order to get ahead and avoid participating in gossips or spreading rumours,
	傷 *Shang* **Harm**	Your fortunes seem like they are being decided upon by two different people with two different agendas. You may feel pushed and pulled back in two different directions. There is lack of unity in your workplace as well as synergy in the people around you. You also seem to spend a lot of time fixing things instead of being productive in your work. Ultimately, things will become better and you may eventually find a path. This will take some time though and you need to be patient. If you are with a partner, keep your dealings sincere and honest as this will keep the relationship healthy.
	杜 *Du* **Delusion**	This is not a fortunate sign as disaster and misfortune will occur without warning without warning and there is nothing you can do to avoid them. Your career will suffer from these and you may be doomed to fail at many things, often though, it is through no fault of your own. This is not the best time to consider a career or relationship change.

景 *Jing* **Scenery**	You have trouble focusing on any one idea, project or goal long enough to achieve anything as you lack the focus in order to carry out anything that you dream of or plan. Remember that less is best and that if you want to truly succeed, you will definitely need to rely on the help of other people. When asking for help though, please be modest about it as it will help your cause in the end. And your health is not as strong as you think. It is time to do a check-up.
死 *Si* **Death**	You seem to be in a constant dilemma as you have so many decisions to make but are still unclear or worst, oblivious on how to or what to do with them. This will be the cause of your downfall for you wait for too long, then opportunities will pass you by. Pay attention, stay alert and be sure to take a step forward confidently when the opportunity arises. This way, you can make the most of your potential and have no regrets.
驚 *Jing* **Fear**	It is not enough to just tell people the truth. Your information alone does not cause transformation and it is tough for you to make it to the top. You are prone to day-dreaming and wishing that you are actually getting things done. This makes it very difficult for you to focus on anything if you want things to change for the better. This is sign is associated with a changing situation and changing fortunes, so make sure that they change this time around,
開 *Kai* **Open**	Your career looks like it is set to be remembered for years to come. Not only are you blessed to be in a great environment around you but you also have lots of supportive friends and family as well. The external conditions around you are filled with resources and you can produce everything you need to get ahead in your life. Wealth, prosperity and happiness will al find you without much effort .

奇門遁甲十干格局篇

庚
GENG

天盤 **Heavenly Stem**	地盤 **Earthly Stem**
庚 *Geng* **Yang Metal**	**庚** *Geng* **Yang Metal**

Structure 格局	Great White Same Palace 太白同宮
Rating 吉凶	Inauspicious 凶
Classic Verse 十干剋應歌訣	太白同宮庚加庚，同儕齟齬官災橫
Transliteration 字譯	Where the Geng meets with Geng, it is known as the Great White Same Palace formation. It denotes disagreements between peers, and the prevailing disasters for officials.
Description 解說	This is one of the most undesirable configurations in the Qi Men. Known as the War Structure, it indicates a rise in unexpected disasters. The individual may experience misfortune and hostile situations. Among the individual's peers, siblings and friends, conflicts and disputes will develop. There are hidden dangers that may plague the individual. Some of these dangers may be obvious and some will be unexpected. Overall, he or she can expect to have their work cut out for them if they want to achieve their ambitions. Even long-held goals may seem like lost causes. This situation can make the individual directionless and disheartened. Due to this, the individual should avoid making any big decisions because the climate is ripe for disasters. Waiting for the situation to develop further and patiently looking for opportunities may turn out better. In general, matters will seldom proceed according to plan. Even when things seem to be going smoothly, they may be sabotaged along the way.

The 8 Doors Analysis:
The following evaluates the effects of **Geng** 庚 and **Geng** 庚 with each Door.

休 *Xiu* **Rest**	The storm has passed just as you had hoped it would, which means that better things are coming your way. Get ready to capitalize on this because anyone's fortunes are always changing like the seasons. There are indications that you have a clear chance to move forward and achieve your goals with little resistance, so get out there and get things done.
生 *Sheng* **Life**	Be true to yourself and make no apologies for who you are and what you stand for. Remember that you are on the right track as you were born this way. The good news is that all your efforts are about to pay off and that whatever you are pursuing will soon be within your reach. You do not need partners or a partnership at this moment as you are better off doing this alone. You already know you have the resources, just look for it and you will find it.
傷 *Shang* **Harm**	Be realistic and do not aim for too high a dream because you will be disappointed in the end. Life will be filled with many obstacles and situations that you will need to overcome as best as you can. To be successful, you have to wait for the perfect moment to make your move. Until then, be patient for and bid your time.
杜 *Du* **Delusion**	Time to take shelter for the weather in your life is about to change drastically. For every lucky break you get, you also have to endure some bad news too. You career fortunes are also about to take a sharp bend. Do be cautious and cultivate a sense of fortitude in order to proceed cautiously. Ask questions and check the details first before making any decision in case you are caught off guard by any problems that will arise later on.

奇門遁甲十干格局篇

GENG

景 *Jing* **Scenery**

Time only flows in one direction and when it is gone, you will never get it back. You may be aware of this if you have failed to take a chance in the past. Not to fear for you will have another chance at success provided you seek a mentor for help. Finding this person will be the key to a brighter future for you. This is not someone you already know, so you need to go out and start networking should you want to increase your luck in finding this person.

死 *Si* **Death**

People cannot always be trusted, unfortunately. As what is said to you may not be what is said behind your back. Choose your friends carefully and always mind what you say and how you say them. Be aware of damaging backstabbing people as this can easily find you trapped and isolated or in a state of conflict with others due to misunderstandings.

驚 *Jing* **Fear**

There are only two things you can use to invest in – time and money. Of the two, time is more important as laziness is never conducive to greatness. You do not capitalize on your time effectively as your attitude is too complacent. You are also just content with achieving the minimal amount of success without having to bother going out to pursue new ones. Put aside your pride and pursue new paths now.

開 *Kai* **Open**

Be careful from whose eyes you see the world through as in tough times, it is important to have the right mentors and advisors to guide you. There will countless situations that will demand your attention, causing you a great deal of anxiety and worry, though this cannot be avoided. You are unable to find any peace of mind at this moment and you are unlikely to find any good life any time soon. To excel on a big level, everything and every detail must be important.

天盤 **Heavenly Stem**	地盤 **Earthly Stem**
庚 *Geng* **Yang Metal**	**辛** *Xin* **Yin Metal**

Structure 格局	White Tiger Stem Formation 白虎干格
Rating 吉凶	Inauspicious 凶
Classic Verse 十干剋應歌訣	白虎干格庚加辛，求財大凶遠行禁
Transliteration 字譯	Where the Geng meets with Xin, it is known as the White Tiger Stem formation. It denotes extremely inauspicious greed for profit. It also indicates a long forbidden journey.
Description 解說	There are unexpected dangers approaching. The formation indicates a high possibility for travel accidents that are related to work. Likewise, traffic accidents may occur. The Two Metals in the formation are equivalent to a sword fight. This indicates that brothers within the household are likely to remain at each others' throats. Additionally, there may a rivalry or unhealthy competitions in the individual's life. There is a chance of a robbery or looting. Personal possessions may be lost.

The 8 Doors Analysis:

The following evaluates the effects of **Geng** 庚 and **Xin** 辛 with each Door.

GENG 庚

	休 *Xiu* **Rest**	No matter the danger and problems – all will be dissolved to your satisfaction. Luck is on your side as you will be safe from harm and danger and the risks you took seem to pay off for you. If you follow your heart, you can be sure of a prosperous and positive outcome – no matter how high you aim. A mentor will be there for you when you need him/her most. This sigh is associated with success.
	生 *Sheng* **Life**	You are truly blessed as the Star of Prosperity shines on you. You are surrounded by Noble People all the time and they are more than willing to mentor and guide you along the way. Whether you wish to stay in your current position or move onto something new, the come outcome will always be good for you.
	傷 *Shang* **Harm**	With a strong spirit and a little financial education, you will be unstoppable as all you have to do is train your mind to think like a successful person. Proceed with caution though for even the smallest details can cause mistakes and sudden incidents to ruin you. Your career fortunes are bad this time, indicating a hidden crisis in waiting. While this sign is not associated with stability and peace, it isn't all that bad either because all the mistakes you make are not failures, merely new lessons learnt.
	杜 *Du* **Delusion**	Frustrated and lonely and often working hard without any due recognition, the good times haven't really arrived yet because many sad events already seem to crop up. This causes undue confusion and frustration in life as external factors continue creeping in. Give yourself the drive you need by cultivating a sense of strength and character and maintain a positive attitude to make it through. Take a step back and observe the situation from afar for you cannot control the situations dealt before you, only merely what you can do with it.

景 *Jing* **Scenery**	With such high expectations in the future, you are bound to be disappointed. Another problem is that you spend too much time inside your own head – talking of imagining what you'd like rather than taking any real action at all. This means you may have a vision but you are unlikely to succeed in bringing it to life. You need to be more practical if you want achieve anything,	
死 *Si* **Death**	You probably don't realize the severity of your situation and yet you remain stubborn. Your tendency to isolate yourself or take a self-righteous stance means that you deprive yourself of the support of others. This is never an effective strategy as you will continue to face a difficult road full of twists and bumps that will exhaust you over time. While you will eventually accomplish what you set out to do, any measure of success won't come easily or in the near future for you.	**GENG**
驚 *Jing* **Fear**	our expectations are too high and they are unlikely to be met and you will be faced with many obstacles that cannot be moved or ignored either. Financial loss by investment is possible and you can easily become involved in damaging conflicts. Stay away from arguments and confrontations with others. This is not the best time to make an investment.as safe financial planning is absolutely necessary.	
開 *Kai* **Open**	Your leadership has brought you this far. Now that you are standing at the top of the mountain with a brilliant view. Enjoy it. Your career fortunes are very favourable and there are no problems in the horizon for you in the near future. This is a great position to be In but do remember that all good things must come to an end. The basis of great leadership is your courage – so test and cultivate that skill whenever you can in order to help it develop further.	

天盤 **Heavenly Stem**	地盤 **Earthly Stem**
庚 *Geng* **Yang Metal**	壬 *Ren* **Yang Water**

Structure 格局	Small Structure 小格
Rating 吉凶	Inauspicious 凶
Classic Verse 十干剋應歌訣	小格上格庚加壬，音信阻隔迷路人
Transliteration 字譯	Where the Geng meets with Ren, it is known as the Small Structure formation. It denotes that messages are impeded and that a person is losing his or her way.
Description 解說	The Ren 壬 Water indicates flowing movement while Geng 庚 is the Deity of Obstruction. As such, this formation indicates that the flow is suddenly obstructed. Production levels may be suddenly stopped and enjoyment may be unexpectedly ended. When it comes to work-related travel opportunities, disaster may happen along the way. In the workplace, projects will fail if they are not in line with the individual's unique talents. Projects that are within his or her skill level are more likely to turn out well. A risk of losses means that current possessions must be safeguarded. Greed will also lead to the loss of possessions or monetary losses. Additionally, the individual may feel like they are tied down to a set path in life.

The 8 Doors Analysis:
The following evaluates the effects of **Geng** 庚 and **Ren** 壬 with each Door.

休 *Xiu* **Rest**	The picture does not look beautiful. Good things seem to fade quickly as not everyone can enjoy the best of luck and every lucky person, there will be an unlucky one. For the way events seem to unfold, you may well feel like this person is you. Expect to meet more than your fair share of resistance in any matter you pursue. Be prepared for the worse-case scenario and put in more effort in solving them this time.
生 *Sheng* **Life**	You win some and you lose some as the saying goes. This saying may well have been written about you no doubt. You might find that you win more than you lost if you can learn to disregard people who seek to criticize or stand in your way. Your instincts are sharp so if something feels right to you, then go for it without seeking the approval of those around you first. Believe in yourself and know that you can't please everyone.
傷 *Shang* **Harm**	The things you are looking for are no longer there for what you have lost may never return. Learning to let go is the key to a better outcome and hence, your projects, plans and schemes are unlikely to pan out because of obstacles and problems that are beyond your control. All of this can be incredibly disheartening, keep the good memories, learn the valuable lessons and move on in a different direction.
杜 *Du* **Delusion**	You are looking good, but going nowhere. This is how you may feel as you try and move forward. Something is empty as it does not seem right. Unforeseeable crisis, which must be dealt with, keep arising but if you keep battling on for long enough, however, then stability will come around. In the short term, success is something that does not come easily.

奇門遁甲十干格局篇

庚
GENG

Qi Men Dun Jia Strategic Execution   253

奇門遁甲十干格局篇

GENG

	景 *Jing* **Scenery**	Emotions often get in the way of logic that underpins wise decision-making. Do not let your emotions control your actions. Perhaps you care too much about how others think of you, or your ego just gets in the way. Because of this, you are unable to look at the cold facts in a realistic and productive way. You are also unsure of the future or what to do as you have too many conflicting ideas, concerns and opinions that hinder you from moving forward in any one definitive direction. Clarity is the solution to your problem. Be clear about what you want and what you need. When you are clear, then you can focus.
	死 *Si* **Death**	You seem to missing out on the details. It is best you seek an independent third party opinion. If you want to see your ideas succeed, then you cannot make this happen on your own and help is required. It is best to temporarily stop your projects or plans and go back to the drawing board. For now, you are prone to procrastination and carelessness and this will lead to wasted opportunities for you. Recruit the help of other talented people around you and find ways to discipline yourself and remain diligent in your duties.
	驚 *Jing* **Fear**	Tough situations are ahead of you as it could be said that you face a character building opportunity buy a very bumpy journey. Difficulties and hardship are things you will get used to dealing. It seems like you are in it all by yourself and that there is no one present that can help you. Find the strength within yourself for only you can get there one step at a time. Don't be tempted to do anything sudden with dreams of becoming rich overnight. And do avoid risks and take the slow and safer route.
	開 *Kai* **Open**	A person with true talent is not afraid of temporary bad luck. A true champion isn't afraid of adversity of challenges and indeed these things shape most victories and bring out the best in people. Don't be frustrated by the fact that you haven't fulfilled all of your ambitions yet. A Nobleman or mentor will be present to back you up and give you the help you need to keep pushing on and beating the odds. The time will come and the right person will appear and this will lead to a happy outcome for you. Embrace the difficulties as opportunities to confidently move ahead.

天盤 **Heavenly Stem**	地盤 **Earthly Stem**
庚 *Geng* **Yang Metal**	癸 *Gui* **Yin Water**

Structure 格局	Big Structure 大格
Rating 吉凶	Inauspicious 凶
Classic Verse 十干剋應歌訣	大格庚加癸，行人不至官訟非，車禍生育母子悲
Transliteration 字譯	Where the Geng meets with Gui, it is known as the Big Structure formation. It denotes a failed lawsuit due to no witnesses. It also indicates possible car accidents and inauspicious news for an expectant mother and her unborn baby.
Description 解説	This formation is known as the Big Structure 大格. Overall, it is a generally unfavorable configuration. This is due to the Gui Stem's arrival from the Jia Yin 甲寅. The Jia Yin is in opposition to Shen 申. The appearance of Shen and Yin together is known as the merciless-class. Due to this, road accidents and traffic delays are increased. There is a rising risk of danger and injury. Additionally, the formation influences a rise in arguments and disagreements. Legal disputes like lawsuits are increasingly likely. Overall, this is not a good sign and could forecast difficulties in childbirth.

The 8 Doors Analysis:

The following evaluates the effects of **Geng** 庚 and **Gui** 癸 with each Door.

	休 *Xiu* **Rest**	Choose your decisions wisely and don't just go with the spur of the moment. A mindful, focused and hands-on approach to yours plans right now is necessary to steer your career, relationship and/or business on track. Do your best to foresee problematic situations and don't proceed blindly, hoping that nothing will derail you. With this vigilant attitude, success will be yours.
	生 *Sheng* **Life**	Something that worries you and has kept you up all night will actually turn out to benefit you, leading to a happy ending. If you can double your efforts and correctly capitalize on opportunity then fame, wealth and happiness itself are waiting for you. Work hard to see the potential in a problematic situation and always look at things from a new and more optimistic perspective.
	傷 *Shang* **Harm**	This sign is only associated with average outcomes. Decisions shape your outcome and you can improve your chances of making the right decisions by running them by people that trust for their unbiased opinion. The truth may hurt, but is better that your resolve matters before it is too late. You must not be hasty. Making an emotional decision here could be disadvantageous. There is also a possibility of you looking your current position, so be prepared for that eventuality.
	杜 *Du* **Delusion**	This sign is associated with bad luck. Therefore, it is always a good idea to think carefully about things before you do them. Because you are prone to overthink things and wait too long before making even a simple decision, this can lead to loss of opportunities, and in most some cases, it can bring damaging and costly errors. Be cautious that you do not become impulsive and make poor decisions when things get out of hand quickly. Hence, it is important to learn to delegate and to trust others to get the job done.

奇門遁甲十干格局篇

GENG 庚

景 *Jing* **Scenery**	Your fortune is unstable and it seems like you even don't have the final say in your own destiny as well. There seems to be too many hurdles in your chosen path as well. Clear your mind and look at your situation with an open mind. In your case, life really is what you make of it because you will be presented with both good and bad options for you to choose from. Bear in mind that whichever path you choose, you will be walking alone as there are not external help forthcoming anytime soon. Do not give up so easily or else or else you will not be rewarded. Do note that the current condition is expected to get worse though.
死 *Si* **Death**	Fortune doesn't smile at you but instead throws obstacles and setbacks at you unfairly. There is very little options available right now unfortunately because you have tolerated this deplorable performance for a long time now. Although luck is not on your side, you could still make things better with the better skills and better mind-set. For now, just try and do what you can to make the most of what is presented to you.
驚 *Jing* **Fear**	You are fighting a losing battle. It is not easy doing things on your own. Everything hits you at once and you have a hard time staying on your feet without any support. You put in 110% but it doesn't do much good unfortunately. You really want to overcome the odds and live up to the challenge, but your courage is worn away. Eventually, you may have to escape or retreat which may not be a bad idea after all.
開 *Kai* **Open**	You are very opinionated but very sensitive. You care too much about whether you win or lose and you have many thoughts but no single, clear focus. If you want to achieve something, you need to take a step back and seek the help of smarter people. Though, be polite in your dealings with others and treat their opinions with as much respect as your own. Your may be also under-skilled, so brush up on your own education and skills in other to further your career goals.

辛

Xin
Yin Metal

天盤 **Heavenly Stem**	地盤 **Earthly Stem**
辛 *Xin* **Yin Metal**	甲 *Jia* **Yang Wood**

Structure 格局	Dragon Tiger Fight 龍爭虎鬥
Rating 吉凶	Inauspicious 凶
Classic Verse 十干剋應歌訣	龍爭虎鬥辛加甲，官司破財靜守住
Transliteration 字譯	Where the Xin meet with Jia, it is known as the Dragon Tiger Fight formation. It denotes financial losses due to lawsuits. It is extremely important to remain patient.
Description 解說	The situation indicated by this formation is highly unstable. It denotes that two strong enemies meet and fight it out. Heaven and earth are shaken as destructive forces come to the forefront. In general, the changes that occur are likely to be for the worst. Even the best of efforts are met with disagreements and miscommunication issues. Due to this, efforts are futile. In the workplace and in life, the individual's talents are unlikely to be recognized by others.

The 8 Doors Analysis:
The following evaluates the effects of **Xin** 辛 and **Jia** 甲 with each Door.

休 *Xiu* **Rest**	Fame, success and happiness are on the cards for you. Your journey to the top is a smooth one, with plenty of opportunities and breaks presenting themselves without too much difficulty on your part. Nevertheless, you will still need to put in some work and make an effort if you're to keep moving forward smoothly and keep the results at the end. Just remember that you can count on many helping hands around you and reaching your goal will be the easy part. It is in keeping it that will be a challenge for you.
生 *Sheng* **Life**	If your friends or advisor loses your money, remember not to blame him/her. On the contrary, take a lot at yourself and ask if you're willing to reduce your risk by getting educated. You mustn't be relying on your luck alone for the upcoming path. You actually need real knowledge and skills to move forward. Naturally, you were very lucky in the past but this doesn't mean the sea will part and you can have whatever you want. Learn how to be independent.
傷 *Shang* **Harm**	Nothing seems to be going you way. It is as if life is holding you hostage and there will countless, traps, troubles, obstacles and accidents that may befall you. Despite your best efforts to escape this, you just can't seem to catch a break. Sometimes, decisions you believe that are wise or opportunities that you think are good will turn out to be disastrous to you. The best you can do is to be cautious and stay alert. Remember to question everything!
杜 *Du* **Delusion**	You will have too many thoughts and too many issues to deal with. Whatever you do will seem to get you nowhere. You will be lost at sea, just like a shipwreck. It almost feels like you are being crush to the core and being trapped in a cage. This is an unfortunate situation for you and the best thing you can do about it is to lay low and be content with what you have for the time being. We must remember that in all our struggles, to feed our spirt as well as our bodies.

奇門遁甲十干格局篇

辛 XIN

	景 *Jing* **Scenery**	The things you are looking for are no longer to be seen by you. What you have actually lost will never return to your path. Learning to let go is of utmost importance to you so you can feel at least a little better about things. Your plans, projects, and schemes are unlikely to pan out the way you want it. All of this will be terribly disheartening to you and you would need to learn your lessons. Move and hold on to the memories.
	死 *Si* **Death**	You lack a sense of spiritual wellbeing. You are like a car without fuel. You are lazy and nobody will be around to tell you otherwise. This situation will make you feeling lonely and hopeless. Don't react too harshly to certain situations. Be realistic and ask yourself what you are capable base on what motivates you. Plan your life and chart your own path. Invest money and time into your education.
	驚 *Jing* **Fear**	It's not enough to just tell people the truth. Your information alone does not cause transformation. It's tough to make it to the top. In your case, you are prone to spending more time daydreaming than actually getting things done properly. This makes it very difficult for you to actually achieve anything. You'll need to be prepared to work out. Make sure you're always in the motive to make a change for the better.
	開 *Kai* **Open**	This sign is associated with good luck. They say you can't have a rainbow without the rain and this saying is especially true in your case. You'll need to suffer and endure some hardships in order to appreciate the better things that life has to offer you later on. Don't just keep thinking about something, when you're dealt with a task – you need to seize the moment and act on it. Every time you can't do something, there will always be someone else who thinks he/she can.

天盤 Heavenly Stem	地盤 Earthly Stem
辛 *Xin* **Yin Metal**	乙 *Yi* **Yin Wood**

Structure 格局	Ferocious White Tiger 白虎猖狂
Rating 吉凶	Inauspicious 凶
Classic Verse 十干剋應歌訣	白虎倡狂辛加乙，家敗人亡莫遠離，勞燕分飛因男起
Transliteration 字譯	Where the Xin meets with Yi, it is known as the Ferocious White Tiger formation. It denotes a crumbling family and therefore, it is important to remain close to each other. It also indicates that a couple may separate due to the presence of another male.
Description 解說	In this formation, Xin 辛 Metal clashes and counters with Yi 乙 Wood. It is called the Ferocious White Tiger 白虎猖狂. As such, it indicates a fierce and violent force lurking in the background. This negative influence intimidates and changes everything around it. When he or she lets their guard down, disasters attack and bring negative consequences with them. Overall, this formation shows danger just around the corner. Due to this, long distance travel carries many dangers. The individual may lose their faith in an outcome or have problems keeping their courage up. Overall, there are uncertainties in the path ahead. Arguments and disputes are likely to occur. Additionally, this formation is generally not ideal for marriage.

The 8 Doors Analysis:

The following evaluates the effects of **Xin** 辛 and **Yi** 乙 with each Door.

休 *Xiu* **Rest**	Although the journey may be long for you, it doesn't mean it needs to be a difficult one. You will be peaceful even if the destination is far away – just try to enjoy the ride while you're at it. Take your time and plan things well, whatever you can envision or predict, you should do it. If you can see it in your mind, you will most likely be able to achieve it. You will also be happy in the long run before reaching your goal. The journey towards your success will be a wonderful one.
生 *Sheng* **Life**	Finally it's your turn to be in the spotlight. You will be given a good opportunity to demonstrate your talents, skills and knowledge. So go ahead and show them and bask in this spotlight of yours. The stage is completely yours! Reveal your talents and start achieving your dreams. Good fortune don't always come so easily so you may want to treasure what you've got. Do your best and all your dreams can come true.
傷 *Shang* **Harm**	The wind is strong and the rain is getting heavier. Once upon time a bright shining sun, now it is covered with thick rainy clouds. You are in it all by yourself and suffering without any support or reassurance. You may be subjected to a degree of bullying from others. You doubt yourself and have fears about the future that will keep you up at night. It's extremely hard to stay ambitious and optimistic with all of this going on. The current path you choose is not your true calling – change while you can!
杜 *Du* **Delusion**	You may feel lost, or you may know what you're actually searching for. It's like a puzzle with a missing piece and unfortunately for you, you will never be able to find it. Your energy level is low and you'll need to pay attention to/check your health. The answers and solutions don't present themselves to you easily. If you stick around and persevere, you might actually find that particular piece of missing puzzle. Things will work out for you in the end but it's simply a matter of time and patience.

景 *Jing* **Scenery**	You dream of the impossible. While you may have the brightest and most wonderful ideas, you look to the practical tools to achieve this dream. A fairly straightforward chain reaction must take place if a dream of yours is to come true. Unfortunately for you, you tend to forget that nothing happens without some good old fashioned hard work. Come up with a practical strategy and you will likely see things materialize.	
死 *Si* **Death**	You will be encountering bad luck. Beware of backstabbing and slandering that will create problems and troubles for you. Don't get involved in any of these activities. You will also need to choose your words carefully so that they can't be twisted or used against you. If you're not careful, you may quite often find yourself isolated. This isolation is usually caused by misunderstandings from other parties. If you choose to stay quiet, you will be able to stay out of trouble and it would seem to be a good strategy for you.	奇門遁甲十干格局篇 辛 XIN
驚 *Jing* **Fear**	You probably don't realize the severity of the situation you're in – yet you will remain stubborn. Your tendency to isolate yourself or take a self-righteous stance means that you deprive yourself of the support of others. This is never an effective strategy. You will face difficult twists and turns in your life and this may exhaust you over a long time. While you will eventually accomplish what you set out to do, victory will not come around so easily.	
開 *Kai* **Open**	Here's some positive news! Not every talented person will get rewarded fairly. Just think of the stories of famous painters who were not able to sell a single painting while they were still alive. Fortunately enough for you, someone will notice this talent of yours. When this happens, things will start to fall into place for you and you can achieve your dreams and goals easily. Grab those chances while you can as those people are your lifelines.	

Qi Men Dun Jia Strategic Execution

奇門遁甲十干格局篇 XIN

天盤 Heavenly Stem	地盤 Earthly Stem
辛 *Xin* **Yin Metal**	丙 *Bing* **Yang Fire**

Structure 格局	Stem Combine Rebelling Officer 干合悖師
Rating 吉凶	Auspicious 吉
Classic Verse 十干剋應歌訣	幹合悖師辛加丙，天庭得明隨門行，合作求財官非驚
Transliteration 字譯	When the Xin meets with Bing, it is known as the Stem Combine Rebelling Officer formation. It denotes co-operation, and the pursuit for profit or an official position.
Description 解說	When the situation is at its worst, there is still a possibility of controlling the problems. The general situation is unstable, but it is possible to take stock of the events and be grateful for the progress that exists. At this time, good news will not automatically appear when wanted. Everything that he or she wants arrives through diligence and consistent progress. The formation shows results materialize only through patience and dedication. Continued perseverance is likely to pay off over the long term. When an auspicious Door is present, the outcome is more likely to be favorable. An inauspicious Door brings about negative outcomes.

The 8 Doors Analysis:
The following evaluates the effects of **Xin** 辛 and **Bing** 丙 with each Door.

休 *Xiu* **Rest**	You can expect good luck all around with the help of a Nobleman. Favorable fortunes will definitely be on your side. The road to success will be smooth and you can expect to be successful easily. No matter what you decide to do, it will be on your good side, so remember to think big. Your reputation and standing with others will be strong and your wealth will increase. The future looks exceptionally bright for you!
生 *Sheng* **Life**	You're a person of great ambitions and great achievements. You can create a good life for yourself. The auspicious stars will shine brightly on your path. This is the kind of outlook that everyone wants to have so you would need to count your blessings. Whatever that you may decide to do in life will ultimately be successful. However ambitious your dreams are, they will come true eventually. All you have to do is to make a start. So roll up your sleeves and get to work.
傷 *Shang* **Harm**	You will have too much to think about and you will be horribly indecisive. You are in this all by yourself and may struggle with feelings of loneliness. Others may not help you right now and they may mean well but they might not understand your chosen path. If you want to make better decision for yourself, you'll need to determine your available options clearly. Learn to see the options from both a short and long-term views. Don't make rash decisions!
杜 *Du* **Delusion**	A good chess player knows that a winning strategy involves both offense and defense. You will need to be aggressive and reactive to situations. You will also need to push forward and remain cautious simultaneously. Problems can arise out of nowhere, therefore you would need to remain prepared and be ready for anything that could come your way. The better you're at planning, the more prepared you will be for the chances to succeed. The more you know, the greater control you have over your life and path.

	景 *Jing* **Scenery**	Your luck is unstable at the moment. Unfortunately, things will not come to you as you may have hoped. Everything you want lies in what seem like an indefinite waiting period. It's best that you get out there and create your own luck. Although it might not be a smooth journey for you, but with a little bit of patience and perseverance, you can slowly (but surely) move towards your ultimate goal. When results don't immediately materialize, don't give up!
	死 *Si* **Death**	You find yourself working aggressively and diligently to build your future but unfortunately, your luck can't be changed. Bad luck will appear to follow you all around. None of the people around you are willing to help you so your future is filled with worries. This is because you are also looking at the wrong network of people for advice. You have indirectly surrounded yourself with mediocre talents. Remember you are only as fast as your slowest teammate. It is advisable for you to continue working hard on your own or simply chart a totally different path.
	驚 *Jing* **Fear**	The resources you need to get things done are all around you and they are made available to you but you don't seem to see this. You would need to look harder! If you don't see this, you will need help in finding the right kind of resources that would work in your favor. If you have plans in mind but are not acting on them for one reason or another, then you'll need to be brave and take more risks.
	開 *Kai* **Open**	The future is full of hope for you. You can expect a successful career, harmonious family and spiritual wellbeing. It seems like every other door will be open and made available to you. Keep moving ahead with a positive mentality and your circumstances will produce more joyful results/moments. This is also known as the virtuous cycle. Enjoy your life and spread the joy to others.

天盤 **Heavenly Stem**	地盤 **Earthly Stem**
辛 *Xin* **Yin Metal**	丁 *Ding* **Yin Fire**

Structure 格局	Restricted White Tiger 白虎受制
Rating 吉凶	Inauspicious 凶
Classic Verse 十干剋應歌訣	辛白虎受制加丁，囚逢天赦利倍盈
Transliteration 字譯	Where the Xin meets with Ding, it is known as the Restricted White Tiger formation. It denotes great clemency for prisoners. It also indicates achieving doubled profits.
Description 解說	The Ding 丁 Fire controls the Xin 辛 Metal in this formation. Due to this, the formation indicates that solutions are available to counter any problem. Unfortunately, these solutions may arrive at the expense of strong relationships. Bridges may be burnt along the way and the individual's personal network may be sullied by disagreements. Business mattes will generate a considerable profit. Even when the individual is at fault in business matters, they will be absolved from the guilt. In order for positive results to be generated, the presence of an auspicious Door is required. When an auspicious Door is lacking, positive results will also be unreachable. Instead, the outcome will most likely be undesirable.

奇門遁甲十干格局篇

XIN 辛

The 8 Doors Analysis:
The following evaluates the effects of **Xin** 辛 and **Ding** 丁 with each Door.

	休 *Xiu* **Rest**	The key word associated with this is 'gentleness.' You're kind and gentle. You'll also use this to turn the bad into good and make the most out of things around you. Others will also recognize this and they'll be keen to help you. Therefore, you would need to control your temper and be nicer to others. With the help of others, you'll be able to overcome plenty of obstacles encountered. Keep looking for the silver lining in everything you do and maintain a positive outlook in life.
	生 *Sheng* **Life**	When at first the progress may not go as smoothly as you might like it to be but if you choose to persevere and go the distance, you'll be able to achieve greatness. Sometimes, you may be tempted to give up on them, but if you stay committed, you'll achieve the payoff that you want at the end. A good turning point is just around the corner. Just move a little further ahead. Keep working hard and things will come to you!
	傷 *Shang* **Harm**	There seem to be leakages all around you. And you may not be able to identify it. Luck will not be on your side and your personal progress, growth and development will be threatened by a high chance of difficulties and obstacles. It may be a good idea to look into giving your time to some charitable work/causes in order to offset some of your own misfortune.
	杜 *Du* **Delusion**	This situation is beyond your control. Don't be frustrated if you can't get the desired outcome that you want. Your career outlook is rather unstable at this point in time. Relationships may also seem changeable. To protect yourself against this, and to most efficiently ride the wave – you'll need to pay close attention to all the details. You've also been taking someone dear to you for granted. Learn to appreciate others and double check everything before proceeding.

景 *Jing* **Scenery**	This isn't a carefree time for you. You'll need to get your act together and move quickly. Many things may worry you and you are doubtful about your plans in life. Other people will be quick to offer advice if you're willing to share your problems with them. If you can listen with an open mind and take criticisms constructively, then new opportunities will be made available to you.
死 *Si* **Death**	You may be prone to going through the motions or functioning on autopilot. You've lost the direction in life and may not know where to turn to. What you do know is how to worry about the future. You are unsure of your family's or your friend's intentions, opinions and wishes for you. Breaking free from bad luck will involve some serious self-reflection and re-evaluating the people in your network/life. Remember to do what is necessary and clarity will be the key to your troubles.
驚 *Jing* **Fear**	Unfortunately, opportunities will be limited for you. You may have been waiting for sometime now but you're yet to see the light at the end of the tunnel. Most people will catch their big break when someone with a higher ranking notices them and lifts them to greater heights. If you can meet this said person, you'll be able to achieve the success you desire on a quicker pace. The right person is probably someone you already know so look around you!
開 *Kai* **Open**	The good news is that you've made it through all the obstacles. The worst is over for you. What may have seemed impossible in the past now seems possible again. It's like clear sky with a beautiful rainbow after a storm/rainy days. You can count on the help of others around you. There will be many talents around you that will be good influence to you. Just ask for help and you'll receive them. This is an auspicious sign.

奇門遁甲十千格局篇

辛 XIN

天盤 Heavenly Stem	地盤 Earthly Stem
辛 *Xin* **Yin Metal**	戊 *Wu* **Yang Earth**

Structure 格局	Trapped Dragon Receives Punishment 困龍受制
Rating 吉凶	Inauspicious 凶
Classic Verse 十干剋應歌訣	困龍受制辛加戊，官司破財，防災靜處。
Transliteration 字譯	Where the Xin meets with Wu, it is known as the Trapped Dragon Receives Punishment formation. It denotes lawsuits, financial losses and grievous separation.
Description 解說	The Wu Stem is representative of "JiaZi 甲子," the Grand Marshall. The Xin 辛 Stem itself comes from Jia Wu 甲午. As Xin 辛 Metal counters Jia 甲 Wood, the Zi 子 and Wu 午 also silently clash with each other. This formation is named Trapped Dragon Receives Punishment 困龍受制. Due to this, it shows that there are direct changes to authority. Colleagues and employees may be disobedient. A coalition of sorts is forming out of sight that forms a direct overthrow to authority. In addition, this formation could lead to an unexpected overthrow. Likewise, financial mismanagement is possible. There is upheaval on the horizon and relationships may be characterized by discord. At times, it may be difficult for the individual to control their emotions. Maintaining a level head is the only way to avoid a disaster, but it will be difficult to stay calm.

The 8 Doors Analysis:

The following evaluates the effects of **Xin** 辛 and **Wu** 戊 with each Door.

休 *Xiu* **Rest**	If you can stick to the tried and tested formula, then you'll be able to expect to thrive in those conditions. The external conditions seem to favor you more as well. However, you'll need to follow a proven system. If you don't have one yet, you'll need to find one immediately. Some investments may seem to have yielded amazing results but not for you this time around. Steer clear from gambling and uncalculated risks. If you could see it clearly in your mind's eye, then you'll be able to achieve the support from your friends and mentors to arrive at a resolve for yourself.
生 *Sheng* **Life**	This sign denotes an optimistic and bright outcome for you right now. It doesn't matter if you're seeking wealth, prosperity or freedom – all these things will be yours. Try not to be complacent and always remember to appreciate all the things in life that you've been blessed with. Remember that slight blemishes do no harm as well.
傷 *Shang* **Harm**	You may look good from the outside but internally, you're going nowhere in life. This is how you may feel as you try to move forward in life. Everything will somehow not seem right and there will be unforeseeable crisis on the horizon. These problems will not stop to haunt you. If you can battle it for long enough, stability will come around to you. Success will not be something that you'll obtain easily.
杜 *Du* **Delusion**	If only a thought could be translated into reality without real action. If a dream could be an instant truth then it will be good for you but this will not be your luck. You can't wish your way towards success and don't confuse yourself between positive thinking and lying to yourself positively. If you want to achieve something, you'd need to get out there and do what it takes to achieve it. You actually need to do your due diligence and study for whatever that you want to achieve in your life. Always remember that there is no such thing as free investments from friends. There won't be free rides for you either!

奇門遁甲十干格局篇

XIN 辛

	景 *Jing* **Scenery**	Miscalculations on your end will lead to unforeseen failures. Perhaps it is an underestimation of risk or an overestimation of the chances of success that will cause you to be in this predicament. Currently, you're unable to capitalize on your talents and will likely to meet a lot of resistance and difficulty in your pursuits. The good news is that there are still people around you who are willing to lend you a helping hand.
	死 *Si* **Death**	Things can't go as smoothly because there are limits to how much an individual can anticipate or control within his/her means. An easy ride can't go on forever and once the good times end, it's difficult to gain it back. You'll encounter a lot of obstacles on your chosen path. Try and be content with what you have. Count your blessings and the best investment for now is to invest in yourself.
	驚 *Jing* **Fear**	Hard work may take you very close to your goals but your life is extremely unpredictable. You might be winning the game one minute but then you might also find that the goal post have been moved or the rules of the game have been changed, in the next. Unforeseen circumstances will arise and your external conditions will change quickly as well. You'll mix with the wrong company and your success is limited.
	開 *Kai* **Open**	You should stop and look back at how far you've come in life. Hard work has gotten you to this position and you have your positive fortune to thank. Use whatever negative events you can to fuel your self-motivation and let it propel you forward. Remember that good relationships with others, even those you disagree with a lot, will do you more good than harm in the long run. Do not hold grudges as it will drain your energy. Make contacts and not enemies.

天盤 **Heavenly Stem**	地盤 **Earthly Stem**
辛 *Xin* **Yin Metal**	己 *Ji* **Yin Earth**

Structure 格局	Enter Prison Self Punishment 入獄自刑
Rating 吉凶	Inauspicious 凶
Classic Verse 十干剋應歌訣	入獄自刑辛加己，奴僕背主訟難理。
Transliteration 字譯	Where the Xin meets with Ji, it is known as the Enter Prison Self Punishment formation. It denotes that justice will be difficult to prevail in lawsuits. It also indicates that servants will betray their lords.
Description 解說	In Qi Men, the Xin 辛 Stem is often regarded as "the sinner" or the "criminal" and the Xu 戌 is the Grave of Wu Fire. This formation is aptly named Enter Prison Self Punishment 入獄自刑. It denotes a loyal servant who turns on their master. Due to this, the individual may find a subordinate or colleague who challenges a master. Likewise, a trusted ally may be secretly plotting the overthrow or upheaval of another. When it comes to business, there is a chance of embezzlement or an unexpected breach of trust. Justice in lawsuits and disagreements will not be served. The individual should take note that there may be betrayals and injustices in the workplace.

The 8 Doors Analysis:
The following evaluates the effects of **Xin** 辛 and **Ji** 己 with each Door.

休 *Xiu* **Rest**	Choose the words you speak with others carefully and show genuine interest in them. Avoid conflict at all costs and sow good seeds and you will be rewarded accordingly. As the saying goes, what goes around comes around. Do good deeds and good things will come to you easily and quickly. It is by treating others well which will bring about a good life to you.
生 *Sheng* **Life**	It is said that if you want to have the rainbow, you'll need to experience the rain first. Remember this if you feel things aren't going your way because there will be periods in your life where fortune doesn't favor you. But fret not, I'll come to you with the right mentors looking after/out you. So network and build a support group that will be beneficial for you towards the path to success. Even though your current situation may seem unremarkable – do not ever give up!
傷 *Shang* **Harm**	Successful people have the ability to make the right decisions quickly and stick to them. You, on the other hand, are prone to handwringing and inconsistency in your decision-making. You'll also encounter setbacks and problems for the time being. Despite your hard work, you may not get the results you desire. This is usually down to you over-analyzing and nitpicking at things. Accept this and consider taking a look at how you deal with your choices in life.
杜 *Du* **Delusion**	You will put plenty of hard work at your workplace and make every effort possible to get ahead but people will always find ways to backstab you. You seem to attract a lot of petty people in your life. They will stick around you for the most part of your life. Even though if you have a Nobleman to help you out, he/she can only do so much for you. Try and persevere and believe in the good in people and derive happiness from that.

景 *Jing* **Scenery**	Your situation may look good and appealing on the surface but it is extremely fickle. Wealth and success can disappear as quickly as they comes. Your vision of the future may not likely come true. You must always remain cautious and alert.	奇門遁甲十干格局篇 辛 XIN
死 *Si* **Death**	If you don't have a team of great mentors right now – all will be lost for you. Your luck is definitely not good. Sadly, your path is not as simple as you think and you'll have to deal with more than your fair share of complications in regards to your endeavors. This will leave you stressed, worried and unable to relax. You may incur great losses when your pursuit fails, hence, while there is still time – seek help!	
驚 *Jing* **Fear**	Your situation isn't kind to you. You may be experiencing rough times in your career. You should take solace in the fact that nothing is ever permanent. For now, just brave the storm and don't make any big or rash decisions. Remember that the odds are not in your favor.	
開 *Kai* **Open**	There is no need to be suspicious or turn into a worrywart. Don't make a big deal out of the same old problems in your own head. This can lead to unnecessary stress and worries. You have very little to worry about in regards to the future as this sign indicates that all the bad will eventually take a turn for the better. Do not worry! You will enjoy many pleasures that life has to offer you because of the challenges you face now. This will serve as lessons to you when you're on the way towards succession.	

天盤 Heavenly Stem	地盤 Earthly Stem
辛 *Xin* **Yin Metal**	**庚** *Geng* **Yang Metal**

Structure 格局	White Tiger Carrying Blade 白虎出刀
Rating 吉凶	Inauspicious 凶
Classic Verse 十干剋應歌訣	白虎出力辛加庚，主客相殘血濺鋒
Transliteration 字譯	Where the Xin meets with Geng, it is known as the White Tiger Carrying Blade formation. It denotes harm between hosts and guests.
Description 解說	This formation indicates the sword and the ax in a dogfight. As such, it shows possible bodily harm and the potential for tyranny to take control. Bloodshed may be possible and arguments are likely to be heated. When disputes break out, it is likely for emotions to broil over the definition of heartbreak. In general, disputes about everything may occur. Relationships may be filled with heart break and turmoil. Health difficulties may relate to diseases or an unexpected wound.

The 8 Doors Analysis:

The following evaluates the effects of **Xin** 辛 and **Geng** 庚 with each Door.

休 *Xiu* **Rest**	The dragon soars into the skies and great fortune begins to shine for you. For some people, golden opportunities can seem like trains. Once you've missed it, it will pass you by but you might also need to wait awhile for it. As you've been waiting patiently, you can now enter a period of your life with unprecedented prosperity. This is all happening for you, if you're willing to act on it. Make the most out of your bright fortunes and happiness and prosperity will be yours for the taking/enjoyment.
生 *Sheng* **Life**	Make your decisions wisely and don't just go with the flow and spur of the moment. A mindful, focused and hands-on approach to your plans right now is what you need to steer your career on the right path. Do your best to foresee problematic situations and don't proceed blindly. Success will be yours with a watchful attitude.
傷 *Shang* **Harm**	This is not a fortunate sign. Disasters and misadventures might befall you. They will usually occur without any warning and there will be nothing you can do about them. Your career will suffer from these situations and you may be doomed to fail at many things. Often times, it's through the fault of your own. This is not the best time to seek a change in career or switch relationships.
杜 *Du* **Delusion**	You will have trouble focusing on any one idea. You will have a lot of ideas but you will need to remind yourself that less is in fact more. And if you want to succeed, you will also need to rely on others. Don't be afraid to seek help outside actively and remain modest as that will help your cause towards success. Remember to ask for help and don't assume people will magically come to your aid.

奇門遁甲十干格局篇

XIN 辛

	景 *Jing* **Scenery**	With every failure or success, you gain experience and learn a valuable life lesson. Be aware of this fact and in the long run, you'll be able to benefit from it. Think things through thoroughly and look before you jump. Always wait for the right moment before you make a move. There will be someone calling or connecting with you to offer you some sound advice. You might want to wait for that connection.
	死 *Si* **Death**	It's time to take shelter – the skies are not very clear for you. There may be negative times ahead. Your career is about to encounter a standstill. What at first may seem like a good chance has become nothing more than a trap for you. Do be cautious. Generate a sense of fortitude and proceed with caution. Remain alert so you won't get caught off-guard.
	驚 *Jing* **Fear**	Unfortunately, people can't be trusted. People may backstab you. As this is an inauspicious sign, you'll need to be aware of these troubles ahead. You'll need to choose your friends wisely and not fall prey to dishonest people. Don't be too naïve when it comes to making friendships. You might also want to caution yourself to speak others appropriately as well. It is easy to find yourself in isolation due to misunderstandings that might occur, so beware!
	開 *Kai* **Open**	Decisions, decisions, decisions. You'll need to make extremely careful decisions. Remember to check out the details and weigh your options clearly. Clarity is a key word for you. You'll usually find that there is only one smart decision that needs to be made. Don't consult too many friends as this will only confuse you. Make up your own mind about things and checking out all the facts. And with the right decisions – fame, fortune and prosperity will be yours for the taking. Keep going in the direction and you'll be headed for success in no time!

天盤 Heavenly Stem	地盤 Earthly Stem
辛 *Xin* **Yin Metal**	辛 *Xin* **Yin Metal**

Structure 格局	The Grand Heavens Fu Yin 伏吟天庭
Rating 吉凶	Inauspicious 凶
Classic Verse 十干剋應歌訣	伏吟天庭辛加辛，公廢私就訟自刑
Transliteration 字譯	Where the Xin meets with Xin, it is known as the Grand Heavens Fu Yin formation. It denotes the eradication of the public and private companies in a litigation or lawsuit as a punishment.
Description 解說	With this formation, the individual has to be aware that the worst sabotage is self-sabotage. He or she is more likely to say too much and reveal their secrets. When it comes to outcomes, the individual counts their chickens before they hatch. This leads to a tendency of over-committing to a cause or under-delivering on a project. Hassles will develop in monetary matters that lead to the loss of fortunes. As such, the individual will have many problems to fix in financial matters and may have an inability to exhibit self-control. Overall, this sign is associated with wasted energy and unrewarded efforts. He or she may have goals that are not practical. An unpractical approach results in a risk of failure. Slow steps toward a goal are rewarded by an improved outcome.

The 8 Doors Analysis:

The following evaluates the effects of **Xin** 辛 and **Xin** 辛 with each Door.

	Xiu **Rest**	A cynic may tell you that good things never seem to last. In your case this is utterly true. Your luck will slowly diminish and it'll run out. Anything that has come into bloom will wither through time. During periods when nothing good seems to come into fruition from your efforts, all you can do is keep trying. The key to turning these situations around lies in your ability to ask for help.
	Sheng **Life**	Remember not to interfere with other people's affairs. It's probably best to keep to yourself and don't ask too many questions about others. This will not be of your concern. Instead, you should find a quiet place and be free from interferences. You might find that some self-reflection will lead you to a clear mindset and you can start planning your life appropriately.
	Shang **Harm**	To advance or to surrender is difficult for you right now. It's almost like you're trap in between a rock and a hard place. Not everyone can share his/her good experience with you. Your career fortunes are diminishing and your luck is running out. These are really bad times for you. Your fortune is unstable and you may even lose out on a very important deal. Try to accept what cannot be changed and let certain things go.
	Du **Delusion**	With a strong spirit and an education in finance, you'll be unstoppable to others. All you have to do is train your mind to think like a successful person. If you get excited too easily, you can fail and miss out on the minor details. Mistakes and sudden incidents might ruin you. Your career fortunes are bad and indicating a hidden crisis looming. You shouldn't see your mistakes as failures and you should see them as new wisdoms instead.

景 *Jing* **Scenery**	Although you may be talented and more than capable, you'll never really make the most out of your gifts. You'll keep wasting your abilities and you can't expect to benefits from them. Also, if you try to make any money from investments, there is a high chance that this can go badly for you unless you do the homework needed. You would need to do your research before you make an investment.	
死 *Si* **Death**	You probably don't realize the severity of the situation that you're in and you'll remain stubborn. Your tendency to isolate yourself or take a self-righteous stance means that you deprive yourself of the support of others. This is never an effective strategy. While you will eventually accomplish what you set out to do, victory will not come to you easily.	辛 XIN
驚 *Jing* **Fear**	Promises will be broken, so don't spend your time trying to argue otherwise. There will be inconsistencies in how things will unfold. Last minute twists and turns will dampen you and your team's spirit. This leads to uncertainty about your future. You should remember that what at first may seem like an ending is often a new beginning.	
開 *Kai* **Open**	You win some, you lose some. This saying applies to you wholeheartedly. You might find that you win more than you lose if you can learn to disregard people who seek to criticize or stand in your way. As another saying goes, a statue was never erected for a critic. Trust your instincts and if something doesn't feel right, don't start seeking approval and advice from others. Learn to believe in yourself!	

天盤 **Heavenly Stem**	地盤 **Earthly Stem**
辛 *Xin* **Yin Metal**	**壬** *Ren* **Yang Water**

Structure 格局	Menacing Snake Enters Prison 兇蛇入獄
Rating 吉凶	Inauspicious 凶
Classic Verse 十干剋應歌訣	兇蛇入獄辛加壬，兩男爭女動墓辰，獄訟不息客遭嗔
Transliteration 字譯	Where the Xin meets with Ren, it is known as the Menacing Snake Enters Prison formation. It denotes that two men fighting for a woman will move the Dragon. It also denotes the occurrence of endless lawsuits.
Description 解說	This formation is highly unfavorable. It denotes the possibility of the individual letting the enemy into their home. As such, havoc and unsettling feelings are likely to pervade the individual's household. There is a chance that they may be deceived. Likewise, carelessness will result in career problems and issues in business matters. There may also be ill feelings among friends and colleagues. Choosing who is an enemy or a friend may be confusing. Overall, this may be a troublesome time.

The 8 Doors Analysis:
The following evaluates the effects of **Xin** 辛 and **Ren** 壬 with each Door.

休 *Xiu* **Rest**	A hostile environment and harsh challenges prevent your efforts to climb the ladder. Since it's not always possible to solve problems or dodge obstacles, sometimes the best thing to do is to make the effort to side-step them before they hit you in the face. Research, planning, and preparation will let you accurately anticipate upcoming difficulties. Plan ahead and make a summary of each outcome before it actually happens. If you fail to do these things, you'll surely lead towards failure. Sacrifices are inevitable. You will need to brace yourself for the road ahead.
生 *Sheng* **Life**	If you don't have the knowledge, and if you don't seek the wisdom you need – you will have no chance in making anything out of yourself. You can lose everything in the blink an eye, with one wrong step. You can't change what has happened to you in the past, so don't try to do so. Shape a better future for yourself and let go of all your regrets in life. Look at what you have right now and try to change your fortune. Your brainpower can be strong-willed if you stay positive and make the money that you can make. Remember to learn new skills and increase your knowledge.
傷 *Shang* **Harm**	You will be fighting a lonely battle. It will not be easy doing things on your own. Everything will hit you at once and you will have a hard time supporting yourself. You put in a 110% but it won't do you any good. You do really want to overcome the odds and live up to the challenge but your courage is diminishing. Eventually, you may have to escape or find a way out of this madness.
杜 *Du* **Delusion**	Frustrated and lonely. Hardworking without recognition as well. You will be filled with worries and doubts. The good times haven't been on your side and there will be many negative events occurring along the way. This causes confusion and frustration in your life. External factors affecting your life which will be beyond your control, will be discouraging to you too. Take a few steps back and observe the situation from afar.

辛 **XIN**

奇門遁甲十干格局篇

XIN

景 *Jing* **Scenery**	Be careful of the way you view the world. In tough times, it is extremely important for you to have the right mentors around you. They will be able to guide you accordingly. You will find yourself in critical situations which may demand a lot of your attention and this will cause you anxiety and worry. This can't be avoided by you. For every battle you win, there will be one which you may lose. This constant pulling and tugging makes it difficult for you to stand back and find peace. You're unlikely to find yourself enjoying the good life any time soon. The key to obtaining better luck is not letting anything be on the back burner.
死 *Si* **Death**	It's just not enough to tell people the truth. Your information alone doesn't cause transformation. It's tough for you to make it to the top, especially in your case. You're prone to spending more time day-dreaming and wishing than actually getting things done. This will make it very difficult for you to achieve anything in life. You'll need to roll out of bed and get into work! This sign is associated with a changing situation and changing fortune – make sure those changes are for the betterment of you.
驚 *Jing* **Fear**	This sign indicates that there are hidden dangers ahead. Your situation will be deceptively peaceful. It is important that you don't rock the cradle and do anything out of the ordinary. Avoid making any major decisions in this climate because the conditions are poor - externally and internally. The key word to remember for you is: patience.
開 *Kai* **Open**	Trust has no real value to many people, especially those people who will screw others for a few dollars. As your luck cycle is running low, you need to know who you can actually trust. You aren't troubled by any major catastrophic problems but you still tend to worry. Although you are aggressive in your efforts, you will still be rewarded with less than your fair share when all is said and done. In regards to your wealth, material possessions are difficult to obtain for you. You will just gain recognition mostly and your dreams will be unlikely to materialize.

天盤 **Heavenly Stem**	地盤 **Earthly Stem**
辛 *Xin* **Yin Metal**	癸 *Gui* **Yin Water**

Structure 格局	Heavenly Prison Elegant Seal 天牢華蓋
Rating 吉凶	Inauspicious 凶
Classic Verse 十干剋應歌訣	天牢華蓋辛加癸，誤入天網動止虧
Transliteration 字譯	Where the Xin meets with Gui, it is known as the Heavenly Prison Elegant Seal formation. It denotes losses due to movements or faults in the Heaven grid.
Description 解說	The Xin 辛 Stem in Qi Men is sometimes known as the Heavenly Prison 天牢. In addition, the Gui 癸 Stem is known as the Elegant Seal 華蓋. Together, this formation is known as the Heavenly Prison Elegant Seal 天牢華蓋. It denotes that the Sun and Moon in the Heavens suddenly become dim. Essentially, the Heavenly net is darkened by the appearance of clouds that trap the brightness. There may be darkness in the heart and mind of the individual that prevents them from seeing the real picture. Additionally, fear and hatred are growing stronger. As such, animosity dominates the actions of the individual. Although the individual may have pure intentions, forces that are beyond their control are holding them back. Their big dreams are impossible to move forward. Despite best efforts, moving forward will be met with obstacles and mishaps. A storm will rage in the individual's life that will lead to continued problems and strife. Dealing with the additional problems will take a great deal of energy. Due to this, it may be difficult to move forward in life or to make progress. The individual may lack in the support that they need to move forward. He or she may have to suffer in silence and learn how to cope alone. In order to insulate the individual from their misfortune, it may be necessary to avoid taking risks. Luck is not on the side of the individual and success will only appear through hard work and dedication.

奇門遁甲十干格局篇

XIN

The 8 Doors Analysis:
The following evaluates the effects of **Xin** 辛 and **Gui** 癸 with each Door.

休 *Xiu* **Rest**	You've been through some rough patches as of late. Don't falter now if you had persevered through it. Better things will see the light of day for you. Continue on with your best efforts and don't let anything sway you from your current/existing objectives. Hold your head up high and remind yourself that you're almost there!
生 *Sheng* **Life**	Nothing really comes for free. Nobody will make you successful or have the responsibility to make you happy. You've got to get out there and put things in motion and make all the necessary efforts. Instead of working blindly, you'll need to come up with a strategic plan to take you where you want/need to be. Be methodical about it all. Help will be found where help is needed. Tread slowly and steadily and you'll be able to achieve your dreams.
傷 *Shang* **Harm**	So many obstructions for you that life may just seem unjust. You may sometimes feel that fate seem to single you out in the game of life and that you've been treated unfairly. There seems to be more bumps in the road for yours than anyone else but you would need to persevere. There are some things you just can't control.
杜 *Du* **Delusion**	It's all too easy for you to rush in and do things without first drawing up a thorough plan. If you are aware of this pitfall, then you can get your ideal results with minimal difficulty. Work systematically. Proceed calmly and focus on one step at a time and victory will be yours.

景 *Jing* **Scenery**	You have ambitions and ideas but they all seem to be impractical. It's all very well to have schemes, but unless you get out there and set the ball rolling, then they are doomed to exist only in your head. Take note of successful people around you and the way they take action instead of simply talking or thinking about taking action. Do more, talk less.	
死 *Si* **Death**	Your plans will need to be put on hold. Your future is full of dark clouds looming and also uncertainty is in the air. This doesn't mean you should give up – far from it. What it means is that you should continue to work hard and accept that this may be a thankless task at the moment, though this would be through no fault of your own.	奇門遁甲十干格局篇 辛 XIN
驚 *Jing* **Fear**	This sign is inauspicious. You may be a victim of bullying. You doubt yourself and have fears about the future which will cause you sleepless nights. It's hard for you to stay ambitious and optimistic with all this going on around you. It is terribly unlikely that you will be able to bring dreams to life or experience prosperity. The current chosen path may not be your true calling. You can still change it while you can.	
開 *Kai* **Open**	This sign is associated with good fortune. The coast looks pretty clear and the wind is blowing in your favor. It's the right time if you wish to sail on to better things ahead. You can expect a future filled with wealth, fame, good standing/ranking in society and self-satisfaction. All you have to do is choose a destination and start making a move to towards it.	

壬

Ren
Yang Water

天盤 Heavenly Stem	地盤 Earthly Stem
壬 *Ren* **Yang Water**	甲 *Jia* **Yang Wood**

Structure 格局	Green Dragon Enters Prison 青龍入獄
Rating 吉凶	Moderate 半吉
Classic Verse 十干剋應歌訣	青龍入獄壬加甲,女產嬰童男發達
Transliteration 字譯	Where the Ren meets with Jia, it is known as the Green Dragon enters Prison formation. It denotes a pregnancy, and also prosperity for men.
Description 解說	The appearance of this formation shows dangers and challenges both domestic and foreign. It may seem like challenges appear from every angle. Every enemy may attack at once. Overall, the competition may be gathering to attack the individual. As the competition gathers in power, the individual may be dragged into gossiping and rumors. The only way to avoid potential hassles is to take a passive role and avoid getting involved in any difficulty.

The 8 Doors Analysis:

The following evaluates the effects of **Ren** 壬 and **Jia** 甲 with each Door.

休 *Xiu* **Rest**	You are about to experience some pick up in your life's journey to success. You will find that you have a straight road that is paved well and without bumps, and this will make you want to move faster. Speeding is always discouraged and this is more so in your case. There is a chance that along this straight road, something unforeseeable will emerge and try to cross to the other side. If you are speeding, you will undoubtedly collide with this object. You should adopt a steady but sure pace. You will take a much longer time to get to the end, but at least you will be safe.
生 *Sheng* **Life**	No person is free from the reality of mistakes. Everybody has made some major mistake in his or her life, and if you assume that making mistakes is a weakness in a person, you will inevitably bring yourself more stress and sorrow. Do not assign blame to yourself or to anyone else and cultivate a culture of fear in the workplace. Instead, focus you mind on just doing your part and carrying out your duties according to your capabilities. Do not expect yourself or anyone on your team to be geniuses who can face down any demon. The main point of being human is to learn.
傷 *Shang* **Harm**	This is the time for you to stay at home and keep out of as much trouble as possible. The environment around you changes and circumstances take on a dangerous edge. If you are not careful, these circumstances will negatively affect your life and bring you much suffering. There is little time for you to rejoice and celebrate in any small successes at all. Happiness is gone from your life now and it seems like there is nothing but doom and glum awaiting you. Bad news becomes common and you are not even surprised by your sheer poor fortune anymore. Remain alert and always be cautious.
杜 *Du* **Delusion**	Extreme bad luck befalls you at this point in your life and you cannot seem to attain anything that you desire. Even though you put in effort to bring things together to ensure some sort of satisfactory outcome, you can never get things to fit just the way you want. Therefore, it is wise for you to not be so fussy. Accept whatever can be offered to you at this point because you are not going to get any better any time soon. The situation is far beyond your control and there is virtually nothing you can do to solve the problem. Either you learn to be content, or you slave away even harder trying to attain the impossible.

REN 壬

景 *Jing* **Scenery**	Fate can be cruel. The nature of time also does not help. It only moves forward and there is no flexibility when it comes to time. When bad fate and time collide, what you get is a whole host of missed opportunities and bad luck. Once you fail to seize whatever opportunities come your way, time will make sure to carry those opportunities far away so you never see them again. You should be very concerned at this point because this configuration does not look too favourable for you. Either you will miss many opportunities, or you will have opportunities but will not be able to do anything about it because of bad fortune.
死 *Si* **Death**	People cannot always be trusted no matter how close you are to them. Just because you are friends with someone does not mean that they are necessarily trustworthy or upstanding. Some people possess the capability of masking their flaws with sweet looks or words, coming across as harmless but in actual reality having malicious intentions. You are likely to come across many people like this. They are the kind of bullies who do not do any bullying directly to the face of their victims. Instead, they go behind their backs and ruin their reputation.
驚 *Jing* **Fear**	Two of the most important things to you in your life are time and money. Of the two, time is more invaluable because once it is lost, it cannot be retained. With money, you can always work to earn it back even if you lose it. But there is nothing you can do for time. If you do not use your time wisely and end up lazing your days away, expecting good things to come to you without having to work for it, you will end up suffering in the end because by the time you realise what you have done, it will be too late to do anything about it and you will have lost the most important thing to you.
開 *Kai* **Open**	A person cannot succeed just on smarts alone. Sometimes, passion and determination is more important. Without a strong spirit, you only have your intelligence to carry you forward, making for a very hollow effort. Your pursuits need to be built on a solid foundation of honest, earnest intention. Do not assume that you will be rewarded for your intelligence. The world does not work like that. It is rare to find people who value intelligence for worthy reasons. If by the some chance you are rewarded for your intelligence, take it as a sign that something sinister was behind that event.

天盤 **Heavenly Stem**	地盤 **Earthly Stem**
壬 *Ren* **Yang Water**	乙 *Yi* **Yin Wood**

Structure 格局	Small Snake Day Noble 小蛇日奇
Rating 吉凶	Moderate 半吉
Classic Verse 十干剋應歌訣	小蛇日奇壬加乙，女人柔順男發跡，祿馬光華孕生子
Transliteration 字譯	Where the Ren meets with Yi, it is known as the Small Snake Day Noble formation. It denotes that a man will flourish in their career with a submissive woman partner. It also indicates salary increase and pregnancy.
Description 解說	This formation denotes potential obstacles and drawbacks along the way. Even when things appear to be going smoothly, disasters will occur. This is due to problems in the individuals strategy and overall plan. There are feelings of mistrust and betrayal that exist. These feelings are holding the individual back from what they can succeed. Overall, there is a lack of clarity that is obscuring the underlying cause of any difficulty. The individual may step on toes as they try to take action. Only projects that have been thoroughly discussed will succeed. Otherwise, the individual will make mistakes in their interactions with others. Dealings with other people may be strained because the individual has something in their heart that is holding them back. This problem may be due to blame, hatred or guilt. In general, keeping a low profile makes each project or goal more successful. Proposed plans must be checked by other people before they are put into action. Likewise, proactive attempts at communication are more likely to be successful. Learning how to discuss things first will result in a brighter future.

奇門遁甲十干格局篇

REN

The 8 Doors Analysis:

The following evaluates the effects of **Ren** 壬 and **Yi** 乙 with each Door.

休 *Xiu* **Rest**	Good fortune will come and find you whether you need it or not. You will find success in everything and prosperity will seek you out and fill up your life. You may find all this overwhelming and be stressed out about how you are supposed to adapt to this new change in life. Furthermore, you do not know what to do with your newfound wealth. Do not worry; rejoice instead in the fact that the fates have chosen to bless you. Take whatever you do not need and give it to those who do. You will feel good when you become a charitable person.
生 *Sheng* **Life**	Great success lies just at your fingertips. All you have to do is stretch out to attain it. As long as you make that reach, you will get what you want. Good fortune is on your side and you will find your journey now to be smooth sailing and comfortable. You are a very influential person now and everyone looks up to you for guidance and takes your advice willingly. You are seen as an upstanding member of your community and everyone wants to have you around. Enjoy this time and revel in your good fortune. Make the most of it!
傷 *Shang* **Harm**	You tend to mingle in the affairs of other people. Most people consider you a busybody. You have to ask yourself at this point: what do you even get out of being a meddler? People see you as a nuisance and all try to avoid you. They shun you and keep secrets from you because they do not trust you. Behind your back, they call you a troublemaker and an interferer. You ask many questions about other people but do not learn anything important about them. People do not understand that you ask because you are genuinely concerned. You should change the way you approach people, otherwise they will continue to assume that you simply want gossip.
杜 *Du* **Delusion**	The more you spend, the more debt you have! You want to live a life of luxury but you do not make enough money to sustain such a lifestyle. The minute you make money, you want to spend it on something. This indicates that you have a strong thirst for life and a taste for the finer things. While it is sophisticated of you to want to expect the best, you should not overspend for this will only bring you more suffering in the future. If you save enough money now and continue being hard working, you will eventually have enough money to comfortably experience luxury without burning holes in your pockets.

296　Qi Men Dun Jia Strategic Execution

景
Jing
Scenery

Strategize more effectively to incorporate both defensive and offensive measures in your life. You cannot focus too much on one thing and end up neglecting a very important front. Do not be afraid of being aggressive; no one is going to judge you for trying to protect yourself. React appropriately to different situations. For instance, a mild insult should not illicit an extreme physical response from you. But if you are physically hurt for instance, do not be afraid to report that person or fight back.

死
Si
Death

Dishonesty is a short term investment. People lie to get away with something and save themselves from immediate punishment, but in the long run, those lies return and bite them in the back. You have not been completely honest with yourself or with the people around you and this will interfere with the course of your future. You will have a reputation for dishonesty and your credibility will be very low. People will not want to associate with you. There is not much you can do about this other than to start changing the way you do things.

驚
Jing
Fear

Learn to see the world through realistic eyes and be completely honest with yourself. Sometimes, our perceptions are marred by the influences of other people or by the media. Do not take these outside opinions too seriously. The only outlook that really matters is your own. After all, you will be making decisions for yourself. If you do not learn to be confident in your own opinions, you will forever rely on others. You need to be independent and take charge of your own life now. Be accountable for your own actions and success will come to you.

開
Kai
Open

An abundant life is yours for the taking. Prosperity is at your doorstep, patiently waiting for you to have the courage to go for it. You have a bright future ahead of you both in terms of finances and your social life, but you need to step out of your box and live outside your comfort zone. Learn to speak up and be the centre of attention. There is nothing wrong with being noticed. If you do not start having more of a presence, such good fortune will be wasted on you. You need to keep your reputation up to match with your prosperity.

奇門遁甲十干格局篇

壬 REN

天盤 **Heavenly Stem**	地盤 **Earthly Stem**
壬 *Ren* **Yang Water**	**丙** *Bing* **Yang Fire**

Structure 格局	Water Snake Enters Fire 水蛇入火
Rating 吉凶	Inauspicious 凶
Classic Verse 十干剋應歌訣	水蛇入火壬加丙，官災刑禁連不停
Transliteration 字譯	Where the Ren meets with Bing, it is known as the Water Snake Enters Fire formation. It denotes persistent disasters for officials. It also indicates punishment and imprisonment.
Description 解說	The Ren 壬 Stem clashes with the Bing 丙 Noble within this formation. In Qi Men, the Ren 壬 stem is sometimes referred to as the Water Snake. As such, it is a metaphor for evil, deceit and treachery. With the Bing Stem, individuals encounter three Nobles. These Nobles represent status, power and authority. Due to the configuration, the Water Snake causes fire to be trapped and tied down. This means that the individual may find their authority tied down or temporarily removed. For the individual, this situation may feel like a physical or metaphorical prison. Challenges are invited into their life, so he or she may feel unwanted drama or a sense of unfairness. Due to this, plans are unlikely to proceed as they are supposed to. These plans may even turn out negatively in the end. As such, this formation indicates that opportunities will be missed or not fully capitalized on.

The 8 Doors Analysis:
The following evaluates the effects of **Ren** 壬 and **Bing** 丙 with each Door.

休 *Xiu* **Rest**	No matter what dangers or problems you come across, good fortune will be on your side and help you tackle these issues. Luck is on your side during this time and you should not worry too much about any harm coming your way. Even if someone or something was targeting you, your good fortune will deflect that negativity away from you, allowing you to concentrate on improving your life further. This configuration is auspicious as it is commonly associated with success.
生 *Sheng* **Life**	Great blessings will come to you at this time as this configuration brings about prosperity to you. Good fortune is abundant and you are about to experience one of the more auspicious times in your life. You are surrounded by well-meaning people who are all equipped with the know-how and experience in guiding you to be a better person. You will have good social reputation and skills under this combination and you can use this to your advantage as people will be very willing to help you in your endeavours.
傷 *Shang* **Harm**	Do not hold on to your dreams too tightly, because you will not be able to achieve them under this configuration. Do not dwell on the hold and be bitter about the things you could not achieve because of fate. If you are so gripped by the past, you will only end up being disappointed and sorrowful. The fact is, you will not be able to achieve your dreams with such bad fortune. It is best for you to forget about them and move on; pursue more realistic things. Do not be to upset, for the end of one thing is also the start of something else.
杜 *Du* **Delusion**	Hard work does not always result in recognition. The nature of the world is such that sometimes the best of us are ignore and neglected while the worst are put on a pedestal and praised. This will happen to you and you will feel utterly unappreciated and used by those you trusted. Do not dwell on the injustice of it all and give yourself more stress. Instead, use this opportunity to cultivate stronger character. This learning experience will make you a better person and after this, you will no longer be so affected by the kind of people who have always neglected you.

奇門遁甲十干格局篇

壬 REN

Qi Men Dun Jia Strategic Execution 299

Jing **Scenery**		A strong spirit and financial stability will take you where you need to go. That is all you need to achieve success. You will need to train your mind to make it unbendable and unyielding under pressure. It is highly likely that you will be bombarded with quite a lot of high tension situations and you will need to exercise superior analytical skills. You can achieve all this by seeking out the help of an expert mentor. This person can teach you how to train your mind and show you what needs to be done at crucial times.
死 *Si* **Death**		After a period of extreme difficulties and prolonged strife, you will finally have a clearer idea of what it is you want in life. You will also finally have a clear sense of how to distinguish between what is good and bad for you. With this newfound knowledge, you now know exactly how to make use of your talents and where to channel them to. But this does not mean that your hardships are over. You will not be able to become motivated at first, especially since you are already so fatigued from your previous sufferings.
驚 *Jing* **Fear**		The future is very uncertain right now. You are unsure of what to do and what to look for in life. You are now at a crossroads and each road seems to lead to some darkness. The people around you do not seem to be able to help you in any way and instead, try to mislead and deceive you. The only way to improve this situation is to take some time away and be alone in a quiet setting. Take this time to philosophise on your own without the influence of others and discover your true passions and goals. Every time you seem wary or uncertain about something, take some time away and think in solace.
開 *Kai* **Open**		Insecurity and inadequacy seem to be holding you back from progressing any further in life. You are afraid to take the next step. Risks are considered to be unnecessary jeopardies, when in real life, they are opportunities for a better outcome. You need to develop more confidence in yourself. Seek out a counsellor or mentor whom you trust and get his advice on all matters that trouble. Only through the comforting words of someone wiser will you ever learn to break out of your shell.

奇門遁甲十干格局篇

壬 REN

天盤 **Heavenly Stem**	地盤 **Earthly Stem**
壬 *Ren* **Yang Water**	丁 *Ding* **Yin Fire**

Structure 格局	Stem Combine Snake Punishment 干合蛇刑
Rating 吉凶	Moderate 半吉
Classic Verse 十干剋應歌訣	幹合蛇刑壬加丁，文書牽連貴人行，男吉女兇天羅頂
Transliteration 字譯	Where the Ren meets with Ding, it is known as the Stem Combine Snake Punishment formation. It denotes some kind of documentation in place, and being saved by a Nobleman. If the combination meets with the Heavenly Web, the outlook would be auspicious for men but inauspicious for women.
Description 解說	The formation indicates possible confusion and ambiguity. This is due to it being the Ding Fire Stem. As such, it creates the the Heavenly Stem Combination with the Ren Yang Water Stem. Since the Ren Stem is known as the Water Snake within the Qi Men, it leads to mixed feelings. There are changes that a trusted person in the equation is bad. The individual may be unable to prevent falling in love with this person. This relationship may be characterized by a mixture of love and hatred. Everyone seems to be hiding something and it is difficult to reveal the truth. Finding true sincerity may be impossible between both parties. Due to this, problems are increasingly likely. The presence of an auspicious Door leads to favorable agreements on paper. When an unfavorable Door is present, it shows possible disagreements.

The 8 Doors Analysis:

The following evaluates the effects of **Ren** 壬 and **Ding** 丁 with each Door.

休 *Xiu* **Rest**	You are definitely not short on ambition, but the problem is you lack the skills to move forward. While you have a good vision of what it is you expect out of life, without the expertise needed to carry out your pursuits, you will not go anywhere. Therefore, before you start out on your journey, you need to prepare yourself and take some time away to really grasp all the skills that are required of you. It may be some time before things move along, but you need to be patient and take as much time as possible to do everything that needs to be done first.
生 *Sheng* **Life**	Security is very much present in your life right now. Everything is stable and you do not have much to worry about. All you need to do is possibly put more effort into reaching higher goals. You have the potential to go very far, but if you set low goals for yourself, then it is only lesser goals that you will achieve. Make some brave steps and do not be afraid to take risks. After all, good fortune is on your side and you have all the stability and security you need. If you were going to take any risks, this is the best time to do so.
傷 *Shang* **Harm**	Sleepless nights befall you as you are constantly troubled by the many things that you have to deal with. You have problems in all the major aspects of your life and the stress is truly taking its toll on you. You have to remind yourself to not be too easily frustrated. If you are so easily influenced by the negative things that happen in your life, these things will take over your entire being very easily and you will only end up in a perpetual state of fatigue and worry. There is nothing wrong with kicking back and relaxing and trying to not have a care in the world.
杜 *Du* **Delusion**	You seem to be rather oblivious to the state of harm that you are currently in right now. It is no casual matter and you need to start taking charge of your problems. Do not ignore the issue for it may just be aggravated to become worse. Instead, be less stubborn and recognise the tough spot you are currently in. Do not live in denial because of pride. Seek out some help and do not be so self-righteous. You tend to isolate yourself form others and assume to be better than them. Do not deprive yourself of such valuable assistance just because you cannot live with the reality of being outshone by another.

景 *Jing* **Scenery**	Although you have talent and potential, you do not make enough use of your capabilities. This is mostly in part due to your laziness and also your lack of self-belief. You have been told too often in your life that you cannot succeed. Now is the time to ignore those comments and make them officially a thing of the past with no impact on your future. Forget those comments and become your own person. You should not allow what other people say to define who you are. Work harder and have more confidence in your capabilities and success will be yours.	
死 *Si* **Death**	Do not have unrealistic expectations and assume that everything will go your way. You tend to be too idealistic for your own good. If your expectations are so high, you will only be constantly disappointed and let down as your anticipations keep getting shot down by reality. Try to be more practical and focus on things that can be done easily and without much involvement of others. Do something that you can achieve yourself, because you will be disappointed by the under-performance of other people.	REN
驚 *Jing* **Fear**	Life is like a roller coaster that seeks to throw you out of your seat. Your only safety precaution is to buckle up and stay tight in your seat. Do not be impulsive or easily scared into action. Just remain calm and try to be reasonable and level-headed about your actions. Do not try to fight fire with fire, bringing your own chaos to life. You will inevitably damage yourself and those around you. Strap in and hold on tight; be prepared for the literal ride of your life.	
開 *Kai* **Open**	You are well loved by everyone in your life and they are more than eager to help you out in any endeavour that you are go on. Choose whose help you receive, because you want to only go for those who are true experts in what they do. Coupled with their sincerity, the knowledge that these mentors bring to you will help you succeed in life and reach new heights. They will carry you up and give you everything you need. Keep good relations with these mentors and remember to pay back their kindness with favours of your own.	

	天盤 **Heavenly Stem**		地盤 **Earthly Stem**
	壬 *Ren* **Yang Water**		戊 *Wu* **Yang Earth**

Structure 格局	Small Snake Transform to Dragon 小蛇化龍
Rating 吉凶	Auspicious 吉
Classic Verse 十干剋應歌訣	小蛇化龍壬加戊，男人發達，女爲產婦
Transliteration 字譯	Where the Ren meets with Wu, it is known as the Small Snake Transforms to Dragon formation. It denotes a rich man and a pregnant woman.
Description 解說	Overall, this sign is extremely auspicious. It indicates a positive transformation or change. It is likely that a positive turn of events is in order. A situation that seems to be negative may be transformed into positive results. Someone who seems like they are against the individual may suddenly be on the individual's side. Overall, the situation favors individuals who are seeking fame and a positive reputation. He or she can expect support for their work. In general, plans can be executed with few or minimal hiccups along the way.

The 8 Doors Analysis:
The following evaluates the effects of **Ren** 壬 and **Wu** 戊 with each Door.

休 *Xiu* **Rest**	A higher power has come along and cleared the road for you towards success. Your career and personal life will benefit from this period of prosperity and good fortune. People who are in positions of power in your life have made things easy for you because in their eyes, you are a talented and earnest person who deserves good fortune. The once bumpy road that you took has actually helped you become a better person with more skills. Remember the difficulty you used to face and this will keep you in check when success is finally yours.
生 *Sheng* **Life**	Fame, success, and happiness are yours for the taking under this auspicious configuration. You will have a smooth journey to the top and everyone will admire you for all that you have achieved. There will be plenty of opportunities provided to you, both by people who admire you and by forces that cannot be explained. Should you ever stumble and require assistance, remember that you have loyal friends who are willing to help you and go all out for your sake.
傷 *Shang* **Harm**	You can only rely on yourself at this point. This is going to be a one-person battle in which you are your own general. You have to know what you're going to do and plan both your offense and defence positions well. It is not going to be easy doing this alone because all your trials are going to come in one bunch and hit you at once. You will barely have time to register what just happened let alone get back up on your feet. The best you can do is to believe in yourself and stay strong. Confidence is key.
杜 *Du* **Delusion**	The road is troubled and it meanders for a long time before reaching its destination. Even then, the destination is unclear and possibly treacherous. You, as the adventurer in your own life, have to take this road without hesitation. Be brave and walk on it as if it were a good road. Face your challenges head on and be strong-willed when you start to feel like you want to give up. If you come across forks in the road, choose the one you gut tells you to go with. Both paths are probably equally dangerous, but if you follow your hunches, you will have more confidence.

景 *Jing* **Scenery**		Good leaders are the kind of people who would sacrifice their own benefits to see the team grow. They lead by example and all their subordinates greatly admire them because they take care of their team very well. You are such a leader. People have finally recognised your contributions and hard work and want to repay the favours you have done for them. Allow them to treat you well, because you definitely deserve this. Relax and take some time to reflect on all the good work you have done so that in the future, you know what to do again.
死 *Si* **Death**		You are a very opinionated person but you tend to be easily offended as well. You are pretty sensitive about things that should not really matter that much. In that sense, you are also a bit of an egomaniac because you care too much about losing face. You are very competitive and winning or losing means the world to you. This makes you a very outstanding individual with strong convictions but it becomes very easy for you to come into conflict with other people. You need to not have such a high opinion of yourself and occasionally take a step back.
驚 *Jing* **Fear**		Promises made to you will be broken. Do not waste time hoping for the impossible. Accept that life is as such. If you keep on arguing, you are only wasting your time and energy, further stressing yourself out and upsetting everyone around you. Of course, this dampens your spirit and you are no longer capable of being the same person with hopefulness and optimism, but it is perhaps for the best. Some people are very cynical about life but they tend to also be more realistic. Being realistic will help you get a better grasp of your place in the world.
開 *Kai* **Open**		Strategy is extremely important in the game of life. The person who plans well and anticipates all the possible outcomes is the person that is most likely to succeed. You may see this as unpleasantly shrewd behaviour, but you need to understand that these are the things that need to be done in order for success to come. Always plan ahead and pre-empt all your challenges a few steps earlier. Do not wait for things to go sour before learning to be prepared. If you do this, you can expect a positive outcome in your life.

天盤 Heavenly Stem	地盤 Earthly Stem
壬 *Ren* Yang Water	己 *Ji* Yin Earth

Structure 格局	Fierce Snake Enters Prison 凶蛇入獄
Rating 吉凶	Inauspicious 凶
Classic Verse 十干剋應歌訣	凶蛇入獄壬加己，官司訟敗禍將罹，妄動必兇順守吉
Transliteration 字譯	Where the Ren meets with Ji, it is known as the Fierce Snake Enters Prison formation. It denotes disasters occurring due to failed lawsuits. If one takes impulsive actions, accidents will occur. If one waits patiently, it will be auspicious instead.
Description 解說	This is a generally negative formation. Due to this, there may be hidden obstacles along the path. The individual may have obstacles in their path and success may seem to be far-fetched. The individual may be framed. Additionally, they may be forced to solve the problems of someone else. Even small issues may lead to large headaches. At times, minor problems will escalate into large issues. Nothing is as easy as it initially seemed to be. Overall, this combination does not favor academic pursuits or scholarly examinations. Although the individual may have many friends, these friends may not pull through when the chips are down. The individual has to work for their own gain since friends will not provide the necessary help.

The 8 Doors Analysis:

The following evaluates the effects of **Ren** 壬 and **Ji** 己 with each Door.

休 *Xiu* **Rest**	Everything around you seems to swell with positivity and you are feeling good about yourself all around. Nothing seems to be able to stop you at this point with such good fortune smiling down on you. Your state in life is so good that other people start to envy you. Noble people however, view you in an admiring eye and extend hands of friendship to you, wanting to keep you as a lifelong friend. They want to assist you in all your endeavours and see you succeed and push to even higher ground.
生 *Sheng* **Life**	Someone is going to come into your life and bring you great joy and benefit. You will befriend or become intimate with this person under the most unassuming of circumstances, and an unbreakable bond will flourish from there. This person is going to bring motivation to you in all your pursuits. They will always be there for you and help you with whatever you need. Take this opportunity to go for the goals that you really want to achieve. You may not have support this genuine and good for a long time.
傷 *Shang* **Harm**	Avoid situations that are harmful in nature and seem to put you in a troubling position. Focus on your safety and respect the fact that there is an order to life. Rules are rules and you need to live by them. Do not try to be smart and go against the rules, for you could create some serious problems for yourself if you do so. Try to supress your impulsive nature and be more patient and understanding for once. Wait for the right conditions to come around before making your move. Do not try and manufacture those conditions yourself.
杜 *Du* **Delusion**	Even though you tried your best to succeed, a favourable outcome will not materialise. It is possible that your best is simply not good enough for the real world. Do not be disheartened, but instead take time off to work on your skills. If you can hone some new talents and skills, you will be able to go back to your pursuits and try to achieve them again, this time with more confidence and preparation. It is possible that you will not meet many helpful people, but that is fine. Just stick to your guns and try to improve yourself.

景 *Jing* **Scenery**	You have been put in an environment that is very conducive for success. You have all the resources you need at this point and already possess some level of talent. The only problem is you might not have anyone to go to if you need help with anything. Your old mentors no longer help you because they think that you should be able to look out for yourself now. Your friends don't help you, partly because they are jealous and also because they think you do not need their help. Do not let this bog you down and think instead of other possible opportunities for success.	奇門遁甲十干格局篇
死 *Si* **Death**	Many people who try to correct a bad habit give up halfway, whether it be drinking, smoking, gambling, or perhaps something more mild such as a bad working ethic. This is because real change requires a lot of motivation and determination. Without a strong spirit, real change cannot come. You will have something in your life that you desperately want to change, but without a strong spirit, you cannot possibly hope to have a good outcome. You will be constantly exhausted and disappointed, so a strong spirit will be exceptionally hard to come by.	壬 REN
驚 *Jing* **Fear**	Health is wealth! You have been neglecting your own personal wellbeing in your pursuit for success. Now that you have become physically weak and the fatigue has settled in to completely take you over, there is little you can achieve because you can barely even get out of bed in the morning. Rest now and reflect on where you went wrong. You cannot keep nursing your problems and at the same time, forget to eat. You cannot try to fix your troubles and create new ones for yourself. That is not the right way to live, and you need as much rest and you need action.	
開 *Kai* **Open**	You are never alone in your troubles and there is always someone there to help you no matter what. You need to know how to ask assistance from these people and not let your pride or ego get in the way. Remember that without these people, you will not have the success you have today. You do not have to fear them or whatever judgements you seem to think will be levelled onto you. Have more faith that the people in your life are good, sincere people with your best intentions at heart. Benefit from their assistance and be grateful to them.	

	天盤 **Heavenly Stem**	地盤 **Earthly Stem**
	壬 *Ren* **Yang Water**	**庚** *Geng* **Yang Metal**

Structure 格局	Great White Catch Snake 太白擒蛇
Rating 吉凶	Inauspicious 凶
Classic Verse 十干剋應歌訣	太白擒蛇壬加庚，刑獄公平剖邪正
Transliteration 字譯	Where the Ren meets with Geng, it is known as the Great White Catch Snake formation. It denotes a fair punishment to determine good and evil.
Description 解説	There are huge hassles and problems in store for the individual. He or she may experience a string of headaches as they are drawn into disputes. Although legal problems will occur, the judgment will be fair. As long as the individual has not engaged in no wrongdoing, the legal problems hold nothing to fear. At the same time, hasty actions are unlikely to lead to positive outcomes. Patient outlooks result in better outcomes overall.

The 8 Doors Analysis:
The following evaluates the effects of **Ren** 壬 and **Geng** 庚 with each Door.

休 *Xiu* **Rest**	Vincent Van Gogh only sold one painting during his lifetime. He is now renowned as one of the best painters ever, but when he was alive his work was largely ignored. Luckily, you do not have to be like Van Gogh. Your talents will be recognised soon and you will be elevated to the status you so rightly deserve. However, you are going to have to make a tough decision in regards to this new success. You make have to make a tough sacrifice or abandon a current commitment, but whatever it is, you are going to be in a dilemma.
生 *Sheng* **Life**	Fairy tales can sometimes come true! In fact, you are practically living in a fairy tale right now. With everything going your way and good fortune following you everywhere you go, it is safe to say that you are in the best time of your life right now. This is a highly auspicious configuration and you will find nothing but sheer happiness and joy under it. Success is yours! Your social life is boosted, your reputation secured, prosperity flowing, and emotional health thriving! The way things look; you are going to be in for the time of your life!
傷 *Shang* **Harm**	You spend your days anxious and on edge, awaiting some kind of horrible outcome in your life pursuits. You are dwelling constantly in this unhealthy state of mind and it very bad for your general psyche. Your physiological state suffers under this tyrannical fear, and you have barely taken any rest at all. You need to calm down and try to find inner peace. Look to the harmony of nature or try to draw inspiration from the good relationships other people have. Whatever it is, you need to find a way to get out of shell and move on to a brighter place before you deal any lasting damage to yourself.
杜 *Du* **Delusion**	Mistakes cannot be avoided in life. Sometimes, they are even necessary to help us move forward. Your problem is that you do not seem to learn from your mistakes. They happen to you and then you brush them off without reassessing or reflecting on anything. This is probably why you are so oblivious to your own personal flaws. You think you are unstoppable in everything you do but the truth is if you only learned from your mistakes, you will realise how far you have left to go before you reach success.

REN 壬

奇門遁甲十干格局篇

REN

景 *Jing* **Scenery**

All of the hard work you have put into bringing your life together is about to be paid off. Good news will arrive soon regarding your endeavours and you will notice the obvious change in fortunes there. Good fortune will not give you the ability to finish whatever you started and bring them to positive closings. Make your decisions carefully and try to close up as many loopholes as you can during this time. With good fortune on your side, this is the best time to tackle all those difficult problems that require extra attention.

死 *Si* **Death**

Trapped between moving forward and taking a step back, you are stuck in limbo wondering what you are supposed to do next. You cry out but no one seems to hear you. Your pleas for assistance are ignored or brushed away. No one seems to take your problems very seriously. You are left floating, drowning, and running on the spot. The world closes in around you and darkness seeps in. True, you are helpless and alone and there is virtually nothing you can do to make yourself feel better, but you can learn to accept your fate and be patient to wait for this suffering to pass.

驚 *Jing* **Fear**

Good things are supposed to come to those who wait. But the problem is, you have been waiting for a long time and nothing has happened for you yet. In fact, things only seem to get worse. You will have laboured for a good outcome but no fruits will come of it. It will be as if you have wasted all your time and energy. You keep going to people to seek solace and ask for advice, but they only tell you to wait longer. You are losing your patience now. It is best for you to put this issue aside and focus all your time and energy on a new issue. Let this new issue consume you and distract you completely.

開 *Kai* **Open**

Plans that have been in place for a long time are about to be utilised to their full potential. The time of confusion and lack of direction is now over and you will have victory in sight as you start bringing your plans to fruition. A change in fortunes will come about and direct your life to a new path towards success. Make good use of this time of good fortune to try and accomplish as many things as possible. Now is the time for you to try everything. Failure does not really matter, but the experience you gain will be invaluable to you in the future.

天盤 **Heavenly Stem**	地盤 **Earthly Stem**
壬 *Ren* **Yang Water**	**辛** *Xin* **Yin Metal**

Structure 格局	Flying Snake Awakens 騰蛇相纏
Rating 吉凶	Inauspicious 凶
Classic Verse 十干剋應歌訣	騰蛇相纏壬加辛，謀望今被欺瞞隱，縱有吉門也不寧
Transliteration 字譯	Where the Ren meets with Xin, it is known as the Flying Snake Awakens formation. It denotes false expectations and restlessness even in the presence of auspicious Doors.
Description 解說	This structure is named the Flying Snake Awakens 騰蛇相纏. The Ren Water Stem is known as "the Snake". As such, it represents ongoing problems. It may indicate ongoing problems, arguments and hassles. The Xin 辛 Stem represents punishment, resentment, emotional pain. Due to this, close friendships may experience disagreements and secret jealousy. The Snake shows lingering problems. Treachery, deceit and unforeseen dilemmas are around the corner. The combination shows that the individual may be tricked or bamboozled. They may be cheated into making decisions that they did not originally want. Even when an auspicious Door is present, things are unlikely to be successful. An individual who is looking for an opportunity is likely to meet with deception or difficulties.

The 8 Doors Analysis:

The following evaluates the effects of **Ren** 壬 and **Xin** 辛 with each Door.

休 *Xiu* **Rest**	Do not give up on your dreams! You have been struggling for a long and hard time and it will be a complete waste of all your time and energy for you to drop everything now that you are so close to getting what you want. It may look like you are nowhere near to getting anywhere with your efforts, but the truth is you only need one final push to get to your destination. Helping hands will come to you at the last minute and pull you to the place you need to be. With their help, you will discover the final step you need to take and once you take that step, success is yours.
生 *Sheng* **Life**	Creativity is your strongest suit and you are truly the kind of person who could churn out original ideas at the snap of fingers! You are surrounded by ample resources and have everything that you need to help you keep that creativity mojo flowing, so seize this opportunity to come up with some of your best ideas and works! Good fortune is on your side and you can be assured of success in everything you try. Do not be afraid to express yourself and go all out with your vision. Be a true revolutionary in the way you work!
傷 *Shang* **Harm**	There is no such thing as perfect. At the end of the day, everybody puts in their best effort but end up getting something that does not quite live up to their desires. This will be greatly disappointing, of course, but there will be other ups and downs in your life that will make this matter seem like small potatoes. Your faith and hope for the future will be shattered and you will very discontent with the fact that you can never what you want despite what you try. This is because good fortune is not on your side right now under this inauspicious configuration.
杜 *Du* **Delusion**	You always tend to over-promise and later under-deliver. This is because you are an idealist with no solid grasp on how reality works. You tend to be naïve and overconfident at the same time, which is a very dangerous combination. This causes major problems with all the developments you want to pursue. You make it a personal goal to impress on the first meeting, and that is way your silver tongue has a mind of its own and makes impossible promises. You need to control your words and try to be more level-headed! You do not want to earn a reputation as an unreliable person.

景 *Jing* **Scenery**	It is always darkest before the dawn. A single candle can light up an entire room of darkness. You may be going through a tough time right now, but if you are patient enough, soon good things will come to you and you will realise that all your fretting and despairing was for nothing. Next time you are down or facing any trials, remember this concept. You need to be pushed down first in order to be brought back up. When your fortune does finally change, great rewards await you for you endurance and patience.
死 *Si* **Death**	Three things are needed for success: good relationships, time, and money. You do not have any of the three. You alienated everyone that could have helped you because you found it too difficult to trust others. As for time, you wasted it all on decision making and planning that now you have no time to act. You also spent all your money buying things that do not have any positive effect on your current pursuits. You are a big spender with no concept of saving. Once you earn money, you squander it all on luxury desserts, cute gadgets, and seasonal clothing.
驚 *Jing* **Fear**	Knowing that you want to succeed in life in not enough. You need to have to guts to take action. One of your biggest problems is cowardice. You have been too conditioned to believe the world is a dangerous place and you are too fragile for it. This is simply not true. You have the potential to be successful, but you cannot find the bravery required to step outside of your comfort zone. The people you mix with are all also like this and this is why you are so used to the idea of being comfortable doing nothing and letting things fall into place on their own.
開 *Kai* **Open**	Spirituality is the key to happiness for most people. This is certainly true in your case. You always feel very connected to the world around, being very observant and sensitive to slight changes and special nuances. You enjoy the company of nature and you are generally a good people person. Now that fortune is smiling down on you, your spiritual connection with the universe is at its peak and you are experiencing high levels of inner joy. Use this time to spread your own personal joy to every other person. Seek out those who look like they need cheering up and teach them how to see the world in a better light.

壬
REN

天盤 **Heavenly Stem**		地盤 **Earthly Stem**	
壬 *Ren* **Yang Water**		**壬** *Ren* **Yang Water**	

Structure 格局	Snake Enters Earth Net 蛇入地羅
Rating 吉凶	Inauspicious 凶
Classic Verse 十干剋應歌訣	蛇入地羅壬加壬，外人纏繞內縈素，門吉星吉尚免身
Transliteration 字譯	Where the Ren meets with Ren, it is known as the Snake Enters Earth Net formation. It denotes problems at home and abroad. If the combination meets with the auspicious Stars and Doors, it denotes that the problems can be avoided.
Description 解說	Luck is not on the side of the individual. Due to this, the individual's secret wish is unlikely to be granted. They may lose wealth or lack the support they need for everything to go according to plan. Nothing may seem to go right. When it comes to making marital commitments, there may be unforeseen problems in delivering a baby or treating an illness. Even when everything seems to be going smoothly, individuals may not be able to see the storm brewing on the horizon. Calm and peaceful environments require the individual to keep an eye open. Even in the midst of calm, difficulties are starting to form. Overall, the journey will be filled with crises, harm and problems. It will be difficult to succeed at any goal.

The 8 Doors Analysis:

The following evaluates the effects of **Ren** 壬 and **Ren** 壬 with each Door.

休 *Xiu* **Rest**	This configuration signifies good tidings for career-minded individuals. Fortune is in your favour and you should seize this opportunity to take bigger risks and invest more in up and coming ventures that you may have been unsure about earlier. Prosperity and wealth will come to you at this point so you should not worry about not having enough capital to proceed with your dreams. If you were to take out loans, be very careful about how much you take because you may not need that much in the end and it will just be a hassle to pay it all back again.
生 *Sheng* **Life**	There is no need to be too paranoid about things and be unreasonably suspicious of others. Your lack of trust is not as subtle as you think it is and other people will take offense at the fact that you consider them dishonourable. Give others the same sympathy you would want them to give you. Do your own part well and you will not have to worry about anyone else, no matter the task. You look to be all set for constant and steady development. As long as you maintain a level head and not go overboard with your theories about other people, you should have a smooth sailing ride.
傷 *Shang* **Harm**	Aggressive action does not always bring about the most effective results. In fact it might turn some people off to your cause as they might think you are far too forceful. This aggressiveness only makes enemies for you and gives people the false impression that you are a very disagreeable person. Even though you only have everyone's best interests at heart, you still need to tone down your forwardness and try to be more diplomatic, lest people start to see you as someone undesirable to work with.
杜 *Du* **Delusion**	The idea that money is evil is wrong. Money does not have the capacity to be evil on its own. Human beings are the ones who bring evilness to money. Do not let these false ideas of the corrupting power of money to dissuade you from trying to be a successful person. Do you really have so little faith in your ability to stay true to your values and not be influenced by money? Go for whatever opportunities are out there for you and turn a deaf ear to those people who try to put a damper on your dreams. They are only afraid of what they themselves would do if they had money. Do not let them tell you what they think you would do.

奇門遁甲十干格局篇

壬
REN

奇門遁甲十干格局篇

壬
REN

景 *Jing* **Scenery**	Lingering problems in your life are likely to delay your plans and make it difficult for you to pursue your goals. These problems need time to be solved; you cannot expect for all of them to be dealt with when you want them to be. You must exercise absolute will and determination at this point and not easily give up. You have the tendency to overestimate the challenge and underestimate yourself. Refrain from doing that and instead believe in yourself. As long as you practice this, you will be able to succeed.
死 *Si* **Death**	Do not treat failure like a disease that must be avoided at all costs. One of your bigger flaws is your inability to allow yourself to fail. You have always been a high achiever and could never accept failure. As a result, you have not had any significant failures in your life. This is dangerous because now that you are out in the real world, it is more advantageous to have been a person who failed many times to be a person who has only ever experienced success. When you come across your first failure, you will be devastated and not know how to deal with it.
驚 *Jing* **Fear**	Before you can be successful in life, you need to learn about yourself first. Right now, you do not have a clear idea of who you are and what you want. You need to go on a journey of self-discovery and learn these truths about yourself first before you even try anything. The sad thing about you is that you do not have enough self-confidence to be firm in what you believe in. even if you do eventually discover what it is you really want in life, you will have trouble taking yourself seriously. Stop second-guessing everything and trust in yourself!
開 *Kai* **Open**	Rome was not built in a day. To achieve success and come up with the best product possible, you need meticulous planning and an inordinate amount of time and energy invested. You will have to give it your all and you will be drained long before any success comes. This is normal and you should get used to it. Once you realise this concept and start looking at it in a positive way, success will come to you easy. All you need to do is work hard and invest enough time in your pursuits.

天盤 **Heavenly Stem**	地盤 **Earthly Stem**
壬 *Ren* **Yang Water**	癸 *Gui* **Yin Water**

Structure 格局	Young Maiden Commits Adultery 幼女奸淫
Rating 吉凶	Inauspicious 凶
Classic Verse 十干剋應歌訣	幼女姦淫壬加癸，家醜外揚風流鬼，門吉星兇福反悔
Transliteration 字譯	Where the Ren meets with Gui, it is known as the Young Maiden Commits Adultery formation. It denotes disclosure of one's dirty tales. If the combination meets with the auspicious Doors and inauspicious Stars, it indicates that blessings will come and go.
Description 解說	When everything seems to be too good to be true, it most likely is. Greed and lust will be at the root at many of the individual's problems. Limiting problems relating to lust or greed will lower the overall difficulties and pain. As the path ahead unfolds, it may lead to continued issues. At times, it may feel like the individual is struggling against the movement of a treadmill. The individual may try to move forward, but efforts will not be rewarded. He or she may face troublesome situations. They may leap into activity impulsively in order to play hero. Due to these knee jerk reactions, the individual will have to deal with accidents, destruction and losses. The only way to bring about success is to lay low through all of the troubles.

The 8 Doors Analysis:

The following evaluates the effects of **Ren** 壬 and **Gui** 癸 with each Door.

休 *Xiu* **Rest**	Just a little bit of adversity in your life will not kill you. Take it in stride and go with the flow. You do not have to worry too much because good luck is on your side and you will be able to overcome these problems easily. In fact, these problems will actually help you build character and contribute to your success. Do not expect life to be sweet and smooth sailing all the time. Instead, expect the worst and when the best finally happens, you will be pleasantly surprised and rightfully rewarded. Follow your gut and do not be afraid of being alone. There will be help for you from your friends and family.
生 *Sheng* **Life**	Hard work and creativity are both sure-fire ingredients for success. With your originality and wit about you, you will strive to be the best in everything you do and this will help you to produce the best work you have ever done in a long time. Additionally, you have good fortune on your side and everyone wants to get to know you better. Do not let your goals take up too much of your focus until you neglect the people in your life. Take time off to get to know them as well and you will find yourself forging some meaningful relationships.
傷 *Shang* **Harm**	Fortunes are unstable for you at the moment. Things will not pan out the way you hoped and even though you try very hard to make things different, the things you do will not hold sway over the power of fate. Much of what you want will only come to fruition after a long waiting period. You may not have the patience for this and this is dangerous because if you give up halfway, you are going to have a hard time going back to your goals. You will have to start from scratch and accept the fact that you have lost most of the work you have done midway.
杜 *Du* **Delusion**	There will be an important decision that needs your immediate and focused attention. It will be difficult for you to make a decision because you find that it is an unsolvable dilemma. There will be sacrifices you will have to make regardless of which option you choose, and you find that this puts you in the tough spot of having to choose the lesser of two evils. Generally, you are not the kind of person who is able to make decisions quickly and correctly. You will find this to be one of the bigger trials of your life.

景 *Jing* **Scenery**	No major catastrophic even is troubling you right now but still you worry over what you are going to do with your life. You find it difficult to work without set goals and you find your current lack of plans to be inadequate. You are left wandering aimlessly and you cannot see the bright side of this. In truth, it is a good time for you to rest and relax. But you are so used to strife that you find it abnormal and even annoying. You keep trying to look for trouble, when in fact you should just be staying at home and taking some time off.
死 *Si* **Death**	For some reason, you seem to be in a constant rush, not stopping to rest or reflect on you current progress. You are too hasty in everything you do. Daily reflection is good for everyone and if you are currently pursuing something important, it is doubly important for you to take some occasional steps back and look at the bigger picture, analysing all mistakes and successes in an objective manner. You will find that this slows down your pace but there is nothing wrong with that. In fact, it will bring you better planning and success.
驚 *Jing* **Fear**	Focus and concentrate! Right now you seem to be in a tough spot, unable to give you attention properly to your troubles. Do not let any distractions take you away from your real problem! They may be fun to indulge in for now, but in the long run you will seriously regret not having dealt with your problems sooner. Stay on target and create a focused vision of what you want. Stick to that and stop allowing your friends to convince you to slack off. They may not have any pressing issues that need taking care of, and that is why they do not understand your predicament.
開 *Kai* **Open**	Some level of risk is always involved in the path towards glory. Those who want to pursue success should not be afraid of taking risks. A person who is afraid of failure is not cut out to have success in any way. They simply want to sit around and wait for other people to bring them up. Do not be this kind of person. Go for your dreams and be assured that good fortune is on your side. Be bold in your decisions and always choose what is right over what is easy. Take the righteous path and uphold your own integrity and values.

奇門遁甲十干格局篇

壬
REN

癸
Gui
Yin Water

天盤 Heavenly Stem	地盤 Earthly Stem
癸 *Gui* Yin Water	甲 *Jia* Yang Wood

Structure 格局	Green Dragon Enters Earth 青龍入地
Rating 吉凶	Auspicious 吉
Classic Verse 十干剋應歌訣	青龍入地癸加甲，吉門謀財婚喜嘉，凶門迫制禍非假
Transliteration 字譯	Where the Gui meets with Jia, it is known as the Green Dragon Enters Earth formation. If the combination meets with the auspicious Doors, it denotes happy pursuits for profit or marriage. When it meets with the inauspicious Doors, it denotes forthcoming disasters occurring with persistence.
Description 解說	This formation turns bad luck into good. Even when things seem at their worst, a positive turnaround is possible. The help of a Noble person will make everything better. There may be new ideas that bring new possibilities to the forefront. Due to this, it may seem like a storm has passed and everything now appears like known. As the clouds part, better opportunities come to the forefront. With new opportunities available, individuals can know that new chances can be capitalized on. Individuals know that their fortunes can turn out for the best when new changes and good times are available. He or she has a chance to move forward and achieve some of their secret goals. There is minimal resistance that appears to stop any goal from succeeding.

The 8 Doors Analysis:

The following evaluates the effects of **Gui** 癸 and **Jia** 甲 with each Door.

休 *Xiu* **Rest**	Prepare yourself for the right moment is coming along in your life soon. When it comes, you will finally have the opportunity to harness your good fortune and use it to your advantage in all your life endeavours. You will experience good luck in general and your fortunes will have it so that your life will be free from any catastrophe. The specific success you seek may not come immediately, but the fact that you have so much more ability to see it through now is an excellent indicator of good things to come for you.
生 *Sheng* **Life**	The love and support that you need for motivation will come easily to you and you will be blessed with good luck. You will find it easy to face your challenges. Take this chance to do as many good things as possible to uplift others to the places that they deserve to be as well. Then together you can bring together a team of truly hard-working and bright people to help further your cause. Because of your great work giving back to your community, you will reap its benefits for many to years to come and even your next generations will be blessed.
傷 *Shang* **Harm**	Success requires sacrifices and if you are not willing to go the extra mile to get what you need, you will not achieve success any time soon. You need to put in sufficient hard work to get satisfactory results. If you are lazy or too self-important, you will never move very far. The future is shaping up nicely for you but it is you who does not want to do what it takes to secure it. Sometimes, making sacrifices can be a very tough decision to undertake. You may need time or some advice from respected elders. Take all the time you need and seek out as many as people as possible, because no matter what, you have to find a way to move forward.
杜 *Du* **Delusion**	You are a fickle person and people find it hard to trust you. They cannot put their faith in you to lead a team or to get things done individually either. You need to change the impression that you give off to people otherwise this could become a permanent obstacle on your road to success. Try being more insistent and strong-willed. Do not mistake such traits for stubbornness or a difficult attitude. In this world, if one is not headstrong and decisive, that person would be looked down on. You need to buck up in this aspect of your life otherwise you will not succeed.

	景 *Jing* **Scenery**	Right now, your luck in your career is not stellar, but it is no bad either. Basically, you are being put in the position of having to guess where you stand and you cannot rely on any external forces to help you along. Either you start working hard and hope to get what you give, or you can take this time to brainstorm and plan for the future. However, the future is not guaranteed and your fortunes may be worse compared to now. The decision you make now is going to be very important for your future so choose wisely.
	死 *Si* **Death**	This sign is associated with a change in luck for the worse. The climate has worsened and is settling for a moodier, darker tone. There is little you can do to improve the state of your endeavours. That being said, it is possible for you to lighten up your mood just by being more involved in charities. Being benevolent to others may just help usher in a beneficial outcome for yourself too. There will be obstacles on this road to trying to be a more charitable person, but you need to learn to ignore them and push through.
	驚 *Jing* **Fear**	What goes around comes around. It will not be enough for you to admit your faults to others. You are going to have to honestly repent and allow whatever retributions fate has deemed appropriate to you to come down upon you. What you did was most dishonourable and the consequences and now coming back to bite you. If you do not accept your due penalty for your actions, you will damn yourself forever. These kinds of situations have lasting effects that can jeopardise a person's life in all aspects.
	開 *Kai* **Open**	It looks like you are set to have a memorable career for years to come. You are fortunate enough to have a great environment around you populated with great people so you should make the most of it and try to excel in everything you do. It will be easy for you to access resources and use them to produce everything you could possibly need. All good things will come to you and you will have one of the best times of your life under this auspicious configuration.

天盤 **Heavenly Stem**	地盤 **Earthly Stem**
癸 *Gui* Yin Water	乙 *Yi* Yin Wood

Structure 格局	Elegant Seal Meets Star 華蓋逢星
Rating 吉凶	Moderate 半吉
Classic Verse 十干剋應歌訣	華蓋逢星癸加乙，凡安貴祿門斷吉
Transliteration 字譯	Where the Gui meets with Yi, it is known as the Elegant Seal Meets Star formation. It denotes that a person will be judged by the fortune and safety of others.
Description 解說	Individuals may find it easy to obtain a promotion. Desires and goals are easy to achieve because the path ahead is smooth. There are rewards ahead that are simple to obtains. Desires and awards are within reach. When it comes to a disagreement, a resolution is possible to achieve. Strategies may be implemented effectively with the aid of this favorable sign. This sign is associated with good and indicates the ability to network in professional circles. Additionally, wealth luck is positive. He or she should remember to choose their words carefully because what someone says shapes the opinion of other people. To have a positive reputation, individuals must strive to endear others toward their cause.

The 8 Doors Analysis:

The following evaluates the effects of **Gui** 癸 and **Yi** 乙 with each Door.

休 *Xiu* **Rest**	No one could stop your epic winning streak. You are absolutely unbeatable at this point and everyone sees you as an absolute guru of your craft. You have nothing to worry about at all and your fortunes are well taken care of. Fate favours you and everything has been planned out to be perfect. Wealth and prosperity will come knocking at your door and you will have endless opportunities to choose from. This is a truly auspicious time for you so make the most of it and cherish this time!
生 *Sheng* **Life**	The storm has passed and you are now experiencing a period of true calm. Get ready for new opportunities and capitalise on the fact that fortune seems to be in your favour now. Fortunes always change and if you do not make the most of it now that it is your favour, it may soon pass again. You have got a good chance of moving forward and achieving your goals so all you need to do is have a proper action plan and follow through accordingly. Success is very achievable now for you so take the opportunity and go for it!
傷 *Shang* **Harm**	You are fatigued and worried as you cannot seem to find the right calling for your life. It is like looking for a needle in a haystack and you are afraid you will never be able to find the right thing before it is too late. But fear not – people will come into your life to turn things around for you. They will guide you to your path and you will see the light with their help. From this point onwards, dispel all your fears and start to take the challenges properly. Once you have achieved that, you will feel much less burdened.
杜 *Du* **Delusion**	There is always hope no matter what happens. Try to keep remembering this so that you can face your trials without any problems. You will be in a very tough spot now and it will seem like all is lost. There is nothing you can do immediately to get a good result. You can only try to stay strong as wave after wave of difficulties crash over you and try to knock you down. Keep your wits about you and exercise a hardy mental state so that you are not so easily defeated by fate.

景 *Jing* **Scenery**	Education is the key to getting you up to par with everything that is happening around you. You have been embroiled in many controversies recently and this is because you have not been exercising good judgement. Your lack of education has affected your ability to reason properly and think rationally rather than emotionally. Perhaps it is time for you to invest in new readings and spend more time participating in activities that will stimulate learning. Otherwise, bad things will continue to happen and you will have no one to blame but yourself.	
死 *Si* **Death**	You tend to speed through life without much regard for others. You do not think about whether being fast and furious is always the most effective way to go. While it may seem like you are getting things done, you do not realise how much health problems you have given yourself. Additionally, the mental strain that you have put on yourself is going to affect you in the long run. You will be plagued by stress and bad moods and it will be difficult for you to relax and have fun. Slow down a little bit and start enjoying life.	
驚 *Jing* **Fear**	Do not expect anything to be handed to you on a silver platter. Being spoon-fed is nothing to be proud of. It is simply a testament to the fact that you are not actually truly talented and need to rely on the molly-coddling of others to move along in life. Be a grown up and do not try to find the easy way out. If you do not start becoming more hard-working, it is guaranteed that you will be damaging your life in the long run. You will never be in the same league as your peers.	
開 *Kai* **Open**	Talented people are sometimes overlooked. Their talents go to waste and they never have the chance to shine and contribute to society despite how much they have to offer. Thankfully, you do not have to go through this. Your opportunity to shine will come and you will have everything it takes to showcase your talent and impress everyone who is expecting something out of you. Do not be shy with what you display; show them everything you have got because such an opportunity may not come by again.	

奇門遁甲十干格局篇

癸 **GUI**

天盤 **Heavenly Stem**	地盤 **Earthly Stem**
癸 *Gui* **Yin Water**	丙 *Bing* **Yang Fire**

Structure 格局	Elegant Seal Rebelling Officer 華蓋悖師
Rating 吉凶	Auspicious 吉
Classic Verse 十干剋應歌訣	華蓋悖師癸加丙，貴賤不利上人行
Transliteration 字譯	Where the Gui meets with Bing, it is known as the Elegant Seal Rebelling Officer formation. It denotes disadvantages for noble and humble people.
Description 解說	This formation indicates that success is unlikely. Due to this, individuals should stick with focusing on their present goals and ideals. Trying to influence future plans or pursuing out of reach goals will only end in problems. Overall, things will proceed sluggishly. Patience will be necessary to reach any outcome. Likewise, this time period is not auspicious for holding an important meeting. It is not ideal for asking for favors from someone else. The only time to accept opportunities is when it is an offer of refuge or advice from a monk. The spiritual assistance of a priest or spiritual person can bring about a positive outcome.

The 8 Doors Analysis:

The following evaluates the effects of **Gui** 癸 and **Bing** 丙 with each Door.

休 *Xiu* **Rest**	Be true to yourself and do not bother making any apologies about who you are to questioning doubters. Despite what other people say, you are on the right track and you do not have to worry about them. They are only trying to bring you down because they are jealous that they cannot get any further. Take it as a sign that you are doing very well if people have to stoop so low to try to take you out. Remember to not let their words have any impact on you. You do not need their approval to do anything.
生 *Sheng* **Life**	Do not be too ambitious to the point that it is impossible for you to get anything done. If you set the bar too high you will only disappoint yourself. If you have all these unrealistic goals, there is no way you can ever achieve anything because fortune is already not in your favour. All your outrageous fantasies will only contribute more suffering to yourself as you start believing that it is your lack of ability that results in your failure, when it is simply because you are not a good goal-setter.
傷 *Shang* **Harm**	It is time for you to take shelter. The weather is getting stormier and a bad season is about to pass over you. Everything slowly starts changing from good to bad and you are convinced that it is because of something wrong you did. The fact is: this is only happening as part of the natural course of the flow of fortune. It has its ups and downs and every person must have their equal share of good fortune and bad fortune. Do not be too concerned about this time in your life because it will soon pass. If you play your cards right and keep goodness in your heart, you may even be rewarded significantly once this spell of bad fortune passes.
杜 *Du* **Delusion**	Before you can become successful in life, you need to first get to know yourself. Unfortunately, this will be difficult because everybody around you seems to have made plans for you on your behalf. They already have an idea of what it is they think you should be doing and want to control your life. Do not let these people get to you. Remember that in the end, no one can force you to do anything and you need to take charge of your own life, otherwise you will never grow.

奇門遁甲十干格局篇

GUI

	景 *Jing* **Scenery**	Fortune is very unstable for you right now. It is advisable that you stay put with your plans and not take any drastic steps right now to ensure that you do not get yourself into a sticky situation. If there really is something you want to pursue right now, it is fine for you to commit to it first as a preliminary step, but you should not start taking action until a new configuration comes into place. Taking action at this time is very risky as your luck is unpredictably veering between good and bad.
	死 *Si* **Death**	You need to get out of your comfort zone and make an important decision about your life now! Stop sitting back and making up excuses for yourself that you are that the dilemma is too difficult or that you are too tired. Either you get working now, or you regret not having enough motivation later. The issue at hand now is a very important one that requires your full attention and if you cannot commit yourself to it, you will find that everything slowly starts to fall apart and your earlier stand to not make a decision will haunt you forever.
	驚 *Jing* **Fear**	Honesty is sometimes not the best policy. In your case, it will end up leading you to a lot of trouble. In the past, you have very cleverly navigated your way around the truth and fashioned the most strategic answers for yourself. This time, you will feel as if you have an obligation to tell the truth. You will think that the person you are confessing to will accept what you say and not punish you for it, but you will be wrong. Even though your conscience screams at you to tell the truth, try to restrain yourself and handle this issue with care.
	開 *Kai* **Open**	A successful person does not allow himself to make excuses to slack off. He does not lazy around and shirk responsibility, assigning accountability to others but not to himself. If you truly want to be successful, follow this model and be the kind of person who works hard and keeps his nose down. Try to remain modest in everything you do and constantly remind yourself that all good things come from hard work. If you stick to this practice and do the best you can in every aspect, you will succeed and it will be the kind of success that is admired by people all around you.

天盤 **Heavenly Stem**	地盤 **Earthly Stem**
癸 *Gui* **Yin Water**	丁 *Ding* **Yin Fire**

Structure 格局	Demon Snake 騰蛇妖嬌
Rating 吉凶	Inauspicious 凶
Classic Verse 十干剋應歌訣	騰蛇天嬌癸加丁，文書官司火不停
Transliteration 字譯	Where the Gui meets with Ding, it is known as the Demon Snake formation. It denotes endless paperwork and lawsuits.
Description 解說	In this formation, Gui 癸 Water counters and clashes with Ding 丁 Fire/ Ding Fire burns and boils Gui Water. Due to this, everything appears to be intertwined. Heated disagreements and disputes are likely to happen. At times, the situation appears to be dicey and uncomfortable. Health hazards, ailments and catastrophes are likely to occur. When it comes to forming a partnership or team, disaster may occur, This formation is not auspicious for collaboration or team oriented developments.

The 8 Doors Analysis:
The following evaluates the effects of **Gui** 癸 and **Ding** 丁 with each Door.

休 *Xiu* **Rest**	Your patience is paid off with good tidings all around. Don't forget to share it with people who matter to you, especially those who have helped you get to where you are right now. It will certainly feel good to you to have all these positivity around you. But this is not the end, so do not feel too comfortable or too complacent about it all. Your Nobleman only helped you open the right door – it is then up to you to prove that you really deserve to enter through that door to get to where you need to be. By doing so, you can be sure of a prosperous future ahead.
生 *Sheng* **Life**	Don't jump the gun and do things without due consideration. Hasty decisions done on your part will only create/lead to great losses. Treasure what you have currently whilst keep pushing for more at a gentle pace. Your endeavors will bring you good news in the end. You just need to remember to follow the right steps. Respect the system. It's good to be hungry for more but not if it causes you to become impulsive. Remember that low and steady wins the race.
傷 *Shang* **Harm**	You will continue to face problems in variety settings/situations. You will find yourself fighting battles on various fronts. Through the appearance of a Noble person, the tides will turn in your favor. You are able to turn challenges into your stepping stone for success. Remember this, logic helps you think and your emotions make you act. Your emotions will drive you to success but you must learn how to control and direct them appropriately. Therefore, take care of your morale and stay motivated to succeed.
杜 *Du* **Delusion**	Things aren't going to go smoothly for you. It might seem like you're living in a house filled with holes during the rain. You might stem one leak only to find another one lurking around in the corner to flood you out. Many problems will require your attention. To resolve this, you'll need to seek out the source of the problems. If you don't realize/discover the source, you'll continue fighting for a long time. Other people don't seem to know what's going on, so don't waste your time trying to seek for their opinion when the only one person who is responsible to get the job done is you.

景 *Jing* **Scenery**	You feel like you're talented and smart, but somehow you don't seem to have the opportunities to show off your talents/skills. While good things come to those who wait, that doesn't happen very often with you. The worry-free times you are used to are over. What is gone is not coming back to you. Adjust your target and don't bite off more than you can chew. Move on and prepare adequately for the difficulties that you may face if you want to make it through these times.	奇門遁甲十干格局篇 **癸** **GUI**
死 *Si* **Death**	Things are going to be difficult for you. Your goals will seem impossible to achieve and this is because you have brave beginnings but weak endings instead. You might be the kind of person who begins a race with an explosive spirit but will later grow tired and slow. Worries and doubts will hamper your progress further. You will need to work on your stamina. Motivation is like the fuel in a car – if you want to make it all the way, you will need to top it up several times on a long trip. Remember that your mind is ultimately your greatest asset.	
驚 *Jing* **Fear**	Life may leave you feeling as though you're on a treadmill. You make every effort to move forward, but you never really seem to go anywhere. You're burdened with bad luck. Be cautious and stay alert to avoid more problems later on in life. In a troublesome situation, don't be tempted to leap in and play the part of a hero because impulsive and knee-jerk reactions will lead to further accidents, loss and even destructions. Lay low until everything settles down.	
開 *Kai* **Open**	Prior planning prevents poor performance. This should be your motto in life. Do your research as much as possible and evaluate everything before making a move. Try and anticipate the problems before they arise. Learn to control your finances as well. This is the key towards building a robust strategy that will eventually bring you prosperity and wealth. The key to success is in the details of your plan. You'll win some and you'll lose some. But as long as you prepare yourself and do your best – you'll succeed.	

天盤 **Heavenly Stem**	地盤 **Earthly Stem**
癸 *Gui* **Yin Water**	戊 *Wu* **Yang Earth**

Structure 格局	Heavenly Yi Combine 天乙會合
Rating 吉凶	Auspicious 吉
Classic Verse 十干剋應歌訣	天乙會合癸加戊，吉門財婚喜，兇迫禍非顧。
Transliteration 字譯	Where the Gui meets with Wu, it is known as the Heavenly Yi Combine formation. It denotes wealth and a joyful wedding ceremony at the auspicious Door. If this combination meets with an inauspicious Gate, it denotes disasters.
Description 解說	This combination indicates good prospects for wealth and relationship related matters. The individual may have sudden opportunities for relationships. Likewise, wealth-related matters may meet with harmony and success. If things appear difficult, the help of a Noble person will make everything easier. The formation denotes a good union and shows that a person's rank will be governed by destiny. The individual can rest assured that fate will decide their standing and wealth. In general, fate and luck will be on his or her side. At times, it may seem like an invisible hand controls fate in an effort to make sure that the minimum effort is required. Overall, the positive situation seems like it will continue over the long term.

The 8 Doors Analysis:

The following evaluates the effects of **Gui** 癸 and **Wu** 戊 with each Door.

休 *Xiu* **Rest**	Clear communication and instructions can minimize a lot of frustration and problems, especially when you have undergone some miscommunication issues recently. You can be thankful that those issues have been resolved and a sense of camaraderie has returned. As this brings a good outcome to you, utilize this time to strengthen the ties and widen your network of contacts. This method will benefit you in the near future.
生 *Sheng* **Life**	You will need to chin up. Things may have been bringing you down lately but if you keep your head up and don't succumb to frustration, your determination and patience will finally pay off. Going slow and steady may actually give you an edge as you are more careful with your actions. Take your time to weigh the pros and cons carefully before every decision is made. Your efforts will not go unnoticed. Your big break is coming!
傷 *Shang* **Harm**	Knowing that you need to make a change will not be enough. You've got to find the guts to do it. Go out and actively gather the opinions of others. Be careful of who you seek advice from. Make sure they are qualified and knowledgeable. Describe your situation and the options you have and see what they would suggest to you. Ask these people their opinions and advice. Listen to what they have to say and don't be afraid to change your mind if their reasoning is sound. This collaborative process may yield answers and ideas you had. If you rush and make hasty decisions on your own right now, this will more than likely lead to failure.
杜 *Du* **Delusion**	You will make some mistakes, but if you learn from those mistakes, those mistakes will be lessons for you. You will be able to gain wisdom from these mistakes/lessons. It would seem that whatever path you choose will be filled with twists and turns for you. You can save yourself from danger and conquer the odds with the help of some great advisors around you. Believe in yourself and don't ever doubt the choices you've decided to make. Don't be afraid to turn to your friends, family and colleagues for support when you are in need.

癸
GUI

	景 *Jing* **Scenery**	Turmoil ahead. You will feel anxieties, worries and doubts as these emotions will take over you. They may be justified or they may be the product of an unhealthy state of mind. When good things start turning bad, the least you can do is maintain inner peace. Fortunes will change and things that once brought you happiness will turn into sorrow and regret. Only a positive resilient attitude will keep you on the road that ultimately leads you to a better outcome. This will be a momentary setback.
	死 *Si* **Death**	You will encounter family troubles with lots of bickering, arguments, and misunderstandings. Your family life is far from harmonious and warm, leading to you feeling depressed and low in spirits. By over-thinking and over-analyzing, you can get yourself into emotional troubles. Nothing will turn out successful for you. Look into ways to bring harmony into your strained relationships and improvements will appear in other areas as a result of it.
	驚 *Jing* **Fear**	Luck is always changing for you. When your luck changes, it will be very clear that it has changed for the worse – mishaps, accidents and bad things will befall you. Suddenly, you will face many obstacles on the path to prosperity and you should prepare yourself to begin hearing bad news routinely. There will undoubtedly be bad times ahead – you should probably brace yourself accordingly!
	開 *Kai* **Open**	Things always reach a turning point, one way or another. Don't need to speculate any further. The situation is not as bad as you may think it is. Eventually things can't get any worse and they will begin to take a turn to become better for you. This would mean that if you've been experiencing misfortune, you should know that it wouldn't last forever. Impulsiveness and harsh decisions will only get you in trouble. If you can respond and react slowly, things will be fine.

	天盤 **Heavenly Stem**	地盤 **Earthly Stem**
	癸 *Gui* Yin Water	己 *Ji* Yin Earth

Structure 格局	Elegant Seal Earth Door 華蓋地戶
Rating 吉凶	Inauspicious 凶
Classic Verse 十干剋應歌訣	華蓋地戶癸加己，音信阻隔避厄宜
Transliteration 字譯	Where the Gui meets with Ji, it is known as the Elegant Seal Earth Door formation. It denotes blocked messages or news. It is suitable for avoiding misfortunes.
Description 解説	There may be communication problems may be obstructed initially. Due to this, personal relationship matters may not going according to plan. There may be hidden agendas and problems on the horizon. He or she may find difficulties in taking their goals further. The individual's interest is not protected and their plans are open to the influence of anyone who cares to look. Overall, there is a lack of trust between every party. It will be generally better to be clear in giving instructions. Without thorough instructions, it is possible for workers to misunderstand the ultimate goal.

The 8 Doors Analysis:

The following evaluates the effects of **Gui** 癸 and **Ji** 己 with each Door.

	休 *Xiu* **Rest**	Seems like one good turn will lead to another for you. Joyous events and favorable occasions are coming to you with the help of Noble people. You will generally find it much easier to achieve a goal (provided if you have one set up in the first place) and you could easily resolve any lingering problems at this time. There will be recognition for your efforts in the end. Your reputation spreads across boundaries. This, of course, will be a fortunate sign.
	生 *Sheng* **Life**	It seems that many things in life will not go your way now. Your circumstances may not be acutely awful but they are more than likely to leave you feeling unfulfilled and underwhelmed. Your career may also suffer a lack of progression and in the long run, you will fail to make strategic changes in your life. This is because you are trying to handle so many things at one go. Do not end up being the jack of all trades but the master of none. You should also take good care of your health.
	傷 *Shang* **Harm**	Opportunities that may seem lucrative at the beginning turns out to be rotten and will create many problems for you. Frustration and depression will kick in due to this. You will need to work on relationship with others and make them matter to you. You must also always proceed with caution when you take any action in life. Expect the worst and plan for disaster so that you are ready to deal with what life is going to hand to you.
	杜 *Du* **Delusion**	With such high expectations of the future, you are bound to be disappointed. Your problem is spending too much time in your own head. Usually talking and imagining what you would like, rather than taking any action. This would also mean you may have a vision but you are unlikely to bring it into fruition. You are too idealistic for your own good. You will need to be more practical if you want to achieve anything in your life.

景 *Jing* **Scenery**	With such high expectations of the future, you are bound to be disappointed. Your problem is spending too much time in your own head. Usually talking and imagining what you would like, rather than taking any action. This would also mean you may have a vision but you are unlikely to bring it into fruition. You are too idealistic for your own good. You will need to be more practical if you want to achieve anything in your life.
死 *Si* **Death**	Tired, doubtful and worrisome. Whatever you do, you don't seem to win. Looking for the right calling or the right place in life seems to be like looking for a needle in a haystack. Bad luck seems to follow you around as well and the best advice for you is to stay quiet and remain at peace with yourself. You can't conquer your external challenges upon self-discovery. Try to find the answer within yourself internally. Listen to your own voice and instinct.
驚 *Jing* **Fear**	This sign is associated with bad luck coming your way. Although the road is bumpy ahead – you'll definitely need to stay on your toes and be weary of oncoming troubles which you may encounter without warnings. Your energy level is also low. This would mean that your progress in life will not be as smooth sailing as you'd like it to be. Factor this in your planning and stay alert at all times. There's no need for you to think too far ahead as it will not help you at all. Live in the present and be alert of everything!
開 *Kai* **Open**	While your path is littered with obstacles, you will be able to conquer every obstacle along the way successfully. This will bring you enormous satisfaction. Although you may have a difficult journey ahead, you also seem to find a way to complete it without qualms. You can obviously see the light at the end of the tunnel and your fighting spirit is strong. As long as you don't lose the energy you have within yourself, you will always be able to achieve what you're set out to do.

奇門遁甲十干格局篇

癸
GUI

天盤 Heavenly Stem	地盤 Earthly Stem
癸 *Gui* Yin Water	庚 *Geng* Yang Metal

Structure 格局	Great White Enters Net 太白入網
Rating 吉凶	Inauspicious 凶
Classic Verse 十干剋應歌訣	太白入網癸加庚，暴力爭訟罪自承
Transliteration 字譯	Where the Gui meets with Geng, it is known as the Great White Enters Net formation. It denotes punishments due to vicious lawsuits brought on by oneself.
Description 解說	The individual's personal strategy is flawed. Without realizing it, personal egos get into the way. He or she may be opinionated or unyielding in searching for the outcome. This rebellious nature may leave the individual open to a competitor. An enemy may penetrate the individual's defenses and may break their will. When influenced by an inauspicious Door, a dispute or violence is likely.

The 8 Doors Analysis:

The following evaluates the effects of **Gui** 癸 and **Geng** 庚 with each Door.

休 *Xiu* **Rest**	You can expect good luck and favourable fortunes thanks to the help of a Nobleman. The road will be smooth and you can expect success to come easily no matter what you decide to pursue. Your reputation and standing with others will be strong and wealth or an increase in income is yours for the taking. The future looks bright indeed.
生 *Sheng* **Life**	This sign is a very auspicious sign for you and you have a future filled with a network of helpful, supportive friends and a smooth path to the things you want. If you can spot this path and take it, then you can expect to find fame, wealth and success for yourself at the end of it. Opportunities are just around the corner. Proceed boldly with faith in yourself and your odds of success. Perseverance is the key here.
傷 *Shang* **Harm**	On the surface, everything looks calm to the untrained eye. What people don't see, however is what lies underneath a crisis. You need to be more alert than ever before, for the possibility of disaster of misadventure, resulting in a damaged reputation, family separation and loss of wealth. Keep things together with a cautious, calm approach and this will help you navigate through the danger. Do some charity work or kind deeds to improve your luck but remember it all has to come from the heart.
杜 *Du* **Delusion**	There is no fairness when it comes to wealth. Either you are a winner or you are loser. Be cautious in whatever you do as backstabbing and comments designed to undermine you are common, thanks to small-minded and petty people around you. You have the support of loyal people, but you still face some tough times ahead. You must learn to read the intentions of others because you will be surrounded by fakers most of them. It is when you experience some bad times in life that you will really know who your real friends are.

奇門遁甲十干格局篇

GUI

	景 *Jing* **Scenery**	It is all too easy to rush in and do things without first drawing up a through plan. If you are aware of this pitfall, then you can get your ideal results with minimal difficulty. You work best when you are working in a systematic way, so think before you act and break down what needs to be done to achieve your goals into a series of steps.
	死 *Si* **Death**	You often have great ideas and a solid vision for the future but it's going to take a lot for these to come true. Other people might seem to find success in their schemes more readily than you while you sometimes feel like you are walking on eggshells, waiting for something to go wrong, with no guide to show you the way forward. Nevertheless, you can still make it if you are alert, cautious and wise. Do not trust others blindly and do your homework.
	驚 *Jing* **Fear**	Ambition and talent are not in short supply as far as you are concerned. But when you try and channel these and produce results or progression in your career, you might find that things aren't as easy as you'd like them to be. The Nobleman and the people around you won't be giving you any help. Your Wealth Luck is also shaky at this point. None of this means that you can't achieve what you want to, but simply that you need to work harder and smarter than most.
	開 *Kai* **Open**	The future is full of hope as you will be basking in the afterglow of a successful career, harmonious family and spiritual wellbeing that are all yours for the taking. Keep a hold of this happy mentality your circumstances produce and it will lead to more happiness in the long run. This is known as a virtuous cycle – the opposite of a vicious cycle – and it is great to find yourself in one, enjoy your life and spread the joy to others. This way, you will continue to benefit immensely from this effort.

天盤 **Heavenly Stem**	地盤 **Earthly Stem**
癸 *Gui* **Yin Water**	辛 *Xin* **Yin Metal**

Structure 格局	Elegant Seal Receive Grace 華蓋受恩
Rating 吉凶	Inauspicious 凶
Classic Verse 十干剋應歌訣	華蓋受恩癸加辛，官司敗訴死罪近，問病大凶悲呻吟
Transliteration 字譯	Where the Gui meets with Xin, it is known as the Elegant Seal Receives Grace formation. It denotes failed lawsuits and the death penalty. It also denotes being grief-stricken and an inauspicious visit to the doctor.
Description 解說	There are likely to be losses before the individual will find any gains. There are malicious people that surrounds the individual. Ill intent and traps will prevent he or she from achieving their goals. Enemies may be working to team up on the individual. There are hidden illnesses and health hazards that prevent the individual from reaching their goals. There are dangers that are concealed the the individual must be extremely cautious about, In addition, insincere helpers may make any task more difficult than it ought to be.

The 8 Doors Analysis:

The following evaluates the effects of **Gui** 癸 and **Xin** 辛 with each Door.

休 *Xiu* **Rest**	At first, progress does not go smoothly and your goals can seem like they are a million miles away. It may be tempting to give up on them, but if you go the distance and stay committed, then your perseverance will pay off as you reach success at the end. A good turning point is just up the corner, so watch out for it. Keep working hard and things will become easier for you, leading to the happy ending you deserve.
生 *Sheng* **Life**	The higher the mountain, the more demanding the climb. This means that your future is full of hope and there is a positive potential in the end of the journey, as you make the difficult climb towards your own personal peak, you will learn many new things and gain new experiences. Sometimes you win and sometimes you learn. Do not worry as you will be happy with the inevitable outcome of your efforts. This is the correct direction for you to continue with confidence.
傷 *Shang* **Harm**	Seems that everything is calm and looking good right now. But there is a hidden danger that you could not see, it is advised that you take extra precaution in your actions and look through every detail. Think twice about a decision by analysing it from a different point of view. Careful planning will help stop you from going down the wrong path. This is a quiet moment and it may not be the best time to make big changes or make big calls.
杜 *Du* **Delusion**	Everything you do seems wrong. It seems like none of your decisions ever pan out the way you envisioned it. You know how to pick yourself up but then something always seems to knock you back off your feet again. This number indicates bad luck in your life at present. You must stay calm and composed so that you can protect yourself and ride out the storm you find yourself in. Some things are just out of your control right now. Control what you still can and cultivate a sense of fortitude by taking a step back for now.

景 *Jing* **Scenery**	Others have a shelf life. Sometimes two of them come along and you may spend too much time deliberating which one to take. Make the decisions quickly and respond to the changing circumstances faster and you will get ahead faster. The window of opportunity is very small. So act fast when you have all the facts.	奇門遁甲十干格局篇 癸 **GUI**
死 *Si* **Death**	Opportunities seem scarce. You have been waiting for some time now and yet the light at the end of the tunnel will seem small. Most people catch their big break when someone higher up takes notice and gives them a hand, or when someone around them helps them to greater heights. If you can meet the right person, then they will help you achieve success faster this way. The right person is someone you already familiar with. Look and you shall find because the solution to your problem could be nearer than you think.	
驚 *Jing* **Fear**	You are looking good but going nowhere. This is how you may feel as you try and move forward. Something is empty and it doesn't feel right. All problems that arise must be dealt with immediately. If you can battle on for long enough then stability will come around. In the short term, success is something that does not come easily,	
開 *Kai* **Open**	If you can stick to the tried and tested, then you can expect to thrive in your current pursuits. The external condition seems to follow favour you more. However, you need to follow a proven system in order to be financially successful. Stay clear from gambling or taking uncalculated financial risks. There will be external support from friends and mentors once you arrive at an absolute resolve yourself.	

天盤 **Heavenly Stem**	地盤 **Earthly Stem**
癸 *Gui* **Yin Water**	**壬** *Ren* **Yang Water**

Structure 格局	Heaven Web End Prison 天網終獄
Rating 吉凶	Inauspicious 凶
Classic Verse 十干剋應歌訣	天網終獄癸加壬，重婚後嫁無後人，合作謀望另換門
Transliteration 字譯	Where the Gui meets with Ren, it is known as the Heaven Web End Prison formation. It denotes a lonely life as a divorcee as a result of an adulterous marriage. This person should always look to others for support.
Description 解說	This highly inauspicious formation shows that nothing will be favorable. Even when the individual tries to help someone else, they will end up getting into trouble. The presence of the Surging Snake Deity in this formation indicates the potential for a spiritual disturbance. A marriage or long-term relationship may suddenly become unfavorable. The individual may feel stuck as they try to juggle trust issues and problems with commitment. Likewise, the individual may have issues with love in their life.

The 8 Doors Analysis:
The following evaluates the effects of **Gui** 癸 and **Ren** 壬 with each Door.

休 *Xiu* **Rest**	Goof tidings and good news is on its way. With only a little more effort, you could turn the good into the great and really reach for the stars. Your problems will dissolve as the path ahead of your is clear. All you need to do now is to find that extra 10% within yourself and keep doing what is right and what is needed to be done. Success awaits you if you can push yourself a little further. All the elements are the place right now, so stay on track.
生 *Sheng* **Life**	You spend too much energy on trivial or irrelevant mattes. Have a little more faith in yourself and your current abilities as self-doubt does not help anyone. You might feel that you have been fighting a losing battle but your competence and capabilities will get noticed soon and you'll get your promotion or break when this happens. Soon your goals will suddenly be within your grasp. Your situation is about to take a turn for the better, so be prepared.
傷 *Shang* **Harm**	If only a thought could be translated into reality without real action. If a dream could become the truth in an instant. Sadly for you, it isn't the way things happen and it always takes real action to generate results. You cannot wish your way to success. Do not confuse yourself between positive thinking and positively bluffing yourself. If you want something, you need to get out there and do what it takes.
杜 *Du* **Delusion**	Hard work may take you very close to your goals but your life is unpredictable. You might be winning the game one minute, only to find that the goal must have been moved or the rules have been changed. When you are close to victory, unforeseeable obstacles arise and your external condition changes very quickly. Your hard work is not as recognized or supported by others as you wish it would be. You mix with the wrong crowd and your success is limited on this path.

奇門遁甲十干格局篇

癸
GUI

奇門遁甲十干格局篇

GUI 癸

景 *Jing* **Scenery**		Things can't always go smoothly as there are limits to how an individual can anticipate or control within his/her means. An easy ride can't go on forever and once the good times end, it is difficult to find them again. You will encounter a lot of obstacles on your chosen path and face many difficulties in your pursuit for relationship, status and wealth. Try and be content with what you have. Count your blessings instead. The best investment for now is to invest in your education, knowledge and skills.
死 *Si* **Death**		Successful people have the ability to make right decisions quickly and stick to them. You, on the other, are prone to inconsistency in your decision making, you will encounter setbacks and problems for the time being. Despite your hard work, you may not get the results you deserve. That is because your think too much and tend to be risk adverse. Accept this and consider taking a look at how you deal with choices at work and in life in general.
驚 *Jing* **Fear**		When you are in a spot of difficulty, nobody seems to offer any help. This is frustrating and unfair for you right now. You put in 110% effort but nothing ever comes out of it the way you intended. You certainly have the desire to get out of your current situation but not the courage or drive – perhaps as a result of being constantly disappointed and worn down. This is an inauspicious sign. Time to take a step back.
開 *Kai* **Open**		Think of a marathon runner – independent, self-motivated, hardworking and persistent. These qualities will help them finish the race eventually. Continue cultivating these qualities in yourself and have success you envision for yourself isn't far off. Think of how far you have come already and allow this thought to continue as long as it is necessary. It is important to finish what you begin. Especially if you are pursuing new knowledge or skill. Your success level increases the moment you increase your personal capacity – be it in knowledge, experience or in a specific skill.

天盤 Heavenly Stem	地盤 Earthly Stem
癸 *Gui* Yin Water	癸 *Gui* Yin Water

Structure 格局	Heavenly Net Four Spreads 天網四張
Rating 吉凶	Inauspicious 凶
Classic Verse 十干剋應歌訣	天網四張癸加癸，行人失伴病訟悔
Transliteration 字譯	Where the Gui meets with Gui, it is known as the Heavenly Net Four Spreads formation. It denotes a person losing a partner. It also indicates the occurrence of diseases and inauspicious lawsuits.
Description 解說	The formation is generally inauspicious so individuals should be wary. There may be more issues in a current problem and things may fail unexpectedly. At this same time, circumstances may lead to the failure in business and relationships. Overall, circumstances will not turn out the way the individual wanted. They may feel physically or emotionally trapped. At times, depression or anxiety may plague the individual. He or she may feel unnecessary worry or stress. They may lose their way or be greeted with a worse situation. When it comes to relationship matters, he or she may find that their relationship disintegrates into a worse situation.

The 8 Doors Analysis:

The following evaluates the effects of **Gui** 癸 and **Gui** 癸 with each Door.

休 *Xiu* **Rest**	You are fortunate because there are many people who love and care for you. All you have to do is to learn to accept these gifts from others graciously. Gratitude is very important. Noble people or mentors are always there to support you. This kind of support is often all that is needed for true happiness. Whether the situation is good or bad, you will always land on your feet and enjoy long lasting wealth, good relationships and a good reputation. Have some faith in yourself and don't worry. Whatever dreams you have in mind, just go ahead and do it.
生 *Sheng* **Life**	This sign is associated with very auspicious luck. While other people might be jealous of your good fortunes, you will do well by keeping a low profile. You always land on your feet and things always seem to swing in your favour. The chances of success are very high, so you should strike and give things a go. If you put in the work, then you are sure to see results. Get out there and make your miracles happen now.
傷 *Shang* **Harm**	You face a lot of challenges and obstacles which leave you tired and irritable. Your temper may get the better of you for it seems like you are getting more than your fair share of strife all the time. You may avoid more trouble when you become less naïve because it seems that you often overestimate your abilities and underestimate the difficulties ahead. You need to be more conservative and realistic when dealing with the challenges set before you. More importantly, you need to gain more knowledge, real working skills and be grounded in practical experience. Then and only then can you enjoy good fortune.
杜 *Du* **Delusion**	This is an unfavourable sign in many ways. Despite projecting a calm, composed image, feeling of depression and doubt rage inside, hidden from others. This inner state combined with repeated external misfortune makes for broken dreams and slow progress. In terms of wealth, financial loss from misguided investments can be expected. You are also prone to gossip which is never productive or beneficial in the long run. There is no need to think too far ahead in your future. Just try and see more in yourself and look cautiously for the next right, risk-free way forward.

景 *Jing* **Scenery**	Miscalculation leads to unforeseen failure. Perhaps it is an underestimation of risk or an overestimation of the chance of success; that you are facing in your current predicament. At present, you are unable to capitalize on your talents and will likely to meet a lot of resistance and difficulty in your pursuits. The good news is that there are still people around you who are willing to lend you a helping hand. But only if you lower down your ego and politely ask to. Their support can help you overcome your challenges.
死 *Si* **Death**	Hard work may take you very close to your goals but your life is unpredictable. You might be winning the game one minute, and losing it the next. When you are close to victory, unforeseeable obstacles arise and your external condition changes very quickly. Your hard work is not recognized or supported by others as you wish it would be. You mix with the wrong crowd and your success is limited on this path.
驚 *Jing* **Fear**	The storm will continue raging on in your life, wreaking continuous havoc and unsettling everything you have worked hard to put into place for your future. Braving this brutal storm will drain you of your energy and time, making you stumble tiredly on your path as you fruitlessly try to avoid obstacles. This is going to be a very trying time for you and you need to be ready to face it. Prepare yourself for a roller coaster ride and try to remember that after a storm, calmness will settle. Look forward to this and in the meantime, continue hoping for the best
開 *Kai* **Open**	Success will come to those who work hard for it and as long as you strive to be the best you can be, nothing can come in your way. People will try to bring you down by speaking behind your back and making you feel bad, but you should just ignore them and move on. A nasty rumour about you might spread because of their efforts, but you should just trust in the fact that you have been an upstanding person long enough for it to not have any real effect. Just be calm and allow fate to handle these people.

奇門遁甲十干格局篇

癸
GUI

JOEY YAP'S
QI MEN DUN JIA
Reference Series

Qi Men Dun Jia Compendium — JOEY YAP

Qi Men Dun Jia Ten Thousand Year Calendar — JOEY YAP

Qi Men Dun Jia 540 Yang Structure — JOEY YAP

Qi Men Dun Jia 540 Yin Structure — JOEY YAP

Qi Men Dun Jia Year Charts — JOEY YAP

Qi Men Dun Jia Month Charts — JOEY YAP

Qi Men Dun Jia Day Charts — JOEY YAP

Qi Men Dun Jia Day Charts (San Yuan Method) — JOEY YAP

Qi Men Dun Jia Forecasting Method (Book 1) — JOEY YAP

Qi Men Dun Jia Forecasting Method (Book 2) — JOEY YAP

Qi Men Dun Jia Evidential Occurrences — JOEY YAP

Qi Men Dun Jia Destiny Analysis — JOEY YAP

Qi Men Dun Jia Feng Shui — JOEY YAP

Qi Men Dun Jia Date, Time & Activity Selection — JOEY YAP

Qi Men Dun Jia Annual Destiny Analysis — JOEY YAP

Qi Men Dun Jia Strategic Executions — JOEY YAP

Qi Men Dun Jia The 100 Formations — JOEY YAP

Qi Men Dun Jia Sun Tzu Warcraft — JOEY YAP

This is the most comprehensive reference series to Qi Men Dun Jia in the Chinese Metaphysics world. Exhaustively written for the purpose of facilitating studies and further research, this collection of reference texts and educational books aim to bridge the gap for students who want to learn, and the teachers who want to teach Qi Men.

These essential references provide practical guidance for all branches under the Qi Men Dun Jia studies including Destiny Analysis, Feng Shui, Strategic Executions and Forecasting method.

These books are available exclusively at:
Store.joeyyap.com

E-mail: order@masteryacademy.com | +603 - 2284 8080

JOEY YAP'S
QI MEN DUN JIA MASTERY PROGRAM

The world's most comprehensive training program on the subject of Qi Men Dun Jia. Joey Yap is the Qi Men Strategist for some of Asia's wealthiest tycoons. This program is modelled after Joey Yap's personal application methods, covering techniques and strategies he applies for his insanely high net-worth clients. There's a huge difference between studying the subject as a scholar and learning how to use it successfully as a Qi Men Strategist. Joey Yap shares with you in this program what he personally uses to transform his own life and the lives of million others. In other words, he shares with his students what actually works and not just what looks good on theory with no real practical value. This means that the program covers his personal trade secrets in using the art of Qi Men Dun Jia.

There are five unique programs, each of them covering one specific application aspect of the Joey Yap's Qi Men Dun Jia system.

Joey Yap's training program focuses on getting the results. Theories and formulas are provided in the course workbook so that valuable class time are not wasted dwelling on formulas. Each course comes with its own comprehensive 400-plus pages workbook. Taught ONCE a year exclusively by Joey Yap, seats to these programs are extremely limited.

Email to : courses@masteryacademy.com or call +603 2284 8080 for more details.

- Getting Whatever You Want from Whatever You've Got™ Spiritual Qi Men™
- Qi Men Forecasting Methods™
- Qi Men Destiny & Life Transformation™
- Qi Men Feng Shui™
- Qi Men Strategic Execution™

Call +6(03) 2284 8080 or
email courses@masteryacademy.com for enquiries

www.masteryacademy.com | +603 - 2284 8080

JOEY YAP CONSULTING GROUP

Pioneering Metaphysics - Centric Personal Coaching and Corporate Consulting

The Joey Yap Consulting Group is the world's first specialised metaphysics consultation firm. Founded in 2002 by renown international Feng Shui and BaZi consultant, author and trainer Joey Yap, the Joey Yap Consulting Group is a pioneer in the provision of metaphysics-driven coaching and consultation services for individuals and corporations.

The Group's core consultation practice areas are Feng Shui and BaZi, which are complimented by ancillary services like Date Selection, Face Reading and Yi Jing Divination. The Group's team of highly-trained professional consultants are led by Principal Consultant Joey Yap. The Joey Yap Consulting Group is the firm of choice for corporate captains, entrepreneurs, celebrities and property developers when it comes to Feng Shui and BaZi-related advisory and knowledge.

Across Industries: Our Portfolio of Clients

Our diverse portfolio of both corporate and individual clients from all around the world bears testimony to our experience and capabilities.

Joey Yap Consulting Group is the firm of choice for many of Asia's leading multi-national corporations, listed entities, conglomerates and top-tier property developers when it comes to Feng Shui and corporate BaZi.

Our services also engaged by professionals, prominent business personalities, celebrities, high-profile politicians and people from all walks of life.

JOEY YAP CONSULTING GROUP

Name (Mr./Mrs./Ms.):_____

Contact Details

Tel:_____ Fax:_____

Mobile :_____

E-mail:_____

What Type of Consultation Are You Interested In?
☐ Feng Shui   ☐ BaZi   ☐ Date Selection   ☐ Corporate Events

Please tick if applicable:
☐ Are you a Property Developer looking to engage Joey Yap Consulting Group?
☐ Are you a Property Investor looking for tailor-made packages to suit your investment requirements?

Please attach your name card here.

Thank you for completing this form. Please fax it back to us at:

Malaysia & the rest of the world
Fax : +603-2284 2213   Tel : +603-2284 1213

www.joeyyap.com

www.joeyyap.com

Feng Shui Consultations

For Residential Properties
- Initial Land/Property Assessment
- Residential Feng Shui Consultations
- Residential Land Selection
- End-to-End Residential Consultation

For Commercial Properties
- Initial Land/Property Assessment
- Commercial Feng Shui Consultations
- Commercial Land Selection
- End-to-End Commercial Consultation

For Property Developers
- End-to-End Consultation
- Post-Consultation Advisory Services
- Panel Feng Shui Consultant

For Property Investors
- Your Personal Feng Shui Consultant
- Tailor-Made Packages

For Memorial Parks & Burial Sites
- Yin House Feng Shui

BaZi Consultations

Personal Destiny Analysis
- Personal Destiny Analysis for Individuals
- Children's BaZi Analysis
- Family BaZi Analysis

Strategic Analysis for Corporate Organizations
- Corporate BaZi Consultations
- BaZi Analysis for Human Resource Management

Entrepreneurs & Business Owners
- BaZi Analysis for Entrepreneurs

Career Pursuits
- BaZi Career Analysis

Relationships
- Marriage and Compatibility Analysis
- Partnership Analysis

For Everyone
- Annual BaZi Forecast
- Your Personal BaZi Coach

Date Selection Consultations

- Marriage Date Selection
- Caesarean Birth Date Selection
- House-Moving Date Selection
- Renovation & Groundbreaking Dates
- Signing of Contracts
- Official Openings
- Product Launches

Corporate Events

Many reputable organizations and instituitions have worked closely with Joey Yap Consulting Group to build a synergistic business relationship by engaging our team of consultants, led by Joey Yap, as speakers at their corporate events.

We tailor our seminars and talks to suit the anticipated or pertinent group of audience. Be it department, subsidiary, your clients or even the entire corporation, we aim to fit your requirements in delivering the intended message(s).

Tel: +603-2284 1213   Email: consultation@joeyyap.com

Chinese Metaphysics Reference Series

The Chinese Metaphysics Reference Series is a collection of reference texts, source material, and educational textbooks to be used as supplementary guides by scholars, students, researchers, teachers and practitioners of Chinese Metaphysics.

These comprehensive and structured books provide fast, easy reference to aid in the study and practice of various Chinese Metaphysics subjects including Feng Shui, BaZi, Yi Jing, Zi Wei, Liu Ren, Ze Ri, Ta Yi, Qi Men and Mian Xiang.

The Chinese Metaphysics Compendium

At over 1,000 pages, the *Chinese Metaphysics Compendium* is a unique one-volume reference book that compiles ALL the formulas relating to Feng Shui, BaZi (Four Pillars of Destiny), Zi Wei (Purple Star Astrology), Yi Jing (I-Ching), Qi Men (Mystical Doorways), Ze Ri (Date Selection), Mian Xiang (Face Reading) and other sources of Chinese Metaphysics.

It is presented in the form of easy-to-read tables, diagrams and reference charts, all of which are compiled into one handy book. This first-of-its-kind compendium is presented in both English and the original Chinese, so that none of the meanings and contexts of the technical terminologies are lost.

The only essential and comprehensive reference on Chinese Metaphysics, and an absolute must-have for all students, scholars, and practitioners of Chinese Metaphysics.

The Ten Thousand Year Calendar (Pocket Edition)	 The Ten Thousand Year Calendar	Dong Gong Date Selection
 The Date Selection Compendium	Plum Blossoms Divination Reference Book	Xuan Kong Da Gua Ten Thousand Year Calendar
 San Yuan Dragon Gate Eight Formations Water Method	Bazi Hour Pillar Useful Gods - Wood	 Bazi Hour Pillar Useful Gods - Fire
Bazi Hour Pillar Useful Gods - Earth	 Bazi Hour Pillar Useful Gods - Metal	Bazi Hour Pillar Useful Gods - Water
 Xuan Kong Da Gua Structures Reference Book	Bazi Structures and Structural Useful Gods - Wood	 Bazi Structures and Structural Useful Gods - Fire
Bazi Structures and Structural Useful Gods - Earth	 Bazi Structures and Structural Useful Gods - Metal	 Bazi Structures and Structural Useful Gods - Water
Xuan Kong Da Gua 64 Gua Transformation Analysis	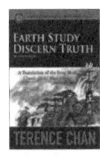 Earth Study Discern Truth Second Edition	 Eight Mansions Bright Mirror
Secret of Xuan Kong	Ode to Flying Stars	 Xuan Kong Purple White Script
Ode to Mysticism	 The Yin House Handbook	Water Water Everywhere

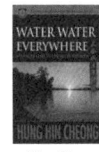

www.masteryacademy.com | +603 - 2284 8080

Chinese Metaphysics Reference Series

SAN YUAN QI MEN XUAN KONG DA GUA
Reference Series

玄空大卦
三元奇門

San Yuan Qi Men Xuan Kong Da Gua Compendium

San Yuan Qi Men Xuan Kong Da Gua Ten Thousand Year Calendar

San Yuan Qi Men Xuan Kong Da Gua 540 Yang Structure

San Yuan Qi Men Xuan Kong Da Gua 540 Yin Structure

Xuan Kong Da Gua Fixed Yao Method

Xuan Kong Da Gua Flying Yao Method

Xuan Kong Da Gua 6 Relationships Method

Xuan Kong Da Gua Five Element Structures

Xuan Kong Da Gua Leaning Star Structures

Xuan Kong Flying Star Natal Chart Analysis 1 - 5

Xuan Kong Flying Star Natal Chart Analysis 6 - 9

Xuan Kong Flying Star Secrets Of The 81 Combinations

Xuan Kong Flying Star Purple White Script's Secret Advanced Star Charts

The **San Yuan Qi Men Xuan Kong Da Gua Series** is written for the advanced learners in mind. Unlock the secrets to this highly exclusive art and seamlessly integrate both Qi Men Dun Jia and the Xuan Kong Da Gua 64 Hexagrams into one unified practice for effective applications.

This collection is an excellent companion for genuine enthusiasts, students and professional practitioners of San Yuan Qi Men Xuan Kong Da Gua studies.

www.masteryacademy.com | +603 - 2284 8080

Joey Yap's BaZi Profiling System

Three Levels of BaZi Profiling (English & Chinese versions)

In BaZi Profiling, there are three levels that reflect three different stages of a person's personal nature and character structure.

Level 1 – The Day Master

The Day Master in a nutshell is the BASIC YOU. The inborn personality. It is your essential character. It answers the basic question "WHO AM I". There are ten basic personality profiles – the TEN Day Masters – each with its unique set of personality traits, likes and dislikes.

Level 2 – The Structure

The Structure is your behavior and attitude – in other words, how you use your personality. It expands on the Day Master (Level 1). The structure reveals your natural tendencies in life – are you more controlling, more of a creator, supporter, thinker or connector? Each of the Ten Day Masters express themselves differently through the FIVE Structures. Why do we do the things we do? Why do we like the things we like? – The answers are in our BaZi STRUCTURE.

Level 3 – The Profile

The Profile reveals your unique abilities and skills, the masks that you consciously and unconsciously "put on" as you approach and navigate the world. Your Profile speaks of your ROLES in life. There are TEN roles – or Ten BaZi Profiles. Everyone plays a different role.

What makes you happy and what does success mean to you is different to somebody else. Your sense of achievement and sense of purpose in life is unique to your Profile. Your Profile will reveal your unique style.

The path of least resistance to your success and wealth can only be accessed once you get into your "flow." Your BaZi Profile reveals how you can get FLOW. It will show you your patterns in work, relationship and social settings. Being AWARE of these patterns is your first step to positive Life Transformation.

www.baziprofiling.com

www.masteryacademy.com | +603 - 2284 8080

THE BAZI
60 PILLARS SERIES

The BaZi 60 Pillars Series is a collection of ten volumes focusing on each of the Pillars or Jia Zi in BaZi Astrology. Learn how to see BaZi Chart in new light through the Pictorial Method of BaZi analysis and elevate your proficiency in BaZi studies through this new understanding. Joey Yap's 60 Pillars Life Analysis Method is a refined and enhanced technique that are based on the fundamentals set by the true masters of olden times, and modified to fit to the sophistication of current times.

www.masteryacademy.com | +603 - 2284 8080

BaZi Collection

Leading Chinese Astrology Master Trainer Joey Yap makes it easy to learn how to unlock your Destiny through your BaZi with these books. BaZi or Four Pillars of Destiny is an ancient Chinese science which enables individuals to understand their personality, hidden talents and abilities as well as their luck cycle, simply by examining the information contained within their birth data.

Understand and appreciate more about this astoundingly accurate ancient Chinese Metaphysical science with this BaZi Collection.

BOOK 1 (English & Chinese versions)
BOOK 2 (English & Chinese versions)
BOOK 3 (English & Chinese versions)
BOOK 4
BOOK 5

Feng Shui Collection

Must-Haves for Property Analysis!

For homeowners, those looking to build their own home or even investors who are looking to apply Feng Shui to their homes, these series of books provides valuable information from the classical Feng Shui therioes and applications.

In his trademark straight-to-the-point manner, Joey shares with you the Feng Shui do's and dont's when it comes to finding a property with favorable Feng Shui, which is condusive for home living.

(English & Chinese versions)   (English & Chinese versions)

Stories & Lessons on Feng Shui Series

All in all, this series is a delightful chronicle of Joey's articles, thoughts and vast experience - as a professional Feng Shui consultant and instructor - that have been purposely refined, edited and expanded upon to make for a light-hearted, interesting yet educational read. And with Feng Shui, BaZi, Mian Xiang and Yi Jing all thrown into this one dish, there's something for everyone.

(English & Chinese versions)

Xuan Kong Nine Life Star series (English & Chinese versions)

Joey Yap's Feng Shui Essentials - Xuan Kong Nine Life Star series of books comprise nine individual titles that provide detailed information about each individual Life Star.

Based on the complex and highly-evolved Xuan Kong Feng Shui system, each book focuses on a particular Life Star and provides you with a detailed Feng Shui guide.

www.masteryacademy.com | +603 - 2284 8080

More Titles under Joey Yap Books

Pure Feng Shui

Pure Feng Shui is Joey Yap's debut with an international publisher, CICO Books, and is a refreshing and elegant look at the intricacies of Classical Feng Shui – now compiled in a useful manner for modern-day readers. This book is a comprehensive introduction to all the important precepts and techniques of Feng Shui practice.

Your Aquarium Here

This book is the first in Fengshuilogy Series, a series of matter-in-fact and useful Feng Shui books designed for the person who wants to do a fuss-free Feng Shui.

Xuan Kong Flying Stars

This book is an essential introductory book to the subject of Xuan Kong Fei Xing, a well-known and popular system of Feng Shui. Learn 'tricks of the trade' and 'trade secrets' to enhance and maximize Qi in your home or office.

Walking the Dragons

Compiled in one book for the first time from Joey Yap's Feng Shui Mastery Excursion Series, the book highlights China's extensive, vibrant history with astute observations on the Feng Shui of important sites and places. Learn the landform formations of Yin Houses (tombs and burial places), as well as mountains, temples, castles, and villages.

The Art of Date Selection: Personal Date Selection (English & Chinese versions)

With the *Art of Date Selection: Personal Date Selection*, learn simple, practical methods you can employ to select not just good dates, but personalized good dates. Whether it's a personal activity such as a marriage or professional endeavor such as launching a business, signing a contract or even acquiring assets, this book will show you how to pick the good dates and tailor them to suit the activity in question, as well as avoid the negative ones too!

Your Head Here

Your Head Here is the first book by Sherwin Ng, an accomplished student of Joey Yap, and an experienced Feng Shui consultant and instructor with Joey Yap Consulting Group and Mastery Academy respectively. Being the second book under the Fengshuilogy series, Your Head Here focuses on Bedroom Feng Shui, a specific topic dedicated to optimum bed location and placement.

If the Shoe Fits

This book is for the ones who want to make the effort to enhance their relationship. Yes, you read it right - EFFORT.

Hence, in her debut release, Jessie Lee humbly shares with you the classical BaZi method of the 10 Day Masters, and the combination of the new-founded profiling system developed by Joey Yap, to understand and to deal with the people around you.

Face Reading Collection

Discover Face Reding (English & Chinese versions)

This is a comprehensive book on all areas of Face Reading, covering some of the most important facial features, including the forehead, mouth, ears and even philtrum above your lips. This book eill help you analyse not just your Destiny but help you achieve your full potential and achieve life fulfillment.

(English & Chinese versions)

Joey Yap's Art of Face Reading

The Art of Face Reading is Joey Yap's second effort with CICO Books, and takes a lighter, more practical approach to Face Reading. This book does not so much focus on the individual features as it does on reading the entire face. It is about identifying common personality types and characters.

Faces of Fortune: The 20 Tycoons to bet on over the next 10 years

Faces of Fortune is Tee Lin Say's first book on the subject of Mian Xiang or Chinese Face Reading. As an accomplished Face Reading student of Joey Yap and an experienced business journalist, Lin Say merged both her knowledge into this volume, profiling twenty prominent tycoons in Asia based on the art of Face Reading.

Easy Guide on Face Reading (English & Chinese versions)

The Face Reading Essentials series of books comprises 5 individual books on the key features of the face – Eyes, Eyebrows, Ears, Nose, and Mouth. Each book provides a detailed illustration and a simple yet descriptive explanation on the individual types of the features.

The books are equally useful and effective for beginners, enthusiasts, and the curious. The series is designed to enable people who are new to Face Reading to make the most of first impressions and learn to apply Face Reading skills to understand the personality and character of friends, family, co-workers, and even business associates.

Annual Releases
2014 Annual Outlook & Tong Shu

| Chinese Astrology for 2014 |  Feng Shui for 2014 | Tong Shu Desktop Calendar 2014 |  Professional Tong Shu Diary 2014 |  Tong Shu Monthly Planner 2014 |  Weekly Tong Shu Diary 2014 |

www.masteryacademy.com | +603 - 2284 8080

Educational Tools and Software

Xuan Kong Flying Stars Feng Shui Software
The Essential Application for Enthusiasts and Professionals

The Xuan Kong Flying Stars Feng Shui Software will assist you in the practice of Xuan Kong Feng Shui with minimum fuss and maximum effectiveness. Superimpose the Flying Stars charts over your house plans (or those of your clients) to clearly demarcate the 9 Palaces. Use it to help you create fast and sophisticated chart drawings and presentations, as well as to assist professional practitioners in the report-writing process before presenting the final reports for your clients. Students can use it to practice their Xuan Kong Feng Shui skills and knowledge, and it can even be used by designers and architects!

BaZi Ming Pan Software Version 2.0
Professional Four Pillars Calculator for Destiny Analysis

The BaZi Ming Pan Version 2.0 Professional Four Pillars Calculator for Destiny Analysis is the most technically advanced software of its kind in the world today. It allows even those without any knowledge of BaZi to generate their own BaZi Charts, and provides virtually every detail required to undertake a comprehensive Destiny Analysis.

This Professional Four Pillars Calculator allows you to even undertake a day-to-day analysis of your Destiny. What's more, all BaZi Charts generated by this software are fully printable and configurable! Designed for both enthusiasts and professional practitioners, this state-of-the-art software blends details with simplicity, and is capable of generating 4 different types of BaZi charts: **BaZi Professional Charts, BaZi Annual Analysis Charts, BaZi Pillar Analysis Charts and BaZi Family Relationship Charts.**

Walking the Dragons with Joey Yap
(The TV Series)

This DVD set features eight episodes, covering various landform Feng Shui analyses and applications from Joey Yap as he and his co-hosts travel through China. It includes case studies of both modern and historical sites with a focus on Yin House (burial places) Feng Shui and the tombs of the Qing Dynasty emperors.

The series was partly filmed on-location in mainland China, and the state of Selangor, Malaysia.

www.masteryacademy.com | +603 - 2284 8080

Educational Tools and Software

Joey Yap Feng Shui Template Set

Directions are the cornerstone of any successful Feng Shui audit or application. The **Joey Yap Feng Shui Template Set** is a set of three templates to simplify the process of taking directions and determining locations and positions, whether it's for a building, a house, or an open area such as a plot of land, all with just a floor plan or area map.

The Set comprises 3 basic templates: The Basic Feng Shui Template, 8 Mansions Feng Shui Template, and the Flying Stars Feng Shui Template.

Mini Feng Shui Compass

The Mini Feng Shui Compass is a self-aligning compass that is not only light at 100gms but also built sturdily to ensure it will be convenient to use anywhere. The rings on the Mini Feng Shui Compass are bilingual and incorporate the 24 Mountain Rings that is used in your traditional Luo Pan.

The comprehensive booklet included will guide you in applying the 24 Mountain Directions on your Mini Feng Shui Compass effectively and the 8 Mansions Feng Shui to locate the most auspicious locations within your home, office and surroundings. You can also use the Mini Feng Shui Compass when measuring the direction of your property for the purpose of applying Flying Stars Feng Shui.

www.masteryacademy.com | +603 - 2284 8080

MASTERY ACADEMY
OF CHINESE METAPHYSICS
Your **Preferred** Choice to the Art & Science of Classical Chinese Metaphysics Studies

Bringing **innovative** techniques and **creative** teaching methods to an ancient study.

Mastery Academy of Chinese Metaphysics was established by Joey Yap to play the role of disseminating this Eastern knowledge to the modern world with the belief that this valuable knowledge should be accessible to anyone, anywhere.

Its goal is to enrich people's lives through accurate, professional teaching and practice of Chinese Metaphysics knowledge globally. It is the first academic institution of its kind in the world to adopt the tradition of Western institutions of higher learning - where students are encourage to explore, question and challenge themselves and to respect different fields and branches of study - with the appreciation and respect of classical ideas and applications that have stood the test of time.

The art and science of Chinese Metaphysics studies – be it Feng Shui, BaZi (Astrology), Qi Men Dun Jia, Mian Xiang (Face Reading), ZeRi (Date Selection) or Yi Jing – is no longer a field shrouded with mystery and superstition. In light of new technology, fresher interpretations and innovative methods as well as modern teaching tools like the Internet, interactive learning, e-learning and distance learning, anyone from virtually any corner of the globe, who is keen to master these disciplines can do so with ease and confidence under the guidance and support of the Academy.

It has indeed proven to be a center of educational excellence for thousands of students from over thirty countries across the world; many of whom have moved on to practice classical Chinese Metaphysics professionally in their home countries.

At the Academy, we believe in enriching people's lives by empowering their destinies through the disciplines of Chinese Metaphysics. Learning is not an option - it's a way of life!

MALAYSIA
19-3, The Boulevard, Mid Valley City, 59200 Kuala Lumpur, Malaysia
Tel : +603-2284 8080 | Fax : +603-2284 1218
Email   : info@masteryacademy.com
Website : www.masteryacademy.com

Australia, Austria, Canada, China, Croatia, Cyprus, Czech Republic, Denmark, France, Germany, Greece, Hungary, India, Italy, Kazakhstan, Malaysia, Netherlands (Holland), New Zealand, Philippines, Poland, Russian Federation, Singapore, Slovenia, South Africa, Switzerland, Turkey, U.S.A., Ukraine, United Kingdom

www.masteryacademy.com | +603 - 2284 8080

Mastery Academy around the world

www.masteryacademy.com | +603 - 2284 8080

Feng Shui Mastery™
LIVE COURSES (MODULES ONE TO FOUR)

An ideal program for those who wants to achieve mastery in Feng Shui from the comfort of their home. This comprehensive program covers the foundation up to the advanced practitioner levels, touching upon the important theories from various classical Feng Shui systems including Ba Zhai, San Yuan, San He and Xuan Kong.

Module One: Beginners Course

Module Two: Practitioners Course

Module Three: Advanced Practitioners Course

Module Four: Master Course

BaZi Mastery™
LIVE COURSES (MODULES ONE TO FOUR)

This lesson-based program brings a thorough introduction to BaZi and guides the student step-by-step all the way to the professional practitioner level. From the theories to the practical, BaZi students – along with serious Feng Shui practitioners – can master its application with accuracy and confidence.

Module One: Intensive Foundation Course

Module Two: Practitioners Course

Module Three: Advanced Practitioners Course

Module Four: Master Course in BaZi

Xuan Kong Mastery™
LIVE COURSES (MODULES ONE TO THREE)
* Advanced Courses For Master Practitioners

Xuan Kong is a sophisticated branch of Feng Shui, replete with many techniques and formulae, which encompass numerology, symbology and the science of the Ba Gua, along with the mathematics of time. This program is ideal for practitioners looking to bring their practice to a more in-depth level.

Module One: Advanced Foundation Course

Module Two A: Advanced Xuan Kong Methodologies

Module Two B: Purple White

Module Three: Advanced Xuan Kong Da Gua

www.masteryacademy.com | +603 - 2284 8080

Mian Xiang Mastery™
LIVE COURSES (MODULES ONE AND TWO)

This program comprises of two modules, each carefully developed to allow students to familiarize with the fundamentals of Mian Xiang or Face Reading and the intricacies of its theories and principles. With lessons guided by video lectures, slide presentations and notes, students are able to understand and practice Mian Xiang with greater depth.

Module One:
Basic Face Reading

Module Two:
Practical Face Reading

Yi Jing Mastery™
LIVE COURSES (MODULES ONE AND TWO)

Whether you're a casual or serious Yi Jing enthusiast, this lesson-based program contains two modules that brings students deeper into the Chinese science of divination. The lessons will guide students on the mastery of its sophisticated formulas and calculations to derive answers to questions we pose.

Module One:
Traditional Yi Jing

Module Two:
Plum Blossom Numerology

Ze Ri Mastery™
LIVE COURSES (MODULES ONE AND TWO)

In two modules, students will undergo a thorough instruction on the fundamentals of ZeRi or Date Selection. The comprehensive program covers Date Selection for both Personal and Feng Shui purposes to Xuan Kong Da Gua Date Selection.

Module One:
Personal and Feng Shui Date Selection

Module Two:
Xuan Kong Da Gua Date Selection

Joey Yap's
San Yuan Qi Men Xuan Kong Da Gua™

This is an advanced level program which can be summed up as the Integral Vision of San Yuan studies – an integration of the ancient potent discipline of Qi Men Dun Jia and the highly popular Xuan Kong 64 Hexagrams. Often regarded as two independent systems, San Yuan Qi Men and San Yuan Xuan Kong Da Gua can trace their origins to the same source and were actually used together in ancient times by great Chinese sages.

This method enables practitioners to harness the Qi of time and space, and predict the outcomes through a highly-detailed analysis of landforms, places and sites.

Feng Shui for Life

This is an entry-level five-day course designed for the Feng Shui beginner to learn the application of practical Feng Shui in day-to-day living. Lessons include quick tips on analyzing the BaZi chart, simple Feng Shui solutions for the home, basic Date Selection, useful Face Reading techniques and practical Water formulas. A great introduction course on Chinese Metaphysics studies for beginners.

Joey Yap's
Design Your Destiny

This is a three-day life transformation program designed to inspire awareness and action for you to create a better quality of life. It introduces the DRT™ (Decision Referential Technology) method, which utilizes the BaZi Personality Profiling system to determine the right version of you, and serves as a tool to help you make better decisions and achieve a better life in the least resistant way possible based on your Personality Profile Type.

Millionaire Feng Shui Secrets Programme

This program is geared towards maximizing your financial goals and dreams through the use of Feng Shui. Focusing mainly on the execution of Wealth Feng Shui techniques such as Luo Shu sectors and many more, it is perfect for boosting careers, businesses and investment opportunities.

Grow Rich With BaZi Programme

This comprehensive programme covers the foundation of BaZi studies and presents information from the career, wealth and business standpoint. This course is ideal for those who want to maximise their wealth potential and live the life they deserve. Knowledge gained in this course will be used as driving factors to encourage personal development towards a better future.

Walk the Mountains! Learn Feng Shui in a Practical and Hands-on Program

Feng Shui Mastery Excursion™

Learn landform (Luan Tou) Feng Shui by walking the mountains and chasing the Dragon's vein in China. This Program takes the students in a study tour to examine notable Feng Shui landmarks, mountains, hills, valleys, ancient palaces, famous mansions, houses and tombs in China. The Excursion is a 'practical' hands-on course where students are shown to perform readings using the formulas they've learnt and to recognize and read Feng Shui Landform (Luan Tou) formations.

Read about China Excursion here:
http://www.fengshuiexcursion.com

Mastery Academy courses are conducted around the world. Find out when will Joey Yap be in your area by visiting
www.masteryacademy.com
or call our office at **+603-2284 8080**.

Online Home Study Courses

Gain Valuable Knowledge from the Comfort of Your Home

Now, armed with your trusty computer or laptop and Internet access, knowledge of Chinese Metaphysics is just a click away!

3 easy steps to activate your Home Study Course:

Step 1:
Go to the URL as indicated on the Activation Card, and key in your Activation Code

Step 2:
At the Registration page, fill in the details accordingly to enable us to generate your Student Identification (Student ID).

Step 3:
Upon successful registration, you may begin your lessons immediately.

Joey Yap's Feng Shui Mastery HomeStudy Course

Module 1: **Empowering Your Home**
Module 2: **Master Practitioner Program**

Learn how easy it is to harness the power of the environment to promote health, wealth and prosperity in your life. The knowledge and applications of Feng Shui will no more be a mystery but a valuable tool you can master on your own.

Joey Yap's BaZi Mastery HomeStudy Course

Module 1: **Mapping Your Life**
Module 2: **Mastering Your Future**

Discover your path of least resistance to success with insights about your personality and capabilities, and what strengths you can tap on to maximize your potential for success and happiness by mastering BaZi (Chinese Astrology). This course will teach you all the essentials you need to interpret a BaZi chart and more.

Joey Yap's Mian Xiang Mastery HomeStudy Course

Module 1: **Face Reading**
Module 2: **Advanced Face Reading**

A face can reveal so much about a person. Now, you can learn the art and science of Mian Xiang (Chinese Face Reading) to understand a person's character based on his or her facial features with ease and confidence.

www.masteryacademy.com | +603 - 2284 8080